Alice and Eleanor

Alice and Eleanor,

A Contrast in Style and Purpose

Sandra R. Curtis

Bowling Green State University Popular Press
Bowling Green, OH 43403

Women's Studies Series
Jane Bakerman, General Editor

Other titles in the series
Child Brides and Intruders
Carol Wershoven

*Communication & Women's Friendships
Parallels and Intersections in Literature & Life*
Janet Doubler Ward
JoAnna Stephens Mink

Copyright © 1994 by Sandra R. Curtis

Library of Congress No.: 93-72172

ISBN: 0-87972-625-3 clothbound

Cover design by Laura Darnell-Dumm

To my children, Danny, Debby and Mich—

May you find a purpose to life that fits your individual style.

and to John—

Who challenges me daily to blend our life's purpose with our personal styles.

Acknowledgements

To my readers, John, Anne and Steve:

Your comments helped refine the style and purpose reflected herein

and

To the Franklin Delano Roosevelt Library Archivists in Hyde Park:

By providing me with copies of the personal correspondence
between Alice and Eleanor, you allowed me
to gain invaluable insights into the relationship
between these two remarkable women.

I offer you all my heartfelt thanks.

Contents

Foreword	i
Chapter One	1
Beginnings	2
Chapter Two	9
Idealized Parents	10
Chapter Three	21
Rebellious and Diligent Youths	22
Chapter Four	29
Blossoming Womanhood	30
Chapter Five	39
Society Debutantes	40
Chapter Six	50
Engagement	51
Chapter Seven	61
Marriage	62
Chapter Eight	76
Early Married Years	77
Chapter Nine	88
Shifting Political Fortunes	89
Chapter Ten	94
Political Warfare	96
Photographs	106
Chapter Eleven	119
Insiders to Exiles	120
Chapter Twelve	130
War and Infidelity	131
Chapter Thirteen	143
Family Conflict Amidst Worldwide Chaos	145

Chapter Fourteen	159
Unconventional Challenges	162
Chapter Fifteen	179
Changing Roles	181
Chapter Sixteen	191
Tragedy and Triumph	192
Chapter Seventeen	201
A Public War of Words	202
Epilogue	215
A Contrast in Style and Purpose	216
Notes	220
Works Cited	225

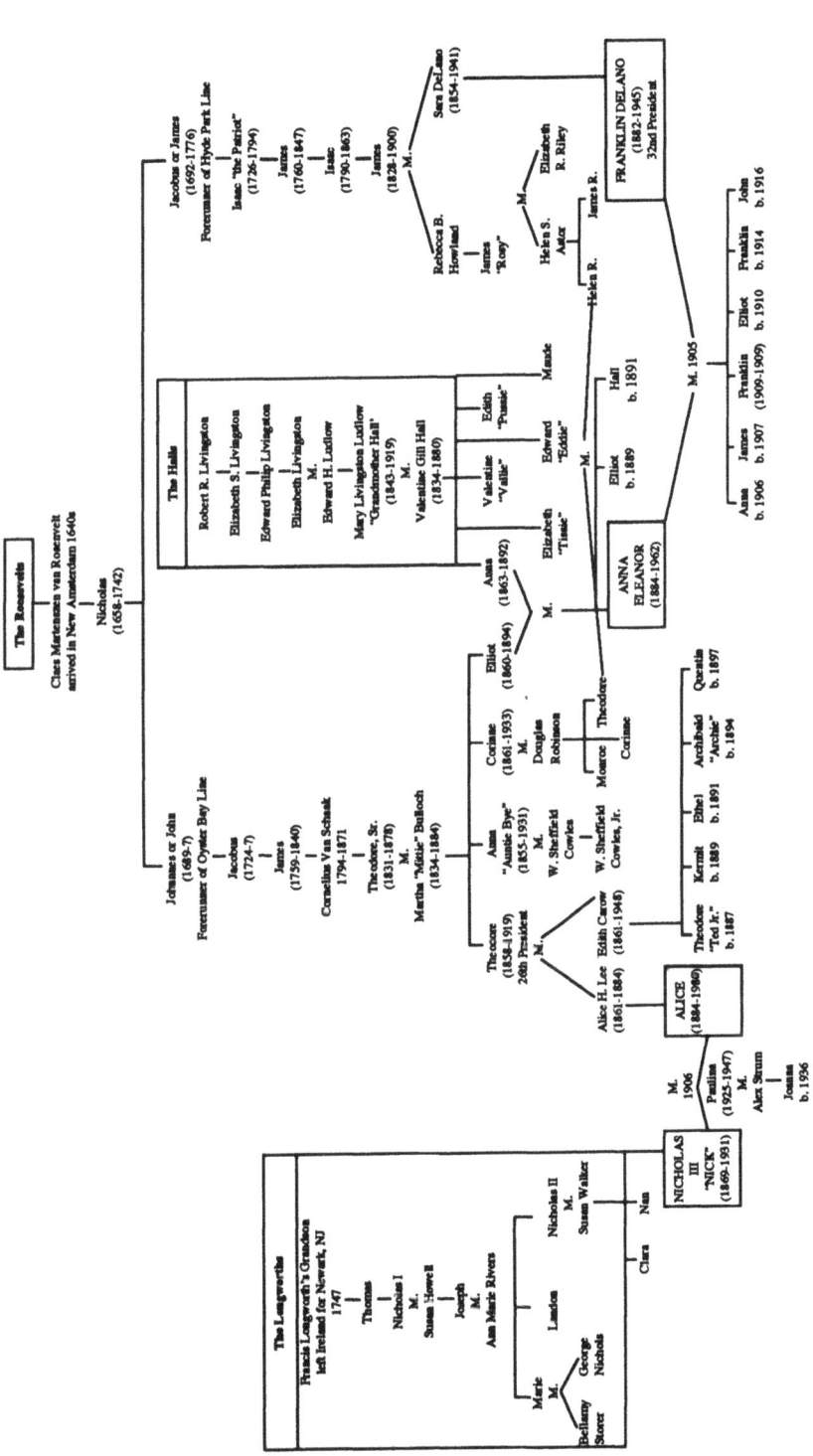

Foreword

The election of 1992 became known as "The Year of the Woman." Three women were elected to the United States Senate, two from California, the most populated state in the nation, and one from Illinois. Their journey to the Senate floor was the continuation of a struggle for women's suffrage and political influence that had preceded their elections by a century. Though Dianne Feinstein, Barbara Boxer and Carole Mosley Braun are trailblazers, bringing women's perspectives to the Senate Chambers, their unique abilities could not have flourished without the pioneering work of the women who came before them, working behind the scenes and leading the marches to prepare the soil for their campaigns to take root.

Alice Roosevelt Longworth and Eleanor Roosevelt were two such feminist pioneers. While each would have disdained the title, they could not escape their status as media stars of their day in a nation enamored with our "First Families." First cousins by birth, polar opposites in personality, political and personal rivals, Alice and Eleanor were intimately connected to the U.S. Presidency for over 45 dramatic years of our country's history. Their story holds an important place in the annals of women in politics.

Alice was the first child of Theodore Roosevelt, 26th President of the United States. Dubbed Princess Alice by an eager press during her father's administration, she developed a reputation as the devilish belle of the ball. Politics consumed her after her marriage to Congressman Nicholas Longworth. Alice became her father's chief political confidant and spent countless hours in the Senate gallery, assiduously following debates on such monumental questions of her day as America's involvement in the League of Nations. In the ironic style typical of her controversial life, Alice's playground became the Senate, even though her husband became Speaker of the House. She lobbied in the Senate chambers, lunched in the Senate cafeteria and played hostess to and poker with the most powerful men of her time. Though Alice influenced many congressional votes, she never cast one herself.

ii Alice and Eleanor

Eleanor emerged from a turbulent childhood as the wife of the nation's most popular and longest serving President, Franklin Delano Roosevelt. As niece of the former Roosevelt president, she earned her reputation as a dogged worker for women's, children's and labor rights. She scorned personal power, preferring to devote herself to achieving empowerment for the disenfranchised. Her dedication earned her the title of "The First Lady of the World" and culminated with her service as chair of the United Nations Commission which drafted the *Declaration of Human Rights*. The U.N. document stands as her crowning achievement, a testament to her courageous life's work.

Before Eleanor's husband became President, she was considered one of the most powerful women during the 1920s and early 1930s in the Democratic party. She drafted legislation, lobbied on behalf of her special interests, but, like Alice, never cast a single congressional vote. Through her work, she became the conscience of her husband's domestic agenda and, in the process, redefined the role of "First Lady."

These two Roosevelt women helped shape the manner in which American women participate in government today. The current female congressional officials are the beneficiaries of Alice's and Eleanor's political legacy. The legacy was by no means harmonious, nor spoken with a unanimous voice. Alice's and Eleanor's styles were not only in contrast to one another, but they were often in conflict, driven by dramatically different purposes. Eleanor committed her life to the cause of social justice while, for Alice, politics assumed a personal dimension. Her commitment was to fulfill her father's legacy. Alice has been likened to a racehorse, quick out of the gate, with little staying power, whereas Eleanor's style reflected a workhorse, enduring over the long haul with persistence and perseverance.

What personal struggles defined Alice and Eleanor? What motivated their involvement in politics? What family influences nurtured their divergent political activities? How did their private lives reflect their public personas? How did they influence events and how did events change them? How did they interact with one another publicly and privately? What guidance can their lives and experience offer? *Alice and Eleanor, A Contrast in Style and Purpose* explores these questions.

While my work encompasses the long lives of each woman, once Eleanor Roosevelt took up residence in the White House, the scope of her national and international influence outweighed any comparison to

Foreword iii

Alice's parochial prestige. As such, the book focuses primarily on the years prior to Eleanor becoming First Lady, rather than her subsequent achievements. The final chapter moves from Franklin's presidency to the post White House years, with an emphasis on the public and private experiences that molded Alice and Eleanor's personal relationship and their political personas.

In her autobiography, Eleanor Roosevelt wrote that the fiction writer can reveal "...what *[s]he* has learned through observation and experience of the inner workings of the souls of *[wo]*men. In an autobiography this is hard to do...The more honest you are about yourself and others,...the more valuable what you have written will be... as a picture of the people and their problems during the period covered ..." *[author's addition]*.

Alice and Eleanor bridges the genres of autobiography and fiction in an attempt to make these women come alive for the reader. Exhaustive biographies have been written about each individually. Both have written their autobiographies. I have taken the liberty of dramatizing their relationship as a prelude to each chapter with the goal of developing an immediacy and vitality absent from the academic works on their lives.

The opening section of each chapter, while developed from actual incidents are, nonetheless, fictional accounts. The only first-person interactions I used between Alice and Eleanor came from correspondence which I had access to courtesy of the Franklin Delano Roosevelt Library in Hyde Park, New York. I am grateful to the archivists who made Alice and Eleanor's limited letters to one another available to me.

In opening each chapter with a fictional account, I hope I have provided a truthful flavor of the dynamic relationship between these two remarkable women and their reflections on one another. I was striving, in Eleanor Roosevelt's words, to reveal the "inner workings" of these two women as they evolved their influential public positions.

Alice and Eleanor, A Contrast in Style and Purpose is a biographical interpretation of the people, events and the times that molded these women's personalities and led them to their unique place in American history.

Sandra R. Curtis

Chapter One

"Take it back!" Eleanor cried, pummeling Alice with a pillow on the bed. "It's blasphemy!"

Alice covered her head with her arms to avoid the blows of her outraged cousin. "It's the truth," retorted Alice, her voice muffled under Eleanor's attack.

By the time their quite pregnant Auntie Bye trudged up the stairs, Eleanor was sitting on top of Alice's head. Gwen Burden, Jessie Sloane, Margaret Dix and Helen Cutting, her friends, watched Eleanor's violent reaction in unabashed astonishment.

"WHAT is the meaning of this, girls?" exclaimed Bye as she pulled a sullen but indignant Eleanor off of Alice.

Alice straightened her mussed hair and her fitted dress, glancing at her friends. They could barely contain their laughter. Eleanor stood with her head hanging limply on her tall thin frame. Her irate expression exaggerated a recessed chin and oversized teeth, and her generally soft blue eyes flared as she stared down at the tips of her shoes. Under the frock that hung loosely from her shoulders, she breathed heavily. The physical exertion had compounded her angry emotional response.

"Alice?" Auntie Bye demanded.

Bye shot a quick glance at the other 14-year-old girls. Too perceptive to miss the knowing looks the adolescents exchanged, she gave them a reproving gaze. Alice's friends huddled together against the wall, guilt etched across their faces.

"We were just discussing the facts of life," Alice answered nonchalantly.

"No one should talk about things like that!" exclaimed Eleanor.

"May I ask where these facts came from?" Bye interrupted the antagonists.

"The Bible," Alice replied. "Everything we said can be found in there."

Eleanor lapsed into injured silence.

"Alice..." said Bye, half accusatory, half amused.

2 Alice and Eleanor

"Well, she'll learn about whores sometime," Alice offered innocently.

Unable to stand the encounter any longer, Eleanor stormed down the stairs to Auntie Bye's sitting room. Her visit was decidedly over. She was ready to return to her Grandmother's house.

Bye shook her head, sadly contemplating the disparate characters of her two nieces. Without admonishing Alice, she said, "It's not a word little girls use."[1]

Beginnings

Alice understood Bye's meaning, for although she and Eleanor were the same age, the two were aware of their differences early in life. On the surface Alice was a self-assured, unruly tomboy. She masked her shyness with adolescent defiance and bravado. In contrast, Eleanor was outwardly shy, awkward and totally lacking in self-confidence. She possessed none of the wise-cracking aplomb nor social ease of her first cousin. From early childhood, Eleanor was acutely aware of her personal deficiencies.

Though Alice teased Eleanor mercilessly, she empathized with her cousin. They had grown up together, in the shadow of tragic parental deaths, shuffled between relatives, each a persistent outsider in her own large family.

Alice and Eleanor were born into the world of society balls and the privileged class. While millions of Americans struggled to earn less than $400 annually, Eleanor's parents travelled in a circle of friends who owned and built million-dollar yachts and mansions. The labor movement was in its infancy. The *laissez-faire* doctrine permeated the business community. Manufacturers wanted to run their factories without government interference. Safety regulations, guaranteed wages, and restricted work hours for adults and children were a barrier to profits.

In the year of both girls' birth, Teddy Roosevelt (TR) was taken on a tour of slum sweatshops by Samuel Gompers of the Cigarmakers Union. The experience led him to develop an enlightened position on working conditions. TR betrayed his class to become the first politician from New York's privileged society to support legislation to limit the entrenched practice of wealthy exploiting the poor. Ironically, his daughter Alice lived her entire life among the privileged class, while his niece, Eleanor, became a champion of the underclass. Eleanor was said to be more like Teddy's daughter than Alice herself. Such "odious comparisons added nothing to family solidarity!" noted Alice lightly, capturing the essence of the cousins' lifelong relationship in one pithy statement.

Alice Roosevelt was born on February 12, 1884, the only daughter of Theodore Roosevelt and his beloved wife, Alice Lee.

Teddy received a telegram about his daughter's birth from his dear, eldest sister, Bye, while on the floor of the New York Assembly in Albany. He was serving his third term as the representative of Manhattan. When a second telegram arrived, he rushed to the train. By the time Teddy arrived at midnight, his boyhood home on Fifty-Seventh Street was almost in mourning. His mother lay dying two floors below his unconscious wife.

Brother Elliot and sister Corinne had gathered at Bye's request. Her given name was Anna, but the family affectionately knew her as Bamie, Bye or Auntie Bye. The entire family depended on her. Bye had been running the household since she was 14. From adolescence, Bye had possessed the common sense, wisdom and nurturing nature that evaded their mother, Mittie, a frivolous southern belle.

Bye had been racing between floors, attending her mother and her sister-in-law, Alice Lee. Teddy's other sister, Corinne, had been in Baltimore for a weekend with her husband, Douglas Robinson. They returned immediately after receiving a distraught telegram from the usually irrepressible Bye. In addition to her nursing duties, Bye had been caring for the Robinson's infant son, her nephew, Ted.

When Corinne and Douglas arrived at 10:30 p.m. on February 13, Elliot (Eleanor's future father) flung the door open in anguish, declaring that a curse lay on the house. Mittie died of typhoid in the early morning hours of February 14. That evening, Alice Lee died of complications attributed to her pregnancy.[2]

Teddy was so bereft by the deaths of his mother and his wife, he left his infant daughter in Bye's care, returned to Albany and immersed himself in legislative work at a furious pace. When his term of office was over, Teddy refused to run for re-election. He fled to the Badlands of Dakota, intent on banishing his young wife from his heart and his mind. In doing so, he also banished his infant daughter. He was

4   Alice and Eleanor

convinced that his sister, Bye, could take care of baby Alice better than he could.

Teddy Roosevelt roamed the Dakotas for the next two years, while Alice flourished in Auntie Bye's care. He invested his abundant energy in ranching, rather than politics, and lost most of his inheritance in the process. On a return trip to New York from his ranch, the Elkhorn, in Medora, Dakota, Teddy bumped into Edith Carow leaving Bye's house. They had been childhood sweethearts. Teddy fell in love again and he became engaged to Edith. He was so conflicted about the engagement, however, he kept it secret, even from Bye, because he did not believe in second marriages. Teddy's rigid Victorian standards dictated that he remain faithful to Alice Lee until they met in heaven. When Teddy and Edith's engagement announcement appeared in the New York society page, Bye wrote a denial.

Six months later, Teddy finally confessed the truth to his sister in a letter from Montana. In the same correspondence, he offered to let Bye keep his young daughter. Alice had grown into a bright-eyed, blond, curly-haired child, the reflection of her young mother. He didn't want Alice around as a constant reminder to Edith that she had been his second choice. Bye, unmarried and in her 30s, was delighted. The matter seemed settled.

However, after Teddy and Edith Carow were married in London in the winter of 1886, Edith insisted that Alice live with them. Whether the choice came out of conscientiousness, or jealousy she felt over Bye's relationship with Teddy, Edith's preference stood. Bye was crushed. Teddy was equally surprised, but the realignment was most traumatic for young Alice. Her father terrified her.

Alice's earliest recollection of her father was at a family gathering held before Teddy's remarriage at their family retreat. Sagamore Hill rose above Oyster Bay on Long Island. During a fox hunt, her father was thrown from his horse. His arm was broken and his face bloodied in the fall. Alice had been waiting in the stables. When Teddy raced up to her after the accident, his toddler ran screaming from the bloody, disfigured apparition coming towards her. His attempt to catch and quiet her only resulted in Alice wailing louder.

Alice met her new mother at Bye's after Theodore and Edith returned from their European honeymoon. She wore her best party dress with her hair set in perfect curls. She recalled descending the stairs at her aunt's house, carrying a bunch of pink roses in her arms to present to Edith Carow Roosevelt.

Giving up her three-year-old niece almost broke Bye's heart. Throughout Alice's life, Bye provided a refuge for her niece, protecting her from the Victorian guilt her father felt over his remarriage, as well as the indifference Edith expressed towards her stepdaughter. Alice recalled the words her aunt often repeated during her childhood, "Remember, darling, if you are very unhappy, you can always come back to me."

Eleanor Roosevelt was born eight months after Alice on October 11, 1884. Her parents were Anna Hall, a leading debutante of New York society in the winter of 1881-82, and Elliot Roosevelt, beloved younger brother of Teddy, Bye and Corinne. He was a charming man accomplished in sports and social skills.

Despite being described as more wrinkled and less attractive than the average baby, Eleanor was a miracle from heaven to her father. Her uncomplicated, safe delivery came as a reprieve from the veil of death that clung to the family since Alice Lee and Mittie's deaths. The baby girl was named Anna Eleanor—Anna after her mother and Bye; Eleanor, after her father, who was nicknamed Ellie and Nell.

During Eleanor's first years of life, she was tenderly and lovingly cared for by her parents as Alice had been by her aunt. And like Alice, she, too, received a traumatic shock in early childhood. Eleanor perceived her father as warm and tender, but Elliot Roosevelt was in reality a nervous, moody wreck, an alcoholic, who lacked direction in his life. He moved from real estate to other business ventures, never truly finding his niche. The only place Elliot felt completely comfortable was in athletic pursuits and at social events. He loved sailing, attending society parties and participating in reckless riding escapades and drinking sprees with his cronies at the Meadow Brook Club.

His wife, Anna, became more and more distraught over Elliot's false promises and their extended separations. Even Teddy, who was completely devoted to his errant younger brother, disdained Elliot's frantic life as a meaningless, unhealthy existence. Both brothers' health had been delicate during childhood, but Teddy overcame his asthma by an obstinate devotion to body building. Elliot never recovered from the fainting, headaches, seizures and nerves he suffered. His illness was

6 Alice and Eleanor

diagnosed as hysteria, but today the symptoms would probably be associated with drug withdrawal.

Their father, Theodore Roosevelt, Sr., believed travel was the cure-all for any problem. At age 14, Elliot took his first voyage to alleviate a health problem. His father took him to England for an autumn holiday. At 15, Elliot was sent to a ranch in Texas to rough it out, riding and hunting on the frontier. Such periodic excursions seemed to make Elliot better for a time.

In the spring of 1887, when Eleanor was two and a half, her mother decided that an extended stay in Europe was necessary not only for Elliot's health, but for the health of their marriage. The family set sail on the *Britannica*. After one day out at sea, the ship collided twice in the fog with another ship, the *Celtic*, killing and injuring many people. The resulting chaos terrorized Eleanor, much as Alice had been terrorized by the sight of her mangled father in the stable. Eleanor's tormented cries mingled with those injured and dying on board. She struggled relentlessly against the men who tried to lower her into a lifeboat where her father waited with open arms in the surging sea. They succeeded in lowering her into the boat, though she never relinquished her struggle. The event was so traumatic that Eleanor had to make a determined effort as an adult to overcome her terror of water in order to swim and sail with her own family.

Despite the tragic accident, Anna remained committed to their travel plans, but Eleanor refused to go. No matter how Elliot pleaded with his daughter, she would not get on another boat. Eleanor was left to spend the summer with her great aunt and uncle, the Gracies. Aunt Gracie was her grandmother Mittie's sister. Eleanor suffered in silence through much of her stay, occasionally wondering aloud where her home would be now that her parents were in Europe. To Aunt Gracie, the little girl seemed hopeless and pathetic in her desire to avoid the water. Whenever they neared the bay, Eleanor would cry, "Baby does not want to go into the water. Not in a boat."

Elliot's health was much improved by the time he and Anna returned six months later. He joined Uncle Gracie's banking and brokerage house and started construction on a large house in Hempstead, Long Island. He rented a nearby bungalow for his family where Eleanor played happily with her kitten, a puppy and the chickens. She and her mother made daily visits to the construction site to supervise the building.

Chapter One

During the following summer of 1888, Alice and Eleanor were together often. They were joined by their extended family. Aunt and Uncle Gracie had built Gracewood on land Teddy had sold them at Oyster Bay. Bye had her own cottage on a nearby property and there were the Robinson cousins as well. Teddy showed the most sympathy for Eleanor, however. She was painfully shy, which kept her isolated from the rest of the "bunnies," as TR called the children.

The four-year-old girls played frequently. They attended reading lessons at their Aunt Gracie's in the morning. Eleanor recalled being fascinated by her aunt's expressive hands, her *B'rer Rabbit* stories and her tales of the vanished plantation life in Georgia. In the afternoons, they went boating, played with blocks and had lunches and tea together. The girls' differences were apparent even in those early days. Baby Lee, as Alice was called, had turned proud and competitive in response to her stern stepmother, Edith, while Eleanor remained gentle, docile and shy.

The short, idyllic period in Eleanor's life ended with two serious riding accidents that summer of 1888. Elliot began riding and drinking with his old crowd. He and Teddy became fiercely competitive. In a polo match between their two riding clubs, Oyster Bay and Meadow Brook, TR tried to outride Elliot. He was thrown from his horse and lay unconscious for several minutes. Teddy didn't fully recover from the fall for several days. Later that summer, Elliot broke his leg riding in a charity circus. The leg was set, but had to be broken and reset. Elliot sought relief from the terrible pain in his old nemesis—drugs and alcohol. He became dependent on morphine, laudanum and cocktails.

Along with the emotional traumas of their early lives, both Alice and Eleanor endured orthopedic problems that required braces for correction. Eleanor battled a back brace for two years, while Alice wore her prescribed leg braces attached to ugly black boots. A bout of polio at age two left one of Alice's legs shorter than the other. The only consistent attention she received from Edith as a young child was a nightly ritual in which her stepmother stretched each foot in "a steel contraption that...resembled a medieval instrument of torture."

Unlike the compliant Eleanor, who bore her brace stoically, the defiant Alice would take hers off and hit other children with them. Metaphorically, words became Alice's braces later in life. They were her spirited personality's vehicle to sting, entertain and lobby, as well as her

8 Alice and Eleanor

mask to hide from painful experiences. The stoicism Eleanor showed in wearing her brace turned to dogged persistence in championing worthy causes, as well as becoming her mask for dealing with life's crises.

Chapter Two

"Jump, Eleanor," called Uncle Teddy, treading water beside the dock in Oyster Bay. "Come on now, you can do it. Give it a big heave ho!"

Eleanor inched toward the end of the dock. Her kneecaps danced violently up and down as cold and fear possessed her. The tall, gangly girl's skin was covered with goose bumps as she peered at her four-eyed uncle in the water below. The screaming and splashing of her cousins around her were drowned out by the horrifying thought that she would disappoint her uncle. Still, the depths of the water held grievous danger. Eleanor couldn't swim.

Two thoughts flitted through her mind, ravaging her with terror. The first was the raging sea around the *Britannica* when her father held out his arms for her to jump. Her second thought was of a donkey ride she had taken with her father in Sorrento, Italy, a few years earlier. She had been afraid to descend a steep hillside. His criticism and acute disappointment still burned in Eleanor's memory, "I never knew you were a coward."

Uncle Ted's voice shattered her mental turmoil. "It's nice and cool, Eleanor. Jump! I'm waiting for you!"

She gulped for a breath, closed her eyes, held her nose and stepped off the dock.

Alice watched from the dock, reliving her own dread at the demands her father continually placed on her. She immediately jumped in after Eleanor, deliberately splashing her younger brother, Ted, Jr., to distract her father. Eleanor bobbed to the surface, gasping for breath. She clawed for her uncle or the dock, anything that might hold her up. Eleanor was rewarded with a dunking from her exuberant uncle.

She sputtered back to the surface, paddling frantic like a puppy. This time, Uncle Teddy shoved her towards the shore.

"That's the way to build character," Teddy laughed. "Tackle every obstacle!"

10 Alice and Eleanor

A sense of relief and exhaustion filled Eleanor as she clambered up the sandy bank. Pride replaced her fear. She had overcome her cowardice.

"Your turn, Alice," Teddy called.

Alice ducked underwater, swimming effortlessly away, pretending not to hear her father. He stroked towards her, treading nearby as she surfaced for a breath.

"Dive, Alice...Now!"

"I can't," she cried.

"*Can't* is not a word in the Roosevelt vocabulary. You saw Eleanor. She can't even swim, but she jumped in! You can dive."

Alice glared at Eleanor, seated at the edge of the water, clutching her lanky knees under her chin. "But I can't!" Tears spilled down her cheeks as Alice made her way to the dock. She pulled herself up the side and inched to the edge.

"Watch out, Edith. Alice is diving. The tide's going to rise again!"[1] Teddy shouted humorously to Edith who rocked baby Ethel, the newest Roosevelt. She kept one eye on Alice and one on Kermit, Ted, Jr.'s younger brother, as he toddled along the water's edge.

Alice hooked her hands together, leaned over from the waist and tremulously pushed off the dock. She landed flat on her belly with a loud smack. Eleanor flinched.

"Bully!" applauded Teddy. Alice swam off angrily to sulk by herself.

Idealized Parents

"In a way we both suffered from being deprived of a parent," Alice explained. "She [Eleanor] had an idealized image of her father and I had one of my mother. But whereas she responded to her insecurity by being do-goody and virtuous, I did [so] by being boisterous and showing off. She got so little enjoyment out of things. If only she had dug in once in a while."

Had either young girl realized that they were struggling with the same insecurities and fears during their childhood, they might have developed a close bond and comforted one another. It was a theme that would be repeated in each of their lives. Eleanor and her mother, Anna Hall, both hurt by the self-destructive behavior of Elliot, might have been allies, but her mother's silence discouraged the bond. Alice's adolescence might have been less flamboyant had she not sought her father's attention so desperately. If he had spoken lovingly of her deceased mother, Alice Lee, instead of refusing to mention his first wife, their bond, too, might have been solidified by their shared loss. Alice and Eleanor suffered from their parents' conspiracy of silence.

They also viewed one another with polite suspicion. Eleanor saw Alice as more sophisticated and socially at ease. Alice tolerated her righteous cousin. She saw Eleanor as a goody-two-shoes, always doing things to please adults. Contrary to Alice's opinion, Eleanor was not a docile child. She craved attention.

Eleanor's overriding need for recognition stemmed from her parents' troubled marriage. While they were loving and devoted to one another, her father's drinking and reckless lifestyle left her mother emotionally bereft. Anna had married at 19 to escape from the oppressive duties that befell her after her father's death. A deeply religious man, he left six children, no will and a child-like wife. As the eldest, Anna had to step into the role of executor, one for which she was utterly unprepared. She was young and beautiful. She wanted to attend parties, not be burdened with financial accounts.

Anna was flattered to be squired about by the handsome, suave Elliot Roosevelt. He was one of the most eligible bachelors in New York. Elliot had recently returned from an around-the-world hunting trip, squandering part of his inheritance in order to hunt elephants and tigers. He embarked on the journey to find himself, traveling to India via England and Italy, then returning home through Ceylon and China.

In Anna, Elliot saw the embodiment of perfection. Eleanor described her mother as "one of the most beautiful women I have ever seen." Though initially hesitant about marrying an unpredictable man, so different from her devout father, Anna succumbed to Elliot's charms. Life with him promised glamour and comfort, filled with joyous, carefree society parties. He would take her away from the serious responsibilities of her immediate family. Their life together began with great promise.

The *New York Times* called Anna and Elliot's marriage on December 2, 1883, one of the most brilliant weddings of the season. Two months later, however, the double tragedy of Mittie's and Alice Lee's deaths struck, ushering in the demise of Anna's gay, promising future. She was precipitously plunged into dealing with Elliot's excesses. The following year, Eleanor's safe delivery brought a respite into their life. The healthy baby offered Elliot a ray of sunshine and initiated the mutual adulation between father and daughter.

As the years passed, Elliot became increasingly neglectful of his wife. Polo, drinking and frantic partying absorbed him. Anna spent more time at her family home in Tivoli along the Hudson River. She withdrew emotionally from Elliot and Eleanor. In her daughter's sad eyes, Anna saw a reflection of the personal sorrow she felt, but could not express. She was unable to give Eleanor the nurturing her daughter needed. Anna lacked emotional support from her husband, which left her no reserves to extend to her child.

Eleanor, however, loved her father unconditionally. She wanted only his loving attention. She had no expectations for him to fulfill, nor standards to maintain or promises to exact. He returned her love with devotion, lavishing attention on her when he was present. When he was absent, he wrote Eleanor emotionally charged letters, filled with hopes and dreams.

In the spring of 1887, while Eleanor stayed with Aunt Gracie after the ocean liner debacle, Alice moved to Sagamore Hill with her father and her "mother." Teddy was his daughter's primary playmate until the birth of her first sibling six months later. Her father had yet to re-enter politics and was pursuing a writing career. He carried his daughter piggyback down to breakfast, spent hours building blocks with her and enchanting her with heroic stories of Davy Crockett, Daniel Boone and other courageous adventurers.

As Edith's stepdaughter, Alice never held the privileged position of firstborn in her father's family. That spot was reserved for Ted, Jr., Edith's first son and Teddy's namesake, who arrived in September 1887. At three and a half years of age, Alice was fascinated by her new brother, "a howling polly parrot that ate Mamma." She set her rocking chair next to his crib with plans to stay forever. Shortly after his birth, however, Alice was sent to visit her maternal grandparents in Boston, a jarring displacement which signalled her precarious family position.

Alice's regular visits with the Lees totaled six weeks a year, three during the spring at their home at Chestnut Hill and three over Thanksgiving at their residence on Beacon Hill in Boston's Back Bay. These times became periods of supreme indulgence for Alice, for she held center stage with her grandparents, unlike in her father's house. Grandma and Grandpa Lee gave her a bright, sunny room, allowed her to jump on the couch and served her creamy soft, buttered bread. Her aunts saved turkey wishbones for her. The maids made them into tiny witchcraft dolls, laying a foundation for her later interest in the occult. Alice got into childish mischief, like hiding in coal bins with neighbor children and sneaking into the pigsty to slap pigs until they squealed. Her greatest pleasure, however, was playing for hours with her mother's cherished doll house.

Throughout Alice's youth, her father never spoke of his first wife. She addressed Edith as "Mother," yet during her evening prayers, Alice's nurse made her recite, "My *mother* who is in heaven." Alice understood that she was not to discuss the *mother* in her prayers, but for such a bright child, the mixed messages left Alice confused and unsure of herself.

Bye, however, salvaged her mother's memory and gave Alice someone to idealize. An incredibly perceptive woman, Bye understood young Alice's need to know about her mother. Through Auntie Bye's wonderful tales of her parents' courtship, wedding, the building of Leeholm (later renamed Sagamore Hill) and their idyllic honeymoon, Alice became enthralled with her mother's beauty and with the way her father had worshipped Alice Lee. Teddy's reluctance to even mention his first wife, coupled with Bye's loving tales, nurtured Alice's romanticized vision of her mother. As Alice grew, even Edith's harsh, jealous descriptions of Alice Lee served to reinforce the idealization of her mother.

Edith never spoke directly to Alice about her mother, either. However, she told stories to Ted, Jr., her firstborn, who gleefully informed Alice that she had a "sweat" (he meant "wet") nurse, not a mother who personally fed and cared for her. Alice heard painful stories about her mother in which Alice Lee was described as devoid of intellectual or emotional depth. Had she lived, Theodore would have become so bored, he would be driven to suicide. Equally hurtful, though untrue, Ted told Alice that their father had proposed to Edith before her mother.[2]

The worst tale Alice learned from her brother, however, was that her father had wanted to leave her with Auntie Bye. Whether for the sake of discretion or fidelity, her father did not want to be reminded of his first wife. Unlike most of Ted, Jr.'s other stories, this one was painfully true.

While Elliot's family suffered from his addictive behaviors, Teddy's family experienced constant financial distress. The loss of half his inheritance on his ranch in the Dakotas kept Edith perpetually managing pennies. TR's writing brought in very little, yet the family still employed several household servants. As gentlefolk, it was unthinkable for them to do without help. Teddy sold off parcels of land to raise necessary money, including the lot where Gracewood was built. The family often joked that in troubled financial times they had best be nice to Alice, for she had a separate inheritance from her maternal grandparents, the Lees.

Eleanor was five when her first sibling was born in the autumn of 1889. Like Alice, she was sent to live with her grandmother, and her brother also became her father's namesake, Elliot, Jr. Unlike Alice's relationship with her father, however, by the time Eleanor's brother arrived, she and her father were allies. They had an impenetrable bond for both experienced themselves as failures in Anna's eyes—Eleanor for her shy sullenness and Elliot for his errant behavior. Each desperately wanted and needed Anna's approval and affection, yet she was unable to give either what they needed most.

The following year, 1890, when Alice turned six, her father was appointed Civil Service Commissioner as a political reward for campaigning in President Benjamin Harrison's election. The family moved from Sagamore Hill to Washington, D.C. TR's salary of $3500 a year did nothing to solve the family's financial problems because they had to rent a house in expensive Washington.

The nation's Capital was emerging from its decadent days after the Civil War. It still had the reputation of being a wicked city, however. When Congress was in session, an army of married men lived in the Capital away from their families. The city's ranks swelled with available female clerks. Behavior was loose. Affairs which would have been clandestine in other places were conducted openly in Washington. Though Alice remembered Washington in the 1890s as a charming village, it hardly fit her description. Mayor "Boss" Alexander Shepherd had made substantial civic improvements. The streets were paved and lit. Parks had been laid out and planted with trees. Most importantly, the city's open sewer had been buried by the time the Roosevelt family took up residence.

Edith suffered from neuralgia as well as recurring pregnancies during the Roosevelts' first Washington years. Alice and her brother, Ted, Jr., were often left to entertain themselves. Between the time they finished school work with their tutors and met their father on his walks back from work at Farragut Square, the youngsters had hours to explore Washington's new parks. They roamed the city's open space as freely as they did the acreage of Sagamore Hill. Had Auntie Bye been in Washington, she undoubtedly would have filled a void in Alice's and her brother's daily lives, but Bye had gone to Paris to help Eleanor's mother.

While Teddy's political star began to shine, his brother's life continued to deteriorate. Elliot was becoming an embarrassment to his family. He sank deeper into depression over his failures. Jealousy consumed him along with self-pity and remorse. He made false accusations about Anna and spent long periods apart from his wife and children. Anna felt abandoned.

She decided they needed to travel again to break Elliot's destructive cycle. The family left for Germany and Italy with Eleanor and Elliot, Jr. in tow during the summer of 1890. Eleanor happily recalled riding with her father in the Venice canals where he sang like a gondolier. Nearly six, she also remembered the stinging humiliation her father heaped on her when she was too afraid to ride her donkey down a steep slope in Sorrento.

Like cousin Alice, Eleanor was brought up to revere physical courage. Both girls' fathers forced unrealistic athletic expectations upon them. While Eleanor struggled to accept the disillusionment she caused her father over the donkey incident, Alice suffered similar physical humiliation. After serving long days on the Civil Service commission, Teddy would take his children on endurance adventures called "scrambles." The goal was to execute point-to-point walks in a straight line, regardless of what was in the way, be it trees, cliffs or water. For Alice, a self-described physical coward, who felt heavy, awkward and timorous, the events were an odious, arduous trial. Teddy's scrambles were distinctly different from the unchaperoned romps Alice enjoyed with her brother Ted, Jr. through Washington's parks.

Eleanor's mother became pregnant again during the family's European trip. Anna set up residence in Neilly, just outside of Paris, with

16 Alice and Eleanor

her two children while Elliot entered a sanitarium in Graz, Austria. Auntie Bye came to await the new baby's birth with Anna, but Eleanor was sent to a convent school in Paris. She felt like she was being punished, banished as her father had been. On the ride to the convent, Anna looked carefully at Eleanor. With her characteristic insensitivity, Anna told her daughter that since she was not pretty, there was nothing for her to be in life except good.

Eleanor, exiled in misery at the convent, failed to be good. She so desperately craved attention that she claimed she swallowed a penny as another girl had actually done. For her lie, she was sent home in disgrace.

While Eleanor's family stayed in Europe, trouble began brewing back in the States between Elliot and his siblings. A scandal surfaced in which Elliot was accused of fathering a child by the family maid, Katy Mann. Despite his brother's protests to the contrary, after reviewing her testimony, Teddy believed Katy's story.

Eleanor's second brother, Hall, was born on June 2, 1891. Bye sailed home with Anna and her three children, but Teddy insisted that Elliot remain and be institutionalized at *Chateau Suresnes* near Paris. Isolated from his family, Elliot began an affair with Florence Bagley Sherman. Teddy advised Anna to divorce his brother, but she refused. As painful as her husband's ordeal was, Anna believed Elliot would be cured.

Anna settled her family on East 61st Street and Madison Ave. in New York. As her emotional distress increased, Anna suffered from severe headaches. Eleanor recalled rubbing her mother's head to soothe the pain. She craved her mother's approval, yet at the same time, Eleanor blamed Anna for her father's exile. She was unaware of the role Uncle Ted played in keeping her father away from the family. Had Eleanor realized that her mother was protecting her father, they might have provided each other with the mutual support they both needed.

Instead, they were antagonists. Eleanor sulked and pouted. She was spiteful and threw tantrums in public. She did things that her mother expressly forbade, like putting sugar on her cereal, stealing candy by the bagful from the pantry and sobbing wildly when her mother tried to take her to children's parties. The trials that mother and daughter endured foreshadowed the impending battle between Teddy and his brother.

In January 1892, Teddy went to Paris to confront Elliot. He browbeat his brother for days, finally securing an agreement in which two-thirds of Elliot's property was assigned to a trust for his family. Elliot also agreed to spend a year in an alcohol treatment center at the Keeley Center in Dwight, Illinois. Teddy demanded a harsh, final stipulation—a two- to three-year probationary period before Elliot would be allowed to rejoin his family. During that time, he would have to prove himself worthy by performing meaningful work. After the confrontation with Teddy, Florence Bagley Sherman, Elliot's mistress in Paris, described her lover as a beaten man. He desperately wanted to prove himself to his family, but he was helpless to fight.

The volatile family situation impacted Eleanor's early education in a manner quite different from Alice's. Given the chaos of Eleanor's early childhood, travel for her father's health, her mother's pregnancies and emotional distress, as well as the humiliating experience of being expelled from the Paris convent, Eleanor's education was severely lacking. She was still not reading by the time she was seven. Maggie Ludlow, a great aunt, was appalled to discover Eleanor's neglected education. She upbraided Anna severely and sent her Alsatian nurse, Madeline, to tutor her great niece.

Madeline terrorized Eleanor for years. She pulled the young girl's hair for minor infractions and berated her unmercifully. Eleanor never mentioned the horrors Madeline inflicted on her until she was 14 years old. Her desire for acceptance and approval were more important than her personal fear of the nurse. If Alice had been subjected to such treatment, she undoubtedly would have howled bloody murder.

In contrast, Alice learned to read early, bragging that she had completed the Bible twice through by the time she was 12. Since her stepmother was a devout Episcopalian, who prayed and read the Bible daily, Alice received a Bible at an early age. She was instructed to read a chapter a day until she had finished it. Alice read at night by candlelight, plowing through more than one chapter of the Bible and numerous books. It became a matter of pride to see how much she could read. Reading became a lifelong habit.

While Anna awaited Elliot's recovery, she tried to structure a normal life for her family in New York. She read regularly to her children. Eleanor sat politely, but never with the rapt attention she had shown when her father read from Dickens' *The Old Curiosity Shop*, or Longfellow's *Hiawatha*.

18 Alice and Eleanor

Alice, too, was enthralled with the ballads her father belted out, like Longfellow's *Saga of King Olaf*, the *Nibelungenlied*, or Kipling's poems and Civil War stories. Like Eleanor, she was less attentive when her "mother" read to her. Edith chose Bible stories, Sir Walter Scott's poetry and Maria Edgeworth's tales. Both Alice and Eleanor developed an early love of poetry from their fathers. Alice could read a poem once and repeat it entirely.[3]

During the fall of 1892, Anna turned part of the upstairs of her home on East 61st into a schoolroom for Eleanor and several other girls. She hired Frederic Roser, a British-style headmaster, to instruct them. Eleanor's first days of school compounded the agony she felt in her family life. She was frozen with shyness and paralyzed by her mother's presence in class. Eleanor humiliated Anna when she stood in front of the class and couldn't, or wouldn't, spell any words she actually knew.

The recession of 1891-92 hit with devastating repercussions to both brothers' finances. Elliot reacted by resuming his unjust accusations against Anna. Teddy, Bye and Corinne began proceedings to have their brother declared unfit. They wanted to make sure that Elliot's children were cared for financially. When the hearings became public, the family was split over whether to continue their joint course of action. For propriety's sake, TR dropped the suit.

After a year of treatment at the Keeley Center, Elliot began working in Abington, West Virginia. His brother-in-law, Dave Robinson, Corinne's husband, had hired Elliot to scout and settle a vast, speculative mining tract he owned. The distance kept Elliot's visits with his children few and far between, but he wrote devotedly to Eleanor.

In the winter of 1892, Anna needed an operation. She wouldn't allow Elliot to be with her, though he begged to see her and promised to stay on his best behavior. Following the surgery, she contracted diphtheria and died on December 7. Neither eight-year-old Eleanor nor her father had an opportunity to resolve their conflicts with Anna. Neither could win her approval by proving themselves. Anna's death symbolized a cruel abandonment.

For Eleanor, her mother's death meant that her father would return. However, Elliot fell apart. He had been driven to prove himself in order to return to the family fold. With Anna gone, he collapsed back into his self-destructive lifestyle. Eleanor and her brothers were sent to live with Grandmother Hall at the family home in Tivoli.

Elliot visited infrequently and though his arrival generally went unannounced, Eleanor would hear her father's voice as soon as he entered the Hall house. She would slide down the banister into his arms before he had time to hang up his hat. At age eight, Eleanor was so eager to please her father, she memorized a Longfellow poem as a surprise for one of his upcoming visits.

Though Elliot's visits could be filled with delight and presents, they could also be harrowing or humiliating experiences. Once he drove the children in a terrifying, reckless ride through Central Park in a hansom carriage. On another occasion, Elliot took Eleanor to the Knickerbocker Club and left her standing outside with his dogs for six hours.

During his long absences, Elliot continued writing Eleanor long, fanciful letters which she reread frequently. She too wrote diligently, signing her letters with the pet name he had given her, Little Nell. Eleanor would wander in the gardens of Tivoli, daydreaming of the time she would make a home for her brothers and her father. They would travel together, just as he promised in his writing. Though Anna had been the world to Elliot, now their family consisted of just Eleanor and his sons. Elliot wrote that he and Eleanor must stay very close together since the boys were so young.

Unfortunately, Eleanor's family tragedy did not end with Anna's death. The following year, Elliot, Jr. and Hall contracted scarlet fever. Hall recovered without complications, but Elliot, Jr. developed diphtheria and died. His son's death plunged Elliot into deep despondency. He spent weeks drinking and taking stimulants. On August 14, 1894, her father's tragic life ended. Elliot leapt out of a parlor window, experienced a convulsive attack, fell and died.

Bye, Corinne and Teddy were all terribly distraught. According to Corinne, Teddy "cried like a little child for a long time." While she recognized Elliot's death was for the best, in her heart, Corinne felt "desperately sad." Her brother's past excesses could not erase the boy they had loved. Just shy of her tenth birthday, Eleanor sobbed herself to sleep that night. Her grandmother did not permit Eleanor to attend her father's funeral, denying her a final goodbye.

Eleanor and Hall went to live permanently with their grandmother, aunts and uncles. Though strict, the next six years of Eleanor's and her brother Hall's lives had the order, permanence and regularity absent from their previous years. It was the first time the children belonged in a stable family home.

The solitary hours at her grandmother's gave Eleanor an opportunity to heal from the emotional storms of her early years. It also offered her the freedom to fantasize about her father, idealizing him as Alice had done to her deceased mother. Eleanor reread Elliot's letters over and over, determined to prove herself worthy of his devotion. She would strive to live up to his expectations. She would pursue a life of discipline and love. She would be noble, studious, brave and loyal. She would remember always to be unselfish, generous, tender and cheerful.

Chapter Three

"Eleanor darling!" Uncle Teddy cried, pouncing on his niece with such a vigorous bear hug that he tore the gathers from her dress and the buttonholes from her petticoat.[1] "Where has your grandmother been hiding you?"

Eleanor's face flushed as she struggled to conceal her exposed petticoat. Alice nudged Ted, Jr., both grimacing to hold back their giggles.

"Why, you're as skinny as a coyote in the Badlands. Don't they feed you in Tivoli? Well, never mind. We'll fatten you up. Simple, coarse food and plenty of it,"[2] he laughed, "plus ice cream and lemonade, and lots of exercise. What do you say to that?"

Eleanor looked timidly around at her cousins, finally letting her eyes rest on her aunt, Edith. "It's so nice of you to invite me for the weekend. I hope I won't be too much trouble."

"I thought we're going swimming?" Ted, Jr. shouted impatiently.

"An absolutely perfect day for a race down Cooper's Bluff!" his father laughed. "Alice, take Eleanor up to your room so she can change. Be back in five minutes."

Alice's sharp blue eyes met Eleanor's soft gray ones. Without saying a word, she led her cousin to her room, the smallest one on the second floor. Before leaving, Alice reminded Eleanor, "Five minutes. Father doesn't like to be kept waiting."

Eleanor descended a few minutes later to find her uncle roaring about on all fours to the delightful squeals of his children. They dodged and weaved to escape his grasping paws. He stopped as soon as his niece appeared.

"Cooper's Bluff," he ordered, leading the charge out of the house.

As she peered down the steep, 200-foot sandbank at the end of Cove Neck, terror seized Eleanor. Teddy gave each child a hand to hold, then led the charge down the bank. Kermit came first, dragging Ted, Jr., then Eleanor and Alice behind him.

"Don't let go!" Teddy called.

22   Alice and Eleanor

Too ashamed to protest, Eleanor went along. Edith, pregnant again with Archie, had to restrain her toddler, Ethel, from chasing the line of screaming children.

Once launched, the children's flying legs and arms blurred with the sand churning under their feet. They tumbled down to the water in a giggling, sputtering heap.

"Stagecoach on the raft—everybody in!" Teddy bellowed, grabbing Kermit under his arm. He raced into the water and tossed his son off the raft. Kermit squealed in mid-air and came splashing back to shore, beaming from ear to ear.

"Ted, you're the whip...Kermit, the coachman...Eleanor, the lead horse, and Alice, the horn. When I say your name in the story, jump in the water and scramble back out. If I say 'stagecoach,' everybody jumps in!"

Later that night, Edith wrote a letter to Bye concerning Eleanor. "Poor little soul, she is very plain. Her mouth and teeth seem to have no future. But the ugly duckling may turn out to be a swan."[3]

Edith's words became prophetic.

Rebellious and Diligent Youths

During their early Washington years, Edith described Alice as a "quiet and mousey person." Alice saw herself as rather chunky, cowardly and lethargic, the slow-witted audience to her younger brother, Ted, Jr., Eleanor viewed her cousin Alice as more competent socially and more skilled athletically than herself, yet Edith's descriptions were closer to the two girls' view of themselves. However, as adolescence approached, any likeness between the "ugly duckling" and the "mousey person" rapidly diverged.

Teddy Roosevelt's political star was rising in the 1890s, but his money problems had not ceased. Even though Washington D.C. was a small town, the expense of renting a house strained his family's fragile budget. Consequently, every summer, the family returned to Sagamore Hill, taking in daily walks to Oyster Bay, running obstacle courses, riding and reading.

Alice spent the lazy summer days engaged in fantasy play. Neither she nor Eleanor had many peer companions. Their brothers were their primary playmates. Both girls now read extensively. From their own accounts, Alice and Eleanor's preadolescent days were rich with enviable childhood distractions, despite their turbulent early years. Eleanor wrote of sliding down the moss-covered roof of the ice house, getting her petticoat stained with grass. Alice frolicked in the orchard, garden and with the family's numerous animals. She transformed herself from one of Cinderella's mice into a prince or a princess riding astride the mythical horse, Pegasus, who encircled the sun. She declared the family orchard her own and made her siblings climb trees and pick fruit for her as their dues.

Alice felt increasingly displaced as Edith's brood grew and her stepmother's health deteriorated. She developed a thick-skinned, defiant attitude in response to Edith's emotional coldness. She was unwilling to be pitied as the poor child who had lost her mother. In addition to problems with her stepmother, Alice was convinced that her father showed more warmth to her cousin Eleanor than he did to her.

Though Teddy felt particularly protective of his brother's children, Grandmother Hall limited Eleanor and her brother, Hall's, visits with the Oyster Bay Roosevelts. She thought Teddy's family was too wild and rambunctious. She was fearful of losing control of her grandchildren, as she had with her own children. Mrs. Hall discouraged a friendship between Alice and Eleanor, as did Edith, albeit for different reasons.

Edith, the daughter of an alcoholic, was particularly embittered towards Elliot. During his life, she feared that his scandals would taint Teddy and, like the popular Social Darwinists of the day, she was determined to protect Alice from any bad blood that might have infected his daughter, Eleanor. Alert to Edith's indifference of her cousin and aware of her father's favoritism, Alice remained aloof during Eleanor's infrequent visits. Not surprisingly, Eleanor experienced Alice as distant and impersonal.

In contrast to her home life, Alice cherished her semiannual visits to her grandparents in Boston. She happily looked forward to staying with the Lees, but she exploded in tears as the time approached for her to return to her father's house. Alice inevitably spent her first night back in her Roosevelt bed crying herself to sleep. In Washington, Alice developed her first real sense of permanent belonging and lifelong roots.

Eleanor settled her first permanent roots at Grandmother Hall's home on 37th Street in Manhattan and at their summer home in Tivoli on the Hudson River. After her mother's death, Eleanor continued her lessons with Mr. Roser. Classes met in the homes of the other girls instead of her mother's upstairs classroom. Eleanor's attitude towards school improved markedly. She developed a desire to succeed. She worked diligently, mastering long division because her father's letters had encouraged her to study. She set high standards for herself, striving to earn acceptance, and therefore, her worthiness, through learning. Eleanor's classmates recognized her achievements and her budding leadership qualities.

In addition to her school work, Eleanor studied French daily with Mlle LeClerq, took music lessons and dance lessons. She learned the waltz, two-step and the polka, plus her grandmother enrolled her in ballet lessons. Mrs. Hall believed that her tall, awkward granddaughter would benefit from the training. Eleanor loved ballet.

Although her life was full and busy, Eleanor was a still bereaved and lonely child. During vacations, she spent hours reading and daydreaming, perched unseen in a favorite tree in their orchard at Tivoli. She often missed meals, engulfed in the romantic literature that fueled her fantasy life.

In a letter to Aunt Corinne, Grandmother Hall declared that Eleanor's short life had "so much sorrow crowded into it."[4] Though aware of the grief in her granddaughter's life, Mrs. Hall imposed her own strict regimen. Rules, study and prayer were her remedy, but what Eleanor needed was a nurturing, supportive environment.

Grandmother Hall's grown children continued to live with her. Their lives lacked discipline and direction. Her daughters, Maude, Pussy, and Tissie, flitted from one unhappy love affair to another. Her sons, Eddie and Vallie, suffered from the same lack of direction and addiction to a meaningless life of sports and drinking as had Eleanor's father. As a consequence, Mrs. Hall kept tight reins on her three grandchildren. Among other restrictions, Mrs. Hall insisted that Eleanor wear short, shapeless dresses that hung straight down from her shoulders, along with black stockings, high button shoes and flannel underwear from November until April. While Eleanor's peers wore longer dresses, she was kept in child-like attire. Eleanor only had two dresses in her wardrobe.

Mrs. Hall spent her days in a dark room, in her dark house, mending and reading. She emerged to issue orders and for the twice-daily prayer sessions which began and ended each day. Eleanor rarely had friends come to visit. Her aunts and uncles encouraged Eleanor to play in Central Park with her friends, skating and amassing a collection of childhood grime. However, if Eleanor's alternate dress had not been laundered, she had to wear the dirty one the next day. Eleanor went poorly clothed not for lack of money like the tenement children in lower Manhattan with whom she would later teach, but, rather, due to her grandmother's neglect.

Eleanor's estrangement from her father's relatives during these years magnified her awkwardness at the Robinson family Christmas parties. The rambunctious Oyster Bay Roosevelts attended as well as her Hyde Park Roosevelt relatives, which included cousin Franklin Delano Roosevelt. The other Roosevelt cousins knew each other well for they saw one another frequently. Eleanor's skating or sledding was limited to her infrequent Central Park outings. She was handicapped by weak ankles and danced poorly despite her lessons. She had no contact with boys her own age except at these parties and her inappropriate dresses, while minimally problematic with her girl friends, were more disastrous with her cousins. They made her look like a grownup in a child's clothes. For Eleanor, the holiday visits were more painful than pleasurable.

Alice, by contrast, thoroughly enjoyed Corinne's parties. They made up some of her happiest childhood recollections, second only to her Boston visits. The children played charades, croquet, picnicked, skated, sledded and played a bruising game called "bumps," which was similar to musical chairs. Alice joined in wholeheartedly, as did Aunt Corinne, who cartwheeled and stood on her head better than any child.

Eleanor's transition from an angry, sullen child to a diligent adolescent sharply contrasted with Alice's shift from a follower of her younger brother's schemes to her full-blown adolescent rebellion. The change began about age ten, intensifying fiercely during her teenage years. Alice's childhood ambition was to grow up as fast as possible and have twin babies. Suddenly, she wanted to own a monkey and wear pants. Her behavior became totally unpredictable. She was completely unwilling to do anything unless forced. Rebellion became a pattern of Alice's life, characterized by defying social conventions, and the traditions of her class.

Concurrent with the onset of Alice's defiant behavior, the year 1894 marked the first political decision Teddy made which he clearly regretted. Edith did not want him to run for Mayor of New York and he acquiesced. Finances weighed heavily on her opinion. She was concerned about moving the family back to New York with its high cost of living. TR's Republican party won the Mayor's office and, a year later, Teddy was offered the position of President of the New York City Police Board. He swallowed his pride and regret at not winning the Mayor's seat himself, resigned his job on the Civil Service Commission and accepted the post of Police Board President. Edith found herself struggling on a limited budget in New York anyway, though not as the wife of the Mayor. With Bye in London helping cousin Rosy Roosevelt (Franklin's half brother) raise his family and serving as his official hostess, the family was able to rent her house on Madison Avenue.

Teddy plunged into his new job with characteristic passion, intent on eliminating the graft and corruption endemic to the ward-style politics of Tammany Hall that controlled New York. Alice recalled her fascination with their excursions to the Mulberry Street police headquarters. She and Ted, Jr. were occasionally taken to see the rogue's gallery display of criminals. She found the burglars' tools and murder weapons delightfully gruesome. Wherever she went, Alice kept a constant vigil, watching for escaped or recently released characters. She grew fascinated by the execution stories of Mary, Queen of Scots, and Lady Jane Grey. Alice was certain that some day she, too, would be hung.

During his year heading the Police Board, Teddy entertained his children with humorous anecdotes, his plans for reform and reorganization, as well as tales of police bravery. He did not dwell on his nocturnal visits into the tenements and police stations, but these unannounced trips built his reputation as a rampant reformer of graft and corruption.

To Alice, her father became the knight-errant fighting the dragon. His life embodied the adventures that filled the stories he regaled his children with during their leisure hours together. When he appeared at dinner in an everyday three-piece suit, everyone knew that he was going out to do battle, not only with criminals, but with the "Boss" of New York City, Senator Tom Platt.

Alice might have developed sensitivities to the underclass, as cousin Eleanor later did, had her father shared his experiences in New

York's slums with the pioneer social reformer, Jacob Riis. A writer and photographer, Riis showed Teddy the sharp discrepancy between life on Madison Avenue and Hell's Kitchen. He helped TR understand that crime was bred from hunger and poverty.

During this period of budding rebellion, Alice's piano teacher described her as a girl from another planet. She fought tooth and nail against writing obligatory letters to her father when the family stayed at Sagamore Hill while Teddy worked in the city. In contrast, when Hall was at boarding school at Groton, Eleanor wrote her brother every day. She wanted him to feel he belonged to someone.

Alice continually challenged her stepmother's iron will. As a young child, Alice had learned by one glare from Edith, that certain behaviors would not be tolerated. As the years passed, the strict discipline, without love, sent Alice on a path of defiance. She would do exactly the opposite of what was expected. Their battles of wills intensified. Edith remained unmoved by Alice's repeated cascade of tears. She insisted on discipline at the expense of pleasure, but no discipline was ever successfully imposed to prevent Alice from enjoyable pursuits.

In the spring of 1897, Alice's family returned to Washington from New York. Teddy was rewarded for his work on McKinley's successful 1896 presidential campaign with an appointment as Assistant Secretary of the Navy. Henry Cabot Lodge and Bellamy Storer, old family friends, overcame McKinley's personal objections to Teddy's appointment. TR had been very vocal in his support of Cuba's desire to oust their Spanish colonial ruler. McKinley didn't want war, but Teddy clearly did.

Alice was 13 years old and hell-bent on independence. She was contrary and obstinate about everything in her life. Her behavior epitomized a fiery adolescent rebellion. Unlike Eleanor, who was earning her self-worth through diligence, Alice marshalled her resources and increased her defiance. Even the school she attended left her disgruntled. It was the only formal education she received in her lifetime.

Alice cultivated friendships with a gang of boys who constantly followed at her heels. She proudly flaunted her membership in their club as the sole girl. They met in the hayloft of a convenient stable. Teddy was stunned when a young fellow came to call for Alice wearing one of his sister's dresses.

28 Alice and Eleanor

Alice grew into a tall, handsome and quintessential tomboy, much to her parents' displeasure. A bicycle, which she received from her Lee grandparents, became her ticket to freedom. Alice recklessly rode from the top of the hill on Connecticut Avenue down to Dupont Circle with her feet up on the handlebars.

Edith warned Alice that she was turning into a guttersnipe, but Alice was oblivious to her parents' criticism. She was enjoying herself, and meant to continue to do so. She was as belligerent as her father and possessed TR's penchant for showing off. Alice was truly her father's heir in this regard.

On the eve of her 14th birthday, 1898, Alice was informed that she was being sent to live with Bye the next day. Her aunt had returned to New York, pregnant for the first and only time. She had shocked the family three years earlier by marrying Commander William Cowles in London. He was the naval attache at the American consulate. A spinster of 40, Bye had met her genial husband, nine years her senior, while she was helping cousin Rosy raise his family.

Alice was stunned by her family's proclamation, for although she loved her aunt dearly, she had made a life for herself in Washington. Her tears and protests went unheeded. Edith was too sick to cope with Alice's wild ways. She had not been well since the birth of their last child, Quentin, in November of the previous year. She suffered from grippe, neuralgia and sciatica. Edith ran a temperature of 101 degrees or higher for a month. A few weeks after Alice was exiled to New York, Edith was operated on for an abdominal abscess.

Bye thought Edith needed a respite from her continual clashes with "the guttersnipe running riot," in order to recover her health. She offered to take Alice in a private conversation with Teddy because she knew Edith disliked outsiders interfering in her private family affairs. Edith consented to the arrangement only after their close friend, Dr. Alexander Lambert, convinced Teddy of the necessity to send Alice to live with Bye.

Bye did not enroll Alice in school. Rather, she set up a schedule of concerts, lectures and reading of books and newspapers for her niece. In addition, Alice was invited to the teas that Bye presided over with worldly guests. A slow transition began to take place, in which Alice metamorphosed from a tomboy into a budding sophisticate.

Chapter Four

"Must I?" Alice pleaded.

"You must," Bye replied firmly. "Mrs. Hall extended the invitation. It would be impolite to refuse."

"Eleanor is such a ninny," pouted Alice.

"She is your cousin. While she may not have the same interests as you or be your best friend, family loyalty requires your cordiality. If you took the time, you might find you have things in common."

Alice rolled her eyes, scrunching up one side of her nose in a well practiced sneer. "Cousin Corinne says the house is grimy and dismal."

"But she goes," Bye replied.

"Her mother makes her," retorted Alice.

"You know very well that my sister does not make her children do anything," smiled Bye.

"Well...it's a horrid house," retorted Alice, "and there's nothing to talk about. Eleanor's so...so...proper. She's not the least bit interested in anything we are. Did you know they eat in silence."[1]

"She's had a difficult life," Bye reminded her.

"Poor thing," Alice mimicked sarcastically.

"Really, Alice." She looked directly at her feisty niece. Alice shrugged her shoulders. "You could try to find something in common with Eleanor. You both love poetry. Share some readings after dinner," Bye suggested.

Alice rolled her eyes with resignation. "Sliding down the banister or a game of bumps would be infinitely more enjoyable."

That evening, Alice dutifully arrived at the Hall's residence on 37th Street. Eleanor welcomed her cousin, self-consciously escorting her into the dining room.

"Not much of a house for playing, is it?" Alice said, glancing around at the unbroken gloom of the dark, ill-kept house.

"It's not a house for children," Eleanor observed. "My aunts and uncles are all grown."

"It's creepy," Alice shuddered. "I can hear the walls shouting, 'Don't do that!' "

"Well, it is my home," replied Eleanor. She looked at her surroundings and sighed. Then she showed Alice to the table. They sat down and ate their meal in silence.

Blossoming Womanhood

The day after Alice arrived in New York to spend the winter and spring of 1897 with Auntie Bye, the *Maine* suspiciously blew up in Havana Harbor. Alice had followed the developments of the drive for Cuban independence with relish. She had listened attentively to her father's pronouncements against the actions of the U.S. government. America should be sending troops, not food, to the starving women and children in refugee camps, Teddy argued. After generations of misrule and anarchy, he advocated overthrowing the Spanish Governor-General Weyler and freeing Cuba's rebel leader, Maximo Gomez.

While McKinley deliberated, Teddy pressed for an American landing on the island. He knew that a war would be cause for building up the U.S. Navy, which was in woeful condition compared to the dominant British Naval Force. He talked non-stop, gesturing violently, arguing to the cigar-smoking President that if he had his way, he would order the whole American navy to Cuba that night.[2]

Undoubtedly, Alice was treated to a few choice conversations about the Cuban situation over tea at Bye's. She conducted her home like a Paris salon, entertaining poets, writers, statesmen and intellectuals alike. Stimulating dialogue over everything from art to politics accompanied tea time. Unable to compete with the extraordinarily rich, Bye catered to taste, not pomp. The example set by her aunt became Alice's desired vocation—to be a witty, *grande dame*. As her life unfolded, Alice succeeded admirably, albeit with her unique twist. She became an unconventional hostess who reveled in creating controversy.

Though Alice and Eleanor saw one another frequently during the winter and spring of 1897, their personality differences had become markedly disparate. Alice's rebellion was being curbed somewhat by Bye's tender loving care, but her demeanor never took on the tone of her cousin's dutiful hard work. Eleanor strove for acceptance under the shelter of Grandmother Hall's umbrella, hardly aware of the events leading up to the war with Spain, an event which profoundly affected cousin Alice's life.

Eleanor's prudishness, illustrated by her conflict with Alice over sex in the Bible, occurred during this period and drew a sharp distinction between herself and Alice. Mrs. Hall's protected environment, plus the chaos and trauma of her parents' deaths, left Eleanor unequipped to engage in the adolescent abandon of her peers. She was appalled when one of her classmates, a preacher's daughter, inked her fingernails or left school unexcused to watch the wedding of the Duke of Marlborough to Consuelo Vanderbilt at St. Thomas' church in the Twombly mansion next door to where their class met.

While Eleanor was toiling dutifully over Dr. Collier's *The Great Events from the Beginning of the Christian Era Till the Present Time*, Alice was reading the Hearst yellow journalistic newspaper, the *Morning Journal*, whose banner headline exhorted the country to "Remember the Maine."

Alice's brother, Ted, Jr., suffered from terrible headaches which worsened at the prospect of his father going to war. He feared being left as the man of the house. Doctor Lambert, the same family friend who talked TR into sending Alice to Bye's, recommended that Ted, Jr. join his sister in New York. He chastised Teddy for pushing his son too hard, potentially towards a nervous breakdown. Dr. Lambert prescribed a regimen of gentle exercise, a balanced diet and a trained nurse under Auntie Bye's supervision. Living with Bye proved helpful to both Alice and her brother. Ted, Jr. recovered, freed from his parents' rigorous demands for achievement, and Alice's obstinacy was curbed.

In 1898, Congress directed the President to demand Spain's withdrawal from Cuba but, before the message was delivered in Madrid, Spain declared war on America. Teddy was ecstatic. He promptly resigned his post to be at the front and redeem his family's honor. He needed to erase the childhood shame he felt when he learned his father had purchased a substitute during the Civil War. The practice was an accepted path for many men of Theodore, Sr.'s social class. To avoid a family conflict with his southern wife, Mittie, Teddy's father paid to have another man fight in his place.

The Secretary of War, Russel Alger, asked Teddy to raise a regiment of volunteer cavalry men to land in Cuba. He proudly accepted. TR's First United States Volunteer Cavalry, nicknamed the Rough

32   Alice and Eleanor

Riders, included polo players, broncobusters, full-blooded Indians and Indian fighters, as well as New York policemen. In New York, Alice and Ted, Jr. cheered Dewey's destruction of the Spanish fleet in Manila Bay. Since Teddy had appointed Dewey to the post, his children claimed the Philippines as their father's own victory. Their voices filled Bye's house with a chant adapted from a hit operetta:

> Unloose the dogs of war
> The enemy will find us unrelenting.
> When our cannons roar,
> The little king of Spain will be repenting.

Teddy visited New York to say goodbye to Alice, Ted, Jr. and his sister, Bye, fully aware that resigning his position also meant severing his political ties. He left his ill wife and six children on May 6, 1898, in order to fulfill his sense of duty. They all knew that he was doing what his conscience dictated. Though the family did not countenance tearful goodbyes, Alice choked up as he kissed them each in turn. She struggled with mixed emotions, knowing that her father was going off like the warrior of his childhood stories. He might return as a hero, or he might not return.

Alice's spirits were buoyed when she returned to Sagamore Hill with Bye and Ted, Jr. Her interest in the occult had grown since her early days in Boston. Alice willed her father's safety and provided Edith with strong emotional support by her unwavering spirit. She always looked on the bright side, while remaining sympathetic to her stepmother's concerns.

The Rough Riders trained in San Antonio, Texas, for a month and then moved on to Tampa, Florida. Teddy had to commandeer a transport ship to take his men across to the island of Cuba. Superior American firepower sank or beached all the Spanish ships that tried to run the blockade of Santiago Harbor. Teddy led the Rough Riders charging up Kettle Hill under enemy fire and became a national hero. He was promoted to Colonel for his heroic battlefield efforts. Spain sued for peace before TR's promotion stripes had time to settle.

The United States victory pushed the country into the role of an imperialist power against McKinley's inclinations. Though the Spanish-American conflict was minor in terms of past and future wars, Spain finally lost any pretense of the military strength it exerted as a colonial power. Teddy Roosevelt was the politician who symbolized America's new status. He had physically led the charge, even though the hill he led his troops up, which became known as San Juan Hill, was merely a gentle slope covered with scrub growth.

Edith and Alice's alliance during Teddy's Rough Rider days was short-lived. They were soon engaged in a battle of their own. Edith informed Alice that she would be enrolled at Miss Spence's boarding school in New York in the upcoming fall term of 1898. The thought filled Alice with dread for she had seen the students marching meekly, two by two down the streets of Manhattan. She ranted, raged and cried, arguing that she would do something to humiliate Edith if her stepmother persisted with the plan.

While Edith and Alice battled over the impending sentence at Miss Spence's, Teddy was fighting a more desperate battle for his men's lives. Malaria and yellow fever became fiercer foes than any Spanish troops he faced. Teddy was convinced that the site of his encampment contributed to the illnesses his men were fighting. He infuriated regular army officers by lobbying to get his camp moved. Finally, his troop was ordered home to Camp Wyckoff at Montauk Point on the eastern tip of Long Island. TR's entire family went to greet him.

As a budding young woman and the Colonel's eldest daughter, Alice became a favorite of the regiment. She hung on the men's every word. The rugged cavalry soldiers were as devoted to her father as she was to them. Impressionable and romantic, Alice fell in love with at least 20 of Teddy's suntanned Rough Riders. They were the embodiment of the adventurers who lived in her father's library. Teddy himself had become the actualized conqueror in his own drama.

In the months that followed, Teddy found that his political career, rather than being ended, had been revitalized. The Republican party boss, Senator Platt, couldn't ignore Teddy's prestige and popularity among rank and file Republicans. They believed he was the only Republican who could win election as Governor of New York. It was the first campaign that Alice was able to see firsthand. She attended a rally for her father in which the crowd was so dense, she was lifted off her feet. She recalled the experience with indescribable excitement.

Teddy was elected New York's Governor in 1898, which resulted in significant changes for the Roosevelt family. From Edith's perspective, their financial problems were finally solved. Teddy received a $10,000 yearly salary, in addition to occupancy of the executive mansion which they moved into on December 30. Though it was a dismal, shabby house with hideous furnishings, it was rent free. The family was not well-to-do enough to bring their own furnishings to liven it up, but they made do, grateful for the large space.

To Alice's great delight, her parents retracted their decision to send her to Miss Spence's at the last minute, even though her uniforms, sheets and towels had been name-tagged. Edith engaged a governess named Miss Gertrude Young, who didn't push Alice very hard. This suited her irreverent student very well. They studied in the breakfast room which was located on the top floor next to the billiard room, looking out a window to the north.

Alice read what she wanted. Her tastes led her to Thomas Huxley, the British biologist, and other post-Darwinists. She began challenging the teachings of the church, which her family attended regularly, claiming Christian dogma was "sheer voo-doo." When the time came for her to be confirmed, Alice refused. She was not rebelling against the family's punishing walks at a five-mile an hour clip in their Sunday best to their father's Dutch Reform Church but, rather, on philosophical grounds.

She dug in her heels, claiming that confirmation went against her grain. Alice expected a monumental battle akin to her boarding school fight, but the big fight never came. Her parents left the decision up to her. She was the only one of their children who was not confirmed. Alice questioned whether she was winning her battle for emancipation, or whether her parents were giving up on her. Ultimately, Alice rejected all religion in favor of magic, myths and archetypes.

In lieu of confirmation, she asked to be let loose in the family library. Her request was granted, but Teddy grilled his daughter every morning over breakfast to relate two things she had learned from her reading the previous day. In her spare time, Alice fantasized about gay society parties, dabbled in magic and got caught up in her father's political career.

For Eleanor, the years between 1894 and 1898 were characterized by the dogged pursuit of achievement. From age ten to 14, her efforts brought her the attention she so ardently craved as a young child but did not receive. Like Alice, she loved poetry and the language of sounds.

Chapter Four 35

She wrote impressive stories and essays filled with intensity. She won medals and acclaim for the poetry she recited and for her dramatic readings. She was fulfilling her father's request to diligently pursue her education.

Eleanor became very attached to her mother's siblings, Aunts Maude, Tissie, and Pussy, as well as her uncles, Eddie and Vallie. While her friends viewed her world as grim, Eleanor's years at Tivoli were a period of emotional sustenance. Her aunts and uncles helped her in sports. Eddie and Vallie, who were superb athletes, spent hours trying to teach her tennis on one of the first lawn tennis courts in the country. They taught her to jump her horse and ride her bike. In the warm months at Tivoli, Eleanor loved rowing down the Hudson to get the mail and paper with Aunt Pussy. She was required to take long walks holding a stick hooked at her elbows, just like her mother and aunts had done.

Though Alice won her fight against attending Miss Spence's boarding school, in 1899 Mrs. Hall decided that Eleanor should leave for Allenswood, a boarding school outside London run by Madame Souvestre. Auntie Bye had attended the same headmistress' school, *Les Ruches*, in Paris. In 1870, the school was forced to close when the Prussians invaded Paris during the Franco-Prussian War. With the help of an ardent English advocate, Lady Strachey, the school was reopened in England as Allenswood. Eleanor's parents had met Madame Souvestre in 1891. It was their wish that Eleanor study at Allenswood, so, at the age of 15, when Alice was rejoining her family in Albany, Eleanor prepared to sail away from her extended family.

Her sheltered existence, dominated by study, was on the verge of great change. Eleanor's self-confidence and her worldly knowledge were about to expand. During her three years at Allenswood, Eleanor learned to think for herself as well as sharpen her social conscience.

She began her schooling in Wimbledon Park outside of London, settling into the rigorous academic life of Allenswood with little knowledge that her Uncle Ted was the most popular Republican governor in a democratic state. She was just as ignorant of the political events that were thrusting Teddy towards the White House. All this would soon be challenged under her Allenswood's headmistress.

Eleanor became the protege of Marie Souvestre, a radical feminist who challenged her students to worthy achievement in realms typically denied to them. Her aim was to make cultivated, worldly women out of her girls. Madame Souvestre promoted questioning, curiosity, and passionate advocacy. She insisted that her young women think for themselves and argue forcefully for their positions. She chastised students who parroted back what they had heard or read and praised independent thinking. The approach was radically different from what Eleanor had learned from her mother and grandmother, who believed that success in society meant conformity.

Politics was a fervent concern of the headmistress. It was not the exclusive purview of men, nor the family history with which Eleanor's grandparents viewed her Uncle Teddy's career. Eleanor had heard a great deal about the sinking of the *Maine* and TR's Rough Riders, recalling the joy and excitement of his return to become New York's Governor. However, the Halls lived outside the political circles of their day and took little interest in public affairs. Politics were discussed within the framework of a family chronicle, not as national events. Uncle Ted's exploits were within the purview of the men, not women.

Not so with Madame Souvestre. The headmistress was an intimate supporter of trade unionists. As the daughter of the highly regarded French philosopher and novelist Emile Souvestre, she was well connected to liberal intellectual circles. Madame was known as a radical free thinker and a passionate humanist, committed to social justice.

Her fervent concern for public affairs and politics was considered dangerous, as was education for women. Patriarchal Victorian society believed a woman's education was the pathway to madness and sterility and women in politics were relegated to providing couches for tired delegates at political conventions. Even with this backdrop, Allenswood thrived under Madame Souvestre's tutelage.

Likewise, Eleanor blossomed during her years at Allenswood. She was conscientious, affectionate and had developed the self-confidence and *savoir faire* necessary for her later years in the public eye. Her ease with the French language thrust her into comfortable conversations with the headmistress. The hours of ballet and posture hikes helped her walk gracefully at her full six-foot height. The leadership qualities recognized by her fellow students at the Roser school found expression at Allenswood. Eleanor eased the transition of new students with her gentleness and eagerness to please.

Among the elite of many countries, Eleanor flourished in

Allenswood's strict environment, occupying a special place among her headmistress's circle. *Totty*, as Eleanor became known, studied history and French with Madame Souvestre and was invited for evenings of poetry reading. She dined across from the headmistress, a ceremonial leadership post at the school.

Their exclusive relationship was attributed to Madame Souvestre's special feeling for Americans, as well as her family ties to Auntie Bye. On a deeper level, both women were deeply attached to their fathers. Corinne Robinson, Auntie Corinne's daughter and a beginning student at Allenswood, saw a motherly relationship between the two. The headmistress recognized that she had a great deal to give to her blossoming young student.

Religion was one area where Madame Souvestre held no sway over Eleanor, other than making her reexamine her beliefs. If Alice had attended Allenswood along with Eleanor, they might have competed for the headmistress' favor. Alice was bright but undisciplined. No young woman got away with less rigorous study, as she herself admitted. Still, Alice epitomized Madame Souvestre's ideal. She was an original thinker. She challenged everything. In addition, they were both atheists. Eleanor was shocked by the position. If her grandmother had suspected such heresy at Allenswood, she would have summoned Eleanor home immediately.

Madame Souvestre's views on religion were not grounded in science. In fact, there was very little emphasis on the subject at Allenswood. Rather, she subscribed to the prevalent anticlerical sentiment in Europe, which argued that right should be done for its own sake. God could not be bothered with the insignificant doings of individuals, nor with rewarding or punishing good or bad behavior. For Alice, dogma and theology didn't mix with the theory of evolution, or myths, archetypes and her interest in the occult.

Given Bye's intimate knowledge of both the headmistress and Alice, she apparently never suggested that Alice attend the London school. In her perceptive wisdom, Bye probably foresaw a clash of wills between this niece and Allenswoods' disciplined environment that would have rivaled the contest between Alice and her father.

At the end of her first year, Eleanor's evaluation reported that she was very satisfactory as a student but that was of small account when compared with "the perfect quality of her soul." Her schoolwork ranged

38 Alice and Eleanor

from good to excellent. She garnered her highest marks in language and literature and recalled one of the proudest moments in her life was making the first team in field hockey. Her selection was not due to athletic ability, but rather, to perseverance and duty, qualities that would have made Uncle Ted very proud.

Historic world events were about to thrust TR and his family onto center stage in American politics. Alice would find herself waiting in the wings to be crowned America's princess. Eleanor would discover not only her own sense of independence and poise, but a strength of character as well.

Chapter Five

"The stories can't be true!" cried Eleanor, pleading for a denial from her grandmother.

"But they are," Mrs. Hall replied firmly. "You must accept it. Elliot ruined my daughter's life. We mustn't let him ruin yours."

Eleanor crumpled into the chair across from her grandmother. The darkness of the room at midday matched her mood. She heard her grandmother's voice through her sobs.

"Control yourself, Eleanor. Blubbering is quite unbecoming for a young lady."

Eleanor dutifully pulled herself together, wiping her eyes. "I want to return to Allenswood."

"It's impossible now. You need a chaperone for the trip and Pussy is quite incapable of going at the moment, as you well know, nor can..."

"I'll hire a deaconess," Eleanor interrupted.

"You'll what?"

"Hire a chaperone, not that I really need one. I'm perfectly capable of making the crossing alone," she replied, pulling herself up to her full height to demonstrate her determination.[1]

While Eleanor made arrangements to cross the Atlantic, amidst the emotional turmoil of coming to terms with the shattered image of her father, her cousin Alice was vacationing in the Adirondack Mountains with her Newport friends.

"Alice, you simply must dance with me," an ardent young man declared approaching her next to the punch bowl.

She drained her cup thirstily, chuckling while she lifted her long auburn hair off her shoulders. "Be a dear and cool my neck, Thomas."

The young man eagerly obeyed, fanning the nape of her neck vigorously. She closed her eyes and sighed.

"This is a heavenly party, don't you think, but it's frightfully hot."

40 Alice and Eleanor

Thomas nodded zealously. The band leader struck his music stand to begin the next number. "You'll have this dance with me," he persisted boldly.

Bobby Goelet passed by, raising a curious eye at the young man attending to Alice. He extended his hand.

"Later, perhaps. I seem to have promised this dance to Bobby," she replied, taking the hand stretched out to her.

As Bobby spun Alice into the middle of the dance floor, she caught a glimpse of Thomas' face. He was crestfallen. She called over her shoulder. "You're a dear to cool me off, though. I won't forget." Thomas' face flushed with hope.

She whispered in Bobby's ear, "You are my knight errant. I am eternally grateful. You saved me from the sweaty clutches of that adolescent boor."

"Where's your compassion? Look at the poor fellow. He's a gentle, earnest, doe-eyed creature whose only fault is that he's in love with you," Bobby teased. "He wants nothing more than half the men in this room who'd like to get you in their grasp."

"I prefer to dance alone," she laughed, "unless I can have a cool, sophisticated partner like you."

Bobby spun her once again. Abruptly the music stopped.

The band leader signalled the crowd for silence. He held a telegraph message in his hand. The solemn look on his face told them he had dreadful news. A pall fell over the ebullient crowd of vacationing youths.

"President McKinley has been shot. He is in critical condition," he announced solemnly.

Shock registered in the faces of the crowd. Hushed whispers began to filter through the artificial silence. Secretive glances darted between Alice and her brother Ted. They affected long faces and furrowed brows. Alice swiftly cocked her head, indicating that they should make their way outside. Once outdoors, they clasped hands joyously and danced a jubilant little jig. Their father was about to become President.[2]

Society Debutantes

The summer after Eleanor's first year at Allenswood coincided with Uncle Ted's Vice Presidential campaign. She had sailed back to New York with Pussy. It turned out to be a desolate period for both Alice

Chapter Five   41

and Eleanor, the only highlight for both girls being separate trips to Bye's new retreat in Farmington, Connecticut. While Alice languished at Sagamore Hill, Eleanor's Aunt Pussy, distraught over a broken love affair, struck out at her niece. She gave voice to Anna's old themes— Eleanor's plainness and lack of desirability. Fortified by a year under Madame Souvestre and her self-assurance intact, Eleanor remained impervious to Pussy's initial attacks.

However, Eleanor's unhappy aunt struck harder. She told Eleanor how her cherished father had ruined her mother's life with his wild ways. He brought grief and shame on the family. Eleanor sought consolation from her grandmother. Unfortunately, she found none. Grandmother Hall confirmed Pussy's account. Eleanor was shattered. She couldn't wait to get back to Allenswood. She took it upon herself to arrange passage for the trip.

The twentieth century dawned with trouble spots brewing around the world. Turmoil punctuated the heated Republican convention as New York sweltered in the summer heat and torrential rains. The Boers were losing against the British in South Africa and the Boxer rebellion commenced in China. The Eiffel Tower dominated the International Exposition in Paris and million-dollar mansions, deemed "cottages," were being erected in Newport, Rhode Island, by society's elite.

During his two-year stint as Governor of New York, from 1898 to 1900, Teddy pushed a tax through the legislature on franchises granted to public service corporations. He ignored the dictates of his party because he felt that corporations making big profits had to pay their fair share of public concerns. Unfortunately, he alienated his party boss, Thomas Platt, in the process. Platt was a loyal servant of big business.

Teddy had decided to run for a second term, but Platt had a different idea. He wanted to shunt the upstart trouble-maker into a dead-end job, the vice-presidency. Edith wholeheartedly supported her husband's run for a second term as Governor. Alice, however, thought Governor-General of the Philippines would be a more exotic post.

Teddy's friend and political mentor, Senator Henry Cabot Lodge, supported Platt. He figured that TR couldn't win re-election without the Republican party behind him. Some speculated that Lodge had his own ambitions for the Presidency and he wanted Teddy out of the way, too.

42 Alice and Eleanor

Teddy Roosevelt found himself boxed into a political corner in 1900. If he didn't accept the nomination as William McKinley's Vice-President, his party would see to it that he never ran for office again. Powerful party leaders, like convention chair Mark Hanna, could not ignore TR's popularity but still considered him a "damned cowboy" and "a madman."

True to her frugal nature, Edith was concerned that as Vice-President, Teddy's salary would be $2000 per year less than as Governor. In addition, the family would have to return to Washington and incur the expense of once again renting a house. The die was cast, however. Teddy Roosevelt was nominated by acclamation. In private, he raged, leaping to his feet. He swung a chair over his head and crashed it to the floor.

While her father stumped the country for the campaign, Alice began conjuring up occult spells for McKinley's demise. She felt her father had been degraded by being forced into the number two spot. Marooned at Sagamore with Edith, she resented not being part of Manhattan's social life. Ted, Jr. had been packed off to Groton like his father. Alice consoled herself by reading about the escapades of society's elite, the Newport 400.

Her only diversion during those solitary months was a visit to Auntie Bye's new home, after Eleanor and Uncle Gracie had visited. The clapboard house at Oldgate predated the Revolution. It had been owned for generations by her husband's family, the Cowles. Eleanor had helped her aunt get the house in order during her visit earlier that summer, transforming it into an English squire's residence.

Bye influenced each girl to grow within her respective domain. Her message to Eleanor was to learn to be content with her role in life. Bye encouraged her niece never to be ashamed of her actions. She should not fear criticism, if she felt satisfied in her own mind that she was doing right, and was unashamed to tell those she loved. Meanwhile, Alice was encouraged to break out from her parents' repressive environment.

Alice and Eleanor shared noble views of their aunt. Alice thought Bye was a brilliant *grande dame*. Though physically crippled with arthritis, people saw only her charm. Alice was certain that had Bye been a man, she would have been president. Eleanor recognized her aunt's executive ability, poise and judgment. Bye was full of animation and always the center of any group. Her home was the meeting place for people from the four corners of the earth. To both young women, Auntie Bye was an inspiration as well as a wise counselor.

Alice experienced sheer joy in her aunt's company. Gaiety, witty conversation and jovial parties filled the rooms when Bye presided over a house, as opposed to her stepmother's solemn austerity. The contrast between her aunt's tenancy at Sagamore Hill compared with Edith's left an indelible mark on Alice. She remembered how much joy filled the family home prior to Teddy's marriage to Edith. More recently, she recalled the tone set by Bye when she stayed with the family during Edith's trip to Texas before Teddy left for Cuba with his Rough Riders.

The Republicans won the election of 1900 with the biggest plurality since Grant's victory in 1872. President McKinley's inauguration at the turn of the century followed tradition. While the President took the oath of office in a glorified public ceremony, the Vice-President was sworn in during an inconspicuous, private ceremony in the Senate Chamber. Teddy was looking forward to a dismal and empty four years. He considered studying law to fill his time.

Alice secretly rejoiced that a hailstorm soaked the crowd, just as the President raised his hand to take the oath of office. She had placed a magic spell on McKinley. It would not be the last hex she placed on a resident of the White House. To others, the President may have been saintly. To Alice, he was an overweight, unhealthy figure of derision. She observed the cabinet officials, their families, their manners and their dress with devouring eyes during dinner and at the following inaugural ball. She unconsciously perched herself on the arm of Mrs. McKinley's chair. No one in Washington possessed the glitter and glamour of Alice's new society friends, the Newport 400, except for Helen and Alice Hay. Secretary of State John Hay's daughters wore old gowns to the Inaugural Ball. Their statement signalled to the impressionable Alice that the ball was not a novelty for which one put oneself out.

The Roosevelt family's concerns in moving back to Washington were not limited to the expenses involved in finding a house they could afford. They had to find one that could accommodate Alice's "coming out." Like every girl of her station in society at the age of 18, Alice would soon be brought out as a society debutante. In New York, the well-trodden debutante trail started with the horse show at Madison Square Garden and climaxed at the Assembly Ball at the Waldorf Astoria. However, the Roosevelts were in Washington. Arrangements

44 Alice and Eleanor

were made to rent the home of their friends, the Bellamy Storers, the following winter. Meanwhile, Edith took the children back to New York.

Alice's budding freedom extended throughout the summer days at Sagamore. She invited friends, visited them and lived gaily. She danced until all hours at the Seawanaka Yacht Club across Oyster Bay. She took up smoking, rejecting the Victorian code of ethics her parents epitomized. Alice spent time with her cousin Helen, Uncle Rosy's daughter, in the Adirondacks, as well as with the Robert Pruyns. As the summer wound to a close, the family congregated in Roosevelt Hospital. Alice had a bone abscess on her jaw that needed operating and Quentin had an ear infection.

Eleanor's fledgling independence and self-assurance were bolstered on her return to Allenswood that fall. The following spring of 1901, Madame Souvestre took her 17-year-old protege on a trip to Europe. Eleanor was responsible for arranging the logistics of the trip, which proved a valuable, as well as immensely enjoyable, learning experience. She developed enough confidence to free herself of the fears that had gripped her during her entire life.

When the Pan-American Exposition opened in Buffalo, New York, the task of performing the official opening fell to the new Vice-President. Teddy asked Alice to accompany Edith and him. She was delighted, viewing the invitation as a sign that her parents now considered her an adult. While her excitement at viewing the exhibits with the French ambassador was genuine, it reflected her newly accepted independence.

On President's Day, September 5, 1901, at the Buffalo Exhibit, Mrs. McKinley, a frail woman who suffered from epilepsy, fainted from the 21-gun salute. The following afternoon the President greeted thousands of citizens waiting in a receiving line at the Temple of Music. Leon Czolgosz inched his way up, his right hand bandaged with a handkerchief. When he reached McKinley, he stuck a revolver into the President's side and fired twice.

McKinley hung on for a week while Alice continued to party with her socialite friends at "camp," a mountain retreat more akin to Newport's million dollar "cottages" than anything her father would have considered camping. She ardently pursued such experiences which subsequently characterized her narcissistic debutante years.

Chapter Five 45

When word finally arrived that the President had died, Alice assumed a distant, uncaring mood. Years later she admitted to feeling "utter rapture" at the news of McKinley's death. To her friends, Alice feigned boredom at the prospect of living in the White House with her father as President. She acknowledged feeling simultaneously resentful, defiant and shy about moving to Washington. Alice's aloofness remained, even when the possibility was raised that her debut could be held in the White House. Alice didn't write to her father after the news of McKinley's death, nor did she see him for several weeks.

Another serious rift had developed between Alice and her parents at the time TR became President. The latest tiff centered on her parents desire to send Alice to the Cathedral School in Washington. She was adamantly opposed to the idea. Alice built a wall around herself, emotionally rejecting her parents before they could reject her. She stayed off and on with Auntie Bye at Oldgate through September and October. The first time she saw her father after he became President was at Bye's. He stopped in on his way to New Haven. Teddy invited Alice to accompany him for the Yale Bi-centennial Celebration. Though her father was as buoyant and zestful as always, unburdened by his high office, the enthusiastic crowds that met him made a strong impression on her. This man, with whom she had viciously locked horns and battled, was the President of the United States.

Alice's only memory of her father's speech in New Haven was sitting next to Mark Twain. He was bedecked in his customary white suit. They travelled back to Washington by rail in a private car, an unaccustomed treat for her. Even a solipsist like Alice, for whom existence resided solely in the self, couldn't help being overwhelmed by the enthusiasm and immense importance of having a father who was President.

Edith encouraged Alice to join the family after spending her customary Thanksgiving in Boston with the Lees. Alice agreed after the Cathedral School idea was dropped and she was promised her "coming out" party in the White House. The possibilities for her future shone bright. Wisely, her parents enlisted Alice's help in getting their musty, gloomy, new residence redecorated. They sat her beside the current Speaker of the House, "Uncle Joe" Cannon. Alice relished her role that evening. She was to convince Uncle Joe to use his considerable influence in allocating funds to replace the mustard-colored carpet in the East Room with a hardwood floor.

The years Alice spent observing her Auntie Bye's and Auntie Corinne's conversational style paid off. Corinne would engagingly put her elbow almost in the soup of a dinner partner, while Bye charmed her companions with the consuming line, "Do tell me all about yourself." Alice adopted both styles in playing up to Cannon. She succeeded in getting his consent. However, the money wasn't appropriated through Congress quickly enough to have the floor installed before her debut.

On the evening of January 3, 1902, the Marine Corps Band, in full dress uniforms of sky-blue tunics with scarlet stripes running down their trouser legs, gave the signal to start the biggest bash since Dolly Madison danced in the East Room. Edith Carow Roosevelt presented Alice to 600 guests. The young debutante, just shy of her 18th birthday, wore a white chiffon dress and carried a bouquet of white roses. After the last guest was greeted, Major Charles L. McCawley, United States Marine Corps (USMC), her father's military aide, led Alice onto the dance floor for the first waltz.

Shortly after midnight, the guests enjoyed a buffet in the State Dining Room. Though convention and her father argued that the party was over, Alice insisted that the band continue playing. The party finally broke up at 2 a.m., after the last waltz to *The Blue Danube*. The newspapers reported that Washington's political old timers complimented Alice's party as being the most successful of memory. Cousin Franklin attended and declared it glorious.

Though Aunt Corinne observed that her niece had the time of her life, Alice only admitted to enjoying herself moderately. She harbored resentment on several counts. Edith had vetoed a formal cotillion dance with its elaborate exchange of partners and expensive favors given by the hostess. With her penchant for austerity and the family's history of money concerns, Edith viewed cotillion favors like brocaded evening bags to be a frivolous waste of money. Her stepmother also refused to serve champagne, a horrid blow to Alice's pride.

The final humiliation was the floor, which she had convinced Uncle Joe she needed. Alice, who loved to dance, found the crash linen floor covering disgraceful. It felt like a sponge and was a perfectly unacceptable surface for waltzes and polkas. Alice claimed that she enjoyed herself far more at sister Ethel's debut in the Blue Room some

Chapter Five   47

years later, even though she felt like a tottering, ancient married woman. At Ethel's coming out party, there were buckets of champagne.

The family was delighted with Alice's success on her initial foray into politics. They would have liked to give her more tasks such as her assignment with Uncle Joe, but Alice preferred to continue her good times. That meant cavorting with her peers and total irresponsibility. Politics would wait until she was a married woman. For the present, she entertained herself by rushing from one amusement to another with the curiosity of a puppy and as little sense of direction. She filled her time taking trains back and forth between Washington and New York, preferring her friends and family in Manhattan. She danced half the night and slept until noon.

Alice has been accused of creating the generation gap of 1901. The press loved her unconventionality. Her personality was every bit as bold as her father's. She moved from a street-wise gamine to a great lady through her wit, intelligence and charm. Her quick tongue responded mischievously and formidably. Gradually, her behavior wore her parents' patience thin.

Alice installed her pet macaw, Eli Yale, in the White House conservatory. She carried her pet snake, Emily Spinach, around her neck. A menagerie of animals accompanied the Roosevelts into the White House, along with stilts, roller-skates and bikes. Once, when Quentin was ill, his brothers and sisters smuggled his pony, Algonquin, into his room. The children played hide and seek, crawled under the tables at official dinners, pinched the guests' knees and begged for food.

Alice often instigated the pranks, preferring to startle people rather than bore them. Such behavior became another of Alice's trademarks. She waltzed in and out of her father's office so frequently that when Owen Wister, author of *The Virginian*, was visiting, he asked Teddy why he didn't control his daughter. TR replied, "I can run the country or I can control Alice, but I can't do both!"

Alice took up smoking, against both Edith's and her father's wishes. Though they couldn't prevent her from this fashionable new habit, they requested that she not smoke under their roof. Alice climbed out the window onto the White House roof where she smoked without disobeying her parents.

She became enamored with the automobile and ordered a four-cylinder touring car for herself. Teddy refused to let her take delivery,

48 Alice and Eleanor

however, withstanding a furious onslaught of tears and pleading. Not even an appeal to her Boston grandparents to buy it for her worked. So, the ever-clever Alice borrowed the car of her new friend Maggie, the Countess Margarite Cassini. Alice took the wheel herself, dispensing with the chauffeur. She scandalized Edith's sensibilities not only by driving to Newport and back alone with Maggie, but by associating with Maggie herself. Rumors abounded that Maggie was the illegitimate daughter of her father, the Russian Count Cassini, and his maid.

Edith was continually appalled when Alice's name appeared in the press. She believed women's names should appear in the paper only for births, marriages and deaths. Alice, however, had become entertainment for the eager public. Her popularity went hand-in-hand with her father's. She inspired cartoons and songs like *Alice, Where Art Thou?* and *Alice Blue Gown*. Her life was covered in minute detail, including her scandalous sightings at the racetrack and with her bookie. Her favorite color, a particular shade of blue-grey, became *Alice Blue*.

The Kaiser of Germany invited Alice to christen his new royal German yacht, the *Meteor*, which was built in New York. He sent his brother, Prince Henry of Prussia, to witness the festivities. The public became enthralled with the notion that the Prince had come to ask for Alice's hand in marriage. Thereafter, she was dubbed Princess Alice.

Alice used her income from the Lees to support her fast-paced lifestyle. However, she couldn't keep pace with her wealthy millionaire friends of the Newport 400. She was continually requesting money from her grandfather, in excess of her allowance. He admonished her for following her friends who had money to burn. Alice would promise to reform but never did. He warned Alice not to let her grandmother know the extent of her extravagances. When Grandmother Lee found out about the car bill which her husband had offered to pay, she put her foot down. She disapproved strongly and was greatly annoyed with Alice.

None of the adults in her life approved of Alice's lifestyle. Not only did her behavior go against Teddy's personal grain, it mocked what he was trying to model for the country. Her sister, Ethel, recalled that the entire family came to consider Alice a hellion. Once she was asked to leave Boston's Copley Plaza Hotel for smoking in the lobby. She was stopped for speeding, regularly bet on the horses and bragged about her winnings.

Chapter Five 49

Alice had become the darling of the media by the time Eleanor returned from Allenswood. She had wanted to spend another year under Madame Souvestre's tutelage, but Grandmother Hall insisted she take her place in the social register. A sensitive conversationalist who spoke with conviction, Eleanor possessed a quiet, sincere and engaging manner. Her persona was diametrically opposed to Alice's.

Eleanor avoided the limelight as ardently as her cousin sought it. While Alice pursued pleasure, Eleanor sought purpose. Alice broke convention for the sheer joy of being unconventional. She delighted in provocative, shocking and scandalous behavior. Eleanor accepted the social conventions of her day, determined to find a role of meaning for herself within its boundaries.

Chapter Six

"Look at Eleanor, standing over there. You can barely see her hiding in the shadows," whispered Alice mockingly as she gaily tossed her hair to the side.

Her partner, cousin Franklin, scanned the distant wall. A lonely girl with long legs, mousey hair and buck teeth stood self-consciously tugging at the ruffled rim of her knee-length dress. While the other girls wore gowns that swept the floor, Eleanor's grandmother insisted she squeeze into a short dress. When the music ended, Aunt Corinne's guests applauded.

Alice leaned over to Franklin."She looks so pathetic. Ask her to dance, FD," she encouraged him. "Everyone should have a good time at these parties. No one should be a wallflower the entire evening."

Franklin smiled. His chiseled good looks and aristocratic build were at Alice's beck and call. He headed obediently across the room towards his other cousin. Eleanor continued fidgeting with her dress, suffering through another of Aunt Corinne's annual Christmas dances.

Alice skittered over to Aunt Corinne, giggling. "Feather Duster's flitting over to dance with Eleanor."

"Alice, must you be so caustic?" her aunt chastised her.

"He still acts like little Lord Fauntleroy," Alice protested. "His mother's made him into a sissy. All fluff and no substance. He'll never amount to anything." Before her aunt could respond, another guest asked Alice for the dance and led her away. She glanced back over her shoulder, winking at her beloved aunt.

Franklin had stopped squarely in front of Eleanor. The music resumed.

"Would you like to dance this one with me, Eleanor?" he asked politely.

Eleanor relaxed, smiling warmly. Her face lit up with charm and gentleness. "Oh, Franklin," she sighed gratefully. "I'd love to!"[1]

Engagement

Eleanor returned to New York at the end of the school year 1902. Almost 18, she spent an isolated summer in Tivoli with her grandmother. The carefree days of study and travel were ended and life's serious nature began to take its place. Her brother, Hall, visited with Uncle Ted's family. Mrs. Hall had relinquished her previous concerns about the boisterous Roosevelts. Perhaps she felt they were more healthy than her own family, for her children were deteriorating rapidly. Both sons were alcoholics. Mrs. Hall strove to keep Vallie in Tivoli with her as much as possible, but he would occasionally bolt to New York for a binge.

When autumn came, Eleanor took up residence at the Hall's 37th Street home with her Aunt Pussy, who was 14 years older. Rather than having a "coming out" party like Alice and the other debutantes of her day, Eleanor's name was merely added to the social register. She began receiving invitations to make the rounds of society lunches, teas, dinners and balls, unaware of what utter agony the experience would be.

She and Pussy gave small lunches and dinners. She met some of her aunt's artist friends, much preferring their informal gatherings than the formal events she attended in the evenings. Eleanor was shamefully aware that she did not live up to her mother's legacy of being the belle of the ball. She found the social schedule trying. During her first winter, the sole object of her life was society and it nearly brought her to a state of nervous collapse.

Pussy was enduring one unhappy romance after another. Eleanor was hardly equipped to handle her uncle Vallie's drunken stupors, particularly in light of what she learned from Pussy about her own father the previous summer. However, the inner strength and self-confidence Eleanor developed during her years at Allenswood helped her cope.

She corresponded regularly with Madame Souvestre, the person who exerted the most positive influence on her life since her father. She sought out her mentor's counsel, drawing strength from her wisdom. Madame's words were timely and appropriate, but hard to follow. "Protect yourself...Give some of your energy, but not all, to worldly pleasures which are going to beckon you. And even when success comes, as I am sure it will, bear in mind that there are more quiet and enviable joys than to be among the most sought-after women at the ball..."

52 Alice and Eleanor

In addition, Eleanor took over the parental role relinquished by her grandmother for her brother Hall. While they saw him off to school together at Groton, Eleanor visited him alone on parents' weekends thereafter and wrote to him daily.

In November of 1902, Eleanor joined many of her Roosevelt relatives at the Madison Square Gardens' Horse Show, the kickoff event for New York society's social season. Her cousin, Franklin, also attended. During the following summer and autumn, they attended many of the same social events. Franklin began to seek out Eleanor's company. Though their fondness for each other was evident to those around them, Franklin did not inform his overprotective and overdependent mother, Sara Delano Roosevelt, of his budding romantic interest in his cousin.

The social season of 1903 was not the agonizing experience the previous year had been for Eleanor. She was appreciated for her conversational ability. She often found herself seated across from the party's host, a position she was accustomed to after her years at Allenswood. Her wide-ranging knowledge made her seem more like 25 than merely 18.

Eleanor and Franklin made a striking couple at parties. He was as tall as the willowy, lithe and elegant companion he pursued. They enjoyed dancing, conversation and reading poetry together, and they made one another laugh. He was charming, enthusiastic, attentive and complimentary, qualities she cherished in her father. He made her feel hopeful. She inspired him. Franklin referred to "E" as an angel in his diary. He found her eyes and hair particularly lovely. More importantly, they shared many interests and dreams.

The headmaster at Groton influenced Franklin in a manner similar to Madame Souvestre's on Eleanor, however, they came from different perspectives. Endicott Peabody believed he was instilling the old-stock Anglo-Saxon Protestants with the character which would make them capable and worthy to serve as America's ruling class. He preached the values of preserving the public order through politics and public service. Franklin's mother found such ideas abhorrent. She wanted her son to lead the life of a country squire, like his father. Yet Eleanor, whose headmistress advocated change to improve the lot of the underclass, reinforced Franklin's idealism. In addition, they both held unabashed enthusiasm for their relative, Teddy Roosevelt. Franklin's brand of politics eventually blended the vision of both his and Eleanor's mentors,

Chapter Six 53

as well as extending the legacy Teddy Roosevelt began.

Eleanor's most gratifying hours during her second social season in New York centered around the volunteer work she did for the Junior League. There she was able to put her idealism and Madame Souvestre's training to practical use. Though the country was brimming with the youthful exuberance epitomized by her Uncle Ted, the President, it was also severely divided between the rich and the poor. Emigrants poured into New York City from Eastern Europe by the thousands. Most lived in cramped tenements on the Lower East Side.

The women's rights movement had made great strides since it was launched by Elizabeth Cady Stanton in 1848. Charlotte Perkins Gilman had called on women to seek economic independence and to use their economic power for social reform. Several debutantes enrolled at Barnard to study sociology and economics after hearing Professor Vida Scudder of Wellesley summon them to staff the settlement houses. The Junior League exemplified how several well-born women were breaking out of their traditional roles. Launched by Mary Harriman and Natalie Henderson, the primary purpose of the League was to provide the settlement houses with such services as enrichment classes.

Eleanor began volunteering at the Rivington Street Settlement house on the Lower East Side. She taught calisthenics and fancy dancing to children while her friend, Jean Reid, daughter of Whitelaw Reid (Ambassador to England), played the piano. Even though Jean took her carriage to Rivington Street, Eleanor always rode public transportation. She wrote Franklin that the hours she spent with the children were the happiest of her day. She admired their spirit and ability to learn and play, despite ten- to 12-hour days working in sweatshops.

Eleanor also joined the Consumer's League that year, headed by Maud Nathan. She investigated working conditions in garment factories and department stores. The Consumer's League fought for better lighting and restroom facilities in these dismal places.

Eleanor's family disapproved of her work, arguing that she ought to spend a carefree summer in idle recreation. That is precisely how Alice spent her time. Teddy continually took his daughter to task for gallivanting with "society" and for not knowing more people like Eleanor. TR greatly admired Eleanor's work and her friends. His chastisements did little to foster a friendship between Alice and Eleanor. Alice reacted indignantly, claiming her "Poor Father" didn't seem to remember that her society friends were the offspring of his own childhood friends.

With Eleanor's work for the Junior and Consumer Leagues, she began a lifetime of work that advanced her uncle's causes and improved the lives of others. Teddy had a penchant for fighting the excesses of the members of his societal birthright, which Alice and her friends pushed to the extreme. While Alice looked back on her coming out years as harmless fun, it is likely that her father felt the same repugnance at Alice's frolics as he had towards his brother Elliot's. The emotional intensity that both Eleanor and Teddy felt for Elliot as father and brother made each shrink from the excesses of Alice's chosen lifestyle. Frivolity and uselessness led to sensuous pleasure at the expense of family and purpose.

Eleanor knew her own inadequacies well enough to realize she could not uphold her mother's reputation as belle of the ball. Yet, she knew she was expected to fulfill her role in the social order. Her volunteer work gave Eleanor's life focus and meaning. Without the strict discipline of an environment like Allenswood, which might have given focus and a purpose to Alice's keen wit and intellect, the President's daughter was never given the opportunity to explore an alternative lifestyle.

Auntie Bye continued to exert her influence on Eleanor, hosting her frequently at her Washington home. Bye's husband had been promoted to admiral and their home became known as the "little White House." When Eleanor visited, she accompanied Bye on her rounds of card-bearing calls. She found the time entertaining, full of wit and *savoir-faire*. The dinners were exciting and the luncheons and teas filled with important, charming people. Alice came to detest such card-calling nonsense; however, it gave Eleanor her first taste of politics. Through her aunt's influence, Eleanor grew fascinated with politics. She began to see how, even without the vote, women could be very influential and powerful.

During their courtship, Eleanor encouraged Franklin to take his school work and his extracurricular interests more seriously. Her influence contributed to his success running for school office, as well as becoming editor of the student newspaper, *The Harvard Crimson*. Likewise, Franklin supported Eleanor's work at Rivington Street and the classes in sociology she attended. He had never been exposed to the overwhelming poverty he saw when he visited Eleanor at Rivington and then escorted her to one of her student's homes. The impact was powerful and lasting. He simply couldn't believe that "human beings lived that way."

Franklin had grown up a pampered and indulged child. He was the only child of the second marriage between his 52-year-old widower father, James Roosevelt, and Sara Delano, who proudly traced her lineage back to William the Conqueror. Franklin was raised with governesses on a rolling estate of 1300 acres called Springwood and in Europe. He had studied with tutors until he went to Groton.

The young couple kept their love a secret until November 22, 1903, when Franklin proposed. He and Eleanor were visiting her brother, Hall, at Groton over the Thanksgiving holiday. Eleanor accepted and they made plans to see one another the following Sunday. In the interim, Uncle Gracie died. Eleanor had truly loved her uncle and his death cast a pall over her joyous engagement. At the same time, Franklin prepared to do battle with his mother over spending Sunday with his sweetheart, instead of her.

A recent widow dependent on her son, Sara moved to Boston to be near Franklin who was in his junior year at Harvard. When he told his mother about his plans to marry Eleanor, she set to work to separate the couple. They were not only too young, but without the emotional foundations or financial security to run an independent household. Though Franklin was seen by his Groton classmates as a smug, spoiled "mama's boy," he showed remarkable strength of character against his mother's efforts to break up his relationship with Eleanor.

Sara Delano's disapproval had a different effect on Eleanor. Her old feelings of self-doubt and her desire for acceptance resurfaced. She strove to gain Sara's confidence, promising to be a loving, devoted daughter. Franklin and Eleanor eventually won the Sunday battle and spent a well-chaperoned weekend together; Sara, however, extracted a promise from them. They were to keep their engagement secret for one year. In the meantime, she distracted Franklin with a six-week Caribbean cruise scheduled during February and March of 1904.

Though Eleanor's work in the slums left relatives like Cousin Susie scandalized, they hardly compared to the outrageous reports of Alice's carryings-on in the rag sheet that pilloried society, the *Town Topics*. Alice and her friend, Maggie Cassini, were colorful targets. The paper pretended a standard of morality that surpassed Edith Roosevelt's, scolding Alice for smoking and attending an embassy luncheon on Sunday. When it was reported that she had stripped to her chemise and pirouetted on a tabletop at a bacchanalian Newport party, someone finally sued the publishing company.

Whether Maggie and Alice were ever called to task over their real, rather than imagined, effronteries is unknown. They were having the time of their lives, joined by a third cohort, Cissy Patterson. The three were the toast of the town. They turned men's heads with their wit, charm and beauty and turned their admirers pocketbooks into flowing rivers. They shamelessly imposed their caprices on everyone. While Alice and her friends were mocking every known social convention of the time, Eleanor and Franklin were being scrupulously chaperoned on their visits together.

James Hazen Hyde, head of the Equitable Life Assurance Society, gave a costume ball in New York in Alice, Maggie and Cissy's honor, spending $100,000 in lavish preparations. Rather than attend, the girls accepted a last-minute invitation to dine with first-term Congressman Nick Longworth at the exclusive Washington Alibi Club. They sent a last-minute wire to Mr. Hyde. The three young women insulted George Westinghouse in the same manner, leaving his party early after he had built an annex onto his ballroom merely to accommodate their guest list.

It is no wonder that Eleanor wrote Franklin that Alice was crazier than ever. She had seen Alice in Bobby Goelet's auto, "quite alone with three other men. I wonder how you would like my tearing around like that." Franklin may have not felt the same as Eleanor, for he enjoyed flirting, engaging in gossip and scandals with his cousin Alice, no less. He even angered his mother by dallying with several older women on his Caribbean cruise. She would have been delighted had he shown interest in any of the young women his own age.

Though societal mores were ripe for challenging, Eleanor's strict code of ethics left no room for raising eyebrows regarding personal matters. Alice recalled a visit to Auntie Bye's at Oldgate when she and Eleanor went rowing together. Eleanor lectured Alice on the types of presents that were acceptable to receive from a man. Flowers, books and cards were acceptable, but jewelry of any kind was absolutely not. Alice recalled listening to her earnest discourse, all the while fingering a modest string of seed pearls an admirer had given her the week before.

Eleanor may have been prompted to discuss the issue after reading reports that Alice had been given a bracelet by Prince Henry which contained a miniature portrait of Kaiser Wilhelm set in diamonds.

Alice was genuinely pleased when she heard about Eleanor and Franklin's engagement. She wrote, "Oh, *dearest* Eleanor—it is simply too nice to be true; you old fox not to tell me before." On accepting Eleanor's invitation to be one of her bridesmaids, Alice responded, "You are an angel to ask me...I should love to...it will be too much fun."

Alice spent as little time as possible at home, for her parents continued to adamantly disapprove of her escapades. After driving from Newport to Boston with her friend Ella Drexel Paul in a record-breaking six hours, she received a letter from her father that accused Alice of losing all regard and affection for the family. The letter filled her with such rage, Alice promptly burned it.

Teddy and Edith thought foreign travel and more political responsibilities might draw Alice away from her hedonistic crowd, as well as giving her more positive outlets for her intelligence. TR sent her with Elihu Root's daughter, Edith, to New Orleans for Mardi Gras and then on a trip to Cincinnati for Ruth Hanna's wedding. Ruth's father, Mark Hanna, was Teddy's old New York political rival, but he wanted to mend fences before his anticipated renomination for the 1904 election. Hanna died prior to the convention and TR insisted that Alice pay a condolence call on Ruth. It was a shrewd political maneuver which made Ruth a long-term ally of TR's.

Controversy swirled around Alice on the international scene when Queen Victoria died. She was invited as a guest of the U.S. Ambassador, Whitelaw Reid, to the coronation of Edward VII with his daughter, Jean, Eleanor's Rivington Street piano accompanist. However, Alice was not royalty and her father recognized that altering state protocol could create an unnecessary international incident. The ambassador could not add guests to the list of dignitaries invited to Westminster Abbey unless the person was related to a reigning sovereign. Alice was only quasi-royal, even though she carried the affectionate title of princess. Therefore, her father declined Reid's invitation and offered Alice a month's trip to Havana instead. She had no choice but to agree, assuring her father she would do as he wished. Protocol interfered this time, but Alice was not likely to let it become a habit in her life.

With Eleanor engaged and contemplating her aunt and uncle's offer

58 Alice and Eleanor

to have a White House wedding, Alice recognized that she, too, must entertain serious thoughts of marriage. She and Maggie competed for the attentions of Count Charles de Cambrun, a direct descendant of Lafayette, in addition to Nick Longworth, the dapper, bald, 34-year-old first-term congressman from Ohio. Unfortunately for Alice, Phillip was only interested in Maggie. At the time, so was Nick.

The Princess didn't like playing second fiddle, even to an accomplished violinist like Nick. She was quite distraught when Maggie told her Nick had proposed, not once but twice. The first proposal came when she and Nick were walking alone together in Lafayette Park. A jealous Alice, the young woman who made a career of mocking society's mores, lectured Maggie on the impropriety of walking alone with a man at night! Nick proposed a second time when he and Maggie were on a sleigh ride. When Nick climbed down to adjust the horse's harness, he demanded an answer from the Russian countess. Her response left the field clear for Alice to pursue Nick. Maggie had grabbed the reins and slapped them down on the back of the horse, leaving Nick standing forlornly in the snow.

International events were also conspiring to eliminate Maggie from contention. The Japanese and the Russians were at war over Russian expansion into Manchuria. The czarist government wanted American support to get rid of the "Yellow Peril," but the President's leanings were with Japan. Maggie's father, the Russian ambassador, had encouraged his daughter's friendship with Alice, in the hopes it would gain him a favorable ear to the President. Nothing of the kind occurred. Teddy thought Nicholas II, the Russian Czar, was an absolute despot, and his ambassador, Maggie's father, the Grand Duke Boris, a pompous fool.

Edith even refused to accept the womanizing ambassador in her home. His presence would be an insult to morality. With the Duke's government in trouble at home, sustaining heavy losses against the Japanese, Maggie was sent back to St. Petersburg, accompanied by her 17 trunks and her maid. President Theodore Roosevelt set in motion a plan to arbitrate a settlement between the two belligerents, an effort that ultimately earned him the Nobel Peace Prize in 1906.

Nationally, another crisis was brewing. While TR toured New England and the Midwest in preparation for his 1904 presidential bid, he denounced trusts and the predatory rich, whose wealth grew at the nation's expense. He used the Sherman Antitrust Act to end a strike organized by the United Mineworkers Union. In a bold and unprecedented move, the President was determined to settle the strike himself. He brought the huge railroad conglomerates together with John Mitchell, the young union leader. Meanwhile, he represented the interests of the American people, the voiceless victims of the strike who needed coal to heat their homes. Teddy's efforts were successful. J.P. Morgan agreed to the creation of an impartial commission which would investigate workers' conditions in the minefields.

The press speculated constantly over Alice's potential mates and she denied none of the rumors. Though the public preferred a titled match, Nick Longworth suited Alice's father perfectly. He had no patience for the modern title pandering that many Americans sought. Nick was an Ohio congressman who had worked his way through the state legislature before coming to Washington. Heir to his family's fortune in Ohio real estate, and 15 years Alice's senior, he seemed a confirmed bachelor.

Nick loved playing poker, drinking and womanizing, as much as he loved playing the violin, a skill at which he had attained professional competence. He had been a Harvard man and a member of the Porcellian club, an exclusive honor that had eluded Franklin.[2] In addition, Nick was a protege of TR's friend and future hand-picked successor, William Howard Taft. Alice was drawn to Nick's ironic wit and sense of fun. He had a talent for improvising verse like Aunt Corinne. They didn't share Nick's interest in classical music. At the time, Alice's level of music appreciation consisted of waltzes and marching bands.

Alice had spent the summer of 1904 casting witches' spells of good fortune in the hope that her father would break the tradition of men who had assumed the office of President but were not re-elected for a second term. Any worries the family had were put to rest on Election Day that fall. TR won by a landslide, the most popular president since Abraham Lincoln. That night, however, he doomed his own political career by handing a statement to the press declaring he would not be a candidate again, or accept another nomination.

On Inauguration Day, Alice posed on the reviewing stand with her father. She stood, waving to greet people she recognized in the crowd. Her father chided her severely to sit down. This was his inauguration, not hers. Their battle over who controlled the limelight was continuing.

60 Alice and Eleanor

Eleanor and Franklin joined the family as guests on the inaugural review stand. They witnessed Uncle Ted's speech in which he expressed his famous line, "All I ask is a square deal for every man." What inspiration that event held for Franklin's political future remains speculation, however, he was an unabashed supporter of cousin Ted. Though born and bred a Democrat, Franklin crossed over to vote for Teddy in the 1904 election. The favor was never returned by the Oyster Bay Roosevelts when Franklin, the Hyde Parker, ran for office.

Along with some 200 other guests, Eleanor and Franklin participated in a sit-down luncheon at the White House and attended the Inaugural Ball. They stayed with Auntie Bye during their visit. Eleanor took advantage of the time to ask Bye for advice on how to deal with her future mother-in-law. Franklin's mother, Sara, was not only intrusive and demanding, but also opinionated, manipulative and overbearing.

Alice was less interested in her father's big moment than she was in making mischief. Nick Longworth had been re-elected for his second term in Congress. Alice engaged a friend, Bertie Goelet, to help design fake historic markers for the many guests who had come to Washington for the inauguration. Bertie backed out at the last minute and refused to help her hang signs around town. She only managed to place one, strategically below Nick's window. It read, "I live here—Nicholas Longworth." Alice successfully maneuvered Nick directly over the sign. He didn't have a clue why the carriages rolling past were roaring with laughter.

Mrs. Longworth found Alice's behavior disrespectful, especially her shameless flirting. Nick's mother would have to get used to such outrageous acts, for Alice had set her sights on Nick and she was maneuvering him towards more than the window.

Chapter Seven

"You clever fox, Eleanor," Alice teased as she and Eleanor rowed up the river. Eleanor struggled to restrain her toothy grin, but her lips parted in a warm chuckle.

"The last time we were here together, rowing like this, you lectured me on acceptable gifts from young gentlemen. So tell me, truthfully now, have you ever received any jewelry from our dear F.D.?" Alice continued in her coquettish manner. Eleanor blushed as her cousin prodded her. "We're all alone on the water. No one else will ever know."

"I'm NOT a fast woman," Eleanor protested, shaking her head.

"Hardly," Alice smiled, confirming the obvious. "But didn't you receive anything other than books, or candy, or flowers from any of your other beaus? Aunt Sally says you were quite the belle in Newport this summer," she teased. Eleanor looked demurely away.

"Come on, you can't deny you enjoyed all the attention."

"It was..." Eleanor said, thoughtfully, "a lovely experience, but not ..."

"Love?" laughed Alice. "What a quaint notion."

"You've never loved anyone," Eleanor said calmly, refusing to be baited by her cousin.

"Isn't he a trifle light-weight for you? You can be awfully serious and Franklin's such a tease and a flirt."

"On the surface, perhaps, but underneath, he has a very serious plan for his life..." Eleanor acknowledged. She paused to enjoy a private thought, adding with a smile, "WE have one..."

"How perfectly romantic," Alice sighed, "but it's not my style. Marriage is voluntary servitude for a lifetime. The world's changing so fast. I don't want to miss a beat."

"That's exactly why you should come to the Junior League with me next time you're in New York. Your presence would make such a difference...Imagine, the President's daughter standing up for the rights of children and the poor!" Eleanor urged Alice, "The world *is* changing and it's up to our generation..."

62 Alice and Eleanor

Alice ceased rowing, stopping her cousin abruptly. She looked directly into Eleanor's usually gentle eyes that flamed with intensity. "You're such a do-goody. Not that I think there's anything wrong with it. It's positively genetic in our family, from grandfather on down.[3] But it's not for me. I'd have to give up my freedom and I'm too self-indulgent for that," she replied.

"It's a matter of balancing priorities," Eleanor offered.

"We're not discussing household accounts," Alice answered, a edge of exasperation in her voice. She rowed on several strokes, then continued speaking calmly. "Dear, sweet Eleanor. Do you think once you're married to Franklin you'll have any freedom at all? Between his mother and the demands of a household..."

"Maybe someday you'll understand..." Eleanor sighed, "if you find someone special to share your dreams...someone, say, like Nick."

Alice looked up at her cousin quizzically. "Even you know?"

"It's not exactly a secret," Eleanor said softly. "He's older, but very polished, even dapper, and quite the ladies' man."

Alice laughed heartily. "You look innocent, but your mind never stops working, does it?" Eleanor blushed. "No one better underestimate you, cousin."

"Nor you, Alice. If you want a man and your freedom, I'm certain you'll figure out how to manage both." She trailed her finger wistfully along the side of the wooden rowboat, her eyes drifting toward the late afternoon sunlight, watching as it danced on the water. She immersed herself in the sounds of the water lapping against the sides of the boat and the oars slicing skillfully beside her, basking in nature's symphony.

"Auntie Bye will be expecting us for dinner," she reminded Alice.

Marriage

Though secretly engaged to Franklin, Eleanor was pursued by several suitors throughout the summer of 1904. She enjoyed the company of Nick Biddle, who was quite taken with Eleanor and an old friend, Bob Ferguson, whom her Aunt Corinne mistakenly thought Eleanor was interested in. When Franklin visited the Robinson's at Dark Harbor, Maine, Eleanor pretended indifference to him. She hoped she would be forgiven her white lies to Aunt Corinne and cousin Corinne when they urged her to take Franklin's interest seriously. Both Howard

Chapter Seven 63

Cary and Caroline Drayton pursued her with invitations to climb and walk, plus dinner and tea.

Franklin entertained other women at his family retreat on the island of Campobello, but he longed for Eleanor's visit. When she finally arrived for the month of August, they spent hours walking, picnicking and enjoying the sunsets. They played tennis despite Eleanor's protests that she was an exceedingly poor player. They sailed and even participated in a play as a benefit for the island library.

By the time Franklin began law school in the autumn, their separations had become unbearable. He enrolled at Columbia instead of his beloved Harvard to be nearer to Eleanor. After the Caribbean cruise with his mother, Sara dropped her visible objection to the young couple's engagement. Franklin usually won her over with his charm, but he could be terribly stubborn. Sara knew he was immovable with regard to his choice of Eleanor, so she switched tactics. She used Eleanor's desire for acceptance, love and devotion to win points with her son. She took Eleanor to teas and lunches and joined her at fittings, all the while urging Eleanor to get Franklin to do her bidding. Eleanor was understanding and generous in soliciting cousin Sara's wishes regarding Franklin, for she wanted to be a dutiful daughter-in-law.

Eleanor's relationship with Franklin was imbued with the hopes and dreams lost with her father. By devoting herself to the man she loved, she would at last have a home of her own. In the process, however, given the constraints of her society, plus the dynamic evolving with Sara, Eleanor's self-doubts returned in force, eroding the self-confidence she had gained at Allenswood.

Though Eleanor and Franklin were guests at Bye's at the beginning of October 1904, the young couple was too absorbed in one another to be caught up in the election fever that surely dominated Oldgate. On October 11, Eleanor's 20th birthday, Franklin presented her with a ring he had selected from Tiffany's. In December, they announced their engagement.

Much to Alice's relief, Eleanor declined Edith's offer to have her wedding at the White House. She stayed with her original plan to be married at the home of cousin Susie Parish on Seventy-Sixth Street in Manhattan. Edith had never warmed to Eleanor and her offer was more out of duty and obligation than caring. The restrictive attitude she nurtured between Alice and Eleanor as children blew into adulthood with a cold, frosty edge. While she included Eleanor in White House festivities, she remained formal, which left Eleanor feeling uncomfortable. Even when invited to stay at the White House, Eleanor preferred to stay with Auntie Bye.

Eleanor did, however, want Uncle Ted to give her away. She set the wedding date after his inauguration on March 17, 1905, when Uncle Ted would conveniently be in New York to lead the Saint Patrick's Day Parade. The President bounded into the house at 3:30 in the afternoon, wearing a top hat and a shamrock in his lapel. According to Alice, he stole the show.

As she descended the circular staircase on her uncle's arm, the guests remarked how much Eleanor looked like her beautiful mother, Anna. The diamond crest that held Eleanor's veil in place had been her mother's. The day was also Anna Hall Roosevelt's birthday. Edith's prophecy about the ugly duckling turning into a swan had come true.

After the solemn ceremony, the crowd followed the President into the double dining room for refreshments, leaving the bride and groom alone except for a few well-wishers. "He wants to be the bride at every wedding and the corpse at every funeral," Alice noted. She well knew the feeling, for both father and daughter enjoyed commanding the limelight. To the family's relief, Alice was perfectly well behaved at the wedding. She may have worked one of her little pagan spells to insure she would catch the bridal bouquet and thereby set in motion her future plans.

Alice knew that she was rapidly wearing out her welcome living under her parents' roof. Her friends no longer competed for Nick Longworth's affection. With Maggie Cassini back in Russia and Cissy Patterson living in Poland with her husband, the Count Gizycka, Alice was free to engineer her plan of attack. Her opportunity came when William Howard Taft, Nick's political mentor and her father's Secretary of War, invited Alice on a visit to the Far East.

Teddy Roosevelt had begun arbitrating a settlement between Japan and Russia. Following the Spanish-American War when the Philippine Islands were ceded to the U.S., William Howard Taft was appointed the first civil governor of the Philippines. His role was to end military rule and prepare the people for self-government. He left a year later to become TR's Secretary of War, but he had promised to return. The President was eager for Taft to revisit the Far East during

Chapter Seven 65

the long congressional recess of 1905. Though it was clearly a political junket, TR wanted Taft to keep his promise, but more importantly, he wanted Taft to stop in Japan and feel out their officials on the Russian-Japanese settlement.

Taft invited Alice to accompany his party. Her parents gladly gave their permission. Edith and TR may have even suggested the idea, for the junket fit precisely into their plans for their errant daughter. Not only would the trip extract Alice from her unruly friends, it would challenge her intellect far more than her previous political excursions. Alice was very excited about the trip and suggested that Nick join the entourage.

He was a member of the House Foreign Affairs Committee, a fellow Ohioan, and Taft's congressman. Their families were old friends from Cincinnati. Knowing that he would be the *de facto* chaperone if he took Alice and Nick along on the voyage, Taft spoke to Nick's mother, Susan Longworth, before he agreed. He warned her that the two would undoubtedly return engaged. Susan Longworth assured her friend Taft that Nick was a confirmed bachelor. She was unaware that Alice had already been a guest at the family home, Rookwood, while she was out of town that spring. In addition, Nick had thrown a costume ball in Alice's honor.

While Alice was maneuvering Nick and Taft, Eleanor and Franklin stayed in Hyde Park for a week following their wedding and then settled into the Webster Hotel while Franklin finished his first year at Columbia law school. Eager to please her mother-in-law, Eleanor plunged into the activities that Sara Delano Roosevelt planned, strictly adhering to the correct social mores for young matrons. In addition, she prepared for their three-and-a-half-month honeymoon in Europe after Franklin completed his law exams. Eleanor's experience organizing travel for Madame Souvestre proved invaluable as she packed trunks, arranged for letters of credit and purchased tickets.

For Alice, who had never been west of the Mississippi, the Far East junket was the experience of a lifetime, as well as a pre-honeymoon. Like Eleanor, she had elaborate packing to do. As the daughter of the Head of State, she had to be well dressed. Alice took every gown and hat she owned, in addition to riding clothes, bathing costumes, accompanying shoes, handbags, jewelry and even her sidesaddle. Managing Alice's three trunks and hat boxes almost drove her maid, Anna, to a nervous breakdown during the voyage.

Teddy and Edith had hoped that allowing Alice to travel would remove her name from the news for a time. Instead, the papers gobbled up every detail of the voyage, at times overshadowing the important groundwork that Taft was doing to insure a peaceful settlement of the Russo-Japanese conflict. "Alice in Wonderland," the papers exclaimed as the special train pulled out of Washington at the end of June, headed on the five-day trip west. The 80-person entourage arrived in San Francisco on July 4th. Alice provided the papers with headlines as she shot fireworks from the train's back platform and took potshots at telegraph poles using her pocket revolver.

Earlier that month, on June 5, Eleanor and Franklin had quietly set sail for England. They spent time with his relatives in Liverpool, then proceeded on to London, where they walked to exhaustion. In Italy, France and Germany, as well as England, they frequented bookstores and visited with family. They shared their favorite sights together from previous trips, filled their days with book bargaining, shopping and dining on specialities of the house, a habit Eleanor had learned from Madame Souvestre. They wrote long, colorful, dutiful letters home to Sara.

Alice sent shockwaves home, not letters. She found San Francisco irresistible. Though the city had not yet been rocked by the devastating 1906 earthquake, Alice hardly slept during her four-day visit. She slipped out on her chaperones in order to visit Chinatown, notorious for its opium dens. Respectable girls dared not tread its streets, but Alice did, reporting that she only skirted the forbidden enclave's fringes. She lunched in the Redwood Grove with the Bohemian Club and at the University of California in Berkeley with University President Wheeler.

After four exciting days, Taft's party boarded the *Manchuria*, a veritable floating palace. The ten-day crossing to Japan was broken up by a stay in Hawaii where, true to form, Alice created a scandal. She asked to see an adult version of the hula, rather than the sanitized one with which the group was entertained. Not only did she try the dance herself, but she remained on Waikiki Beach with Nick and others for so long they missed the boat back to their ship. Alice was enchanted by the tropical splendor and hospitality of the islands.

She made headlines again when it was reported that she had jumped into a jerry-rigged pool on the ship's deck fully clothed. Scandalously, she lured a congressman, Bourke Cockran, to join her. Alice was surprised when the Japanese newspapers splashed the story on their front pages, twisting the event for a more romantic twist. The papers reported that Nick had followed Alice into the pool.

Many years later Alice told Bobby Kennedy that the story would have been news if she had jumped in *without* any clothes! However, fashions being what they were, she hardly saw a difference between her long sleeved, high-necked bathing costume, worn with stockings and the linen skirt and blouse she was wearing.

The line Jack Kennedy made famous when he introduced himself as the man who accompanied Jackie to Paris may have had its origin in Taft's Far East excursion. Mrs. Taft had not accompanied her husband's group, but rather, went on a holiday in England. Having difficulty getting her bags back to the boat for her return voyage to Washington, she blurted out, "I am the wife of the Secretary of War." When she got no response, she exclaimed, "You know, William Howard Taft—the man who is escorting Miss Alice Roosevelt in the Orient." Her bags made it to the boat in no time.

Expectations in Japan were high upon the party's arrival. Everywhere they travelled, Taft's group was met by adoring crowds yelling, "Bonzai, Bonzai!" With the diplomatic *savoir-faire* of a *quid pro quo*, Taft informed the Japanese that the U.S. would not interfere with their control of Korea, since they had no designs on the Philippines.

For five days, Taft's party were guests at endless official parties. Alice described the Japanese ladies attending a garden party at the American Legation as a slightly stoned version of the Ascot scene from *My Fair Lady*. In order to alleviate her boredom at the endless functions, Alice began laying trails of sweets along the white linen table cloths to attract ants.

Taft admonished her for such deeds, fearing Alice's antics would offend their gracious hosts. He also cautioned her about smoking in public and, assuming the role of stand-in father, he queried Alice about whether she and Nick were engaged. She tactfully replied, "More or less." She treated Secretary Taft in much the same manner as she dealt with her father—she gently ignored him.

Taft's official mission with the Japanese was a success. As Roosevelt's Secretary of War worked his way through the diplomatic

68 Alice and Eleanor

circles of Japan, the President was greeting the Japanese envoys at Sagamore Hill. On August 5, 1905, he met with both the Japanese and Russian representatives on the U.S.S. Mayflower, anchored in Oyster Bay.

TR's efforts to hammer out an agreement between the two sides were successfully culminated with the Treaty of Portsmouth, finalized in Portsmouth, New Hampshire. Eleanor and Franklin were ending their honeymoon with the Fergusons, old family friends, in the English countryside near Sherwood Forest when they fittingly heard the news of Uncle Ted's diplomatic triumph. The Ferguson family were part of the Foreign Office and Sir Ronald Ferguson had helped set up the Russo-Japanese meeting. Franklin waved the flag, joyful that everyone was talking about Cousin Theodore as the pre-eminent figure in modern history. He was delighted with the new tone of respect that English public opinion expressed towards America.

The Taft junket continued into the Philippines, hopping from official reception to official reception on island after island. The press continued to keep Alice in the news, inventing tantalizing stories like the proposal of the Sultan of Sula. The news report declared that the four- foot-tall Malay Sultan wanted to add Alice to his harem as his seventh wife. The only thing he actually offered her was a pearl ring.

As the trip progressed, Alice became the recipient of so many gifts from foreign leaders, that her friend Willard Straight composed a satirical poem entitled, *Alice in Plunderland.*

>When Alice came to Plunderland
>The streets were strewn with yellow sand
>The drains were filled with ink
>>of reddish hue for painters hand
>The populace raised thunder and
>The drains I'd hate to think
>>or write it.
>When Alice came to Plunderland
>The Crown Prince sought her lily hand
>The Emperor had a pipe dream
>That this was where his native land
>Could lose the Jap forever and
>Secure a friendship ripe
>With Father.

Alice admitted to being "a frankly unashamed pig," gleefully accepting the gifts, her "loot" as the family called it, with greedy delight.

The main party sailed back to the United States from Hong Kong, but a dozen members, including Nick and Alice, continued on to China. Princess Alice was the sole member of the group invited to stay overnight at the Royal Palace near Peking. The following morning she was presented to the empress dowager, Tz'u Hsi.

A formidable tyrant, the dowager's hatred of foreign devils was notorious. Alice was aware of her hostess's support of the Boxer Rebellion. She personally witnessed the Empress's ruthless power and ironhanded control twice. On the first occasion, the dowager's eunuch servant crawled on his belly to her, received a kick in the stomach and then crawled away in retreat. The second involved the Chinese foreign minister to the U.S. whom Alice had known in Washington. He enjoyed making blandly insolent remarks at Washington dinner parties and invidious comments on America in the press. At the Royal Palace, however, he kowtowed at the Empress' feet while he translated on all fours. He kept his forehead to the ground except when he was speaking.

Alice's father interpreted the dowager's treatment of her minister as a show of power. Though the Americans might perceive the minister as their equal, he would never be HER equal. Alice got the feeling that had the Empress said, "Off with his head," the poor man's head would roll. This tiny, despotic woman made a lasting impression on Alice.

Not only was Alice a guest in the Royal Palace, the Empress bestowed numerous gifts on her American guest, including a Pekinese dog and a picture of herself. It continued to hang on Alice's living room wall 75 years later. After Alice was presented to the dowager, her party toured the palace garden. She was honored by being carried in a yellow, tasseled chair borne aloft on the shoulders of eight men. The tour ended at a huge marble summerhouse built to look like a Chinese junk, situated on the palace lake, where the party had tea and cakes.

From Peking, the small group travelled to Tientsin where they were guests at another Chinese banquet, hosted by a powerful man of the time, General Yan Shih-kai. Due to strong anti-foreigner sentiment, the party was unable to go to Canton. Instead, they headed for Korea.

70 Alice and Eleanor

The visit was anti-climactic after China. Though the party was received in Seoul with heralding bugles and crowded streets lined with imperial guards, the people appeared downtrodden. Alice perceived sadness and dejection, even from the Emperor. She assumed that the Koreans longed for their Chinese Empress as they slipped helplessly and reluctantly under Japanese control.

After days of more official banquets and meetings, Alice was hardpressed to comprehend how real royalty, as opposed to her temporary royal status, tolerated the functions. The most fun she had came on her daily ride atop the native ponies who had an aversion to foreigners. One laid its ears back and bared his teeth while she made faces at it. The pony was securely held by its groom and she was standing ten feet away when she attempted her provocation.

The party returned to Tokyo, en route to Yokohama, where they were to depart for the return trip to San Francisco. Japanese feeling for Americans had soured since their first visit because the negotiated settlement of the Russo-Japanese War did not offer Japan the concessions it had expected. Alice was advised to say she was an Englishwoman on sightseeing excursions. The group met E.H. Harriman's party, who had been investigating railroad properties in Manchuria. He invited them to join his party and sail home on the *Siberia*.

The voyage became the type of madcap prank that exasperated Alice's father. Bertie Goelet, Alice's co-conspirator in the inauguration historic placards scheme, had bet Harriman that the *Siberia* could not beat the ten-day record of travel from west to east set by the *Korea*. Harriman beat *Korea's* time by 27 seconds. He then immediately jumped at another challenge, to beat the previous train record between San Francisco and New York. TR was so outraged by reports that Alice and Nick were guests in the railroad tycoon's lavishly appointed private car and that they were travelling at outrageous speeds, he telegraphed Harriman to stop. TR and Harriman's relationship had been cantankerous since the coal strike, but even a tycoon like Harriman could not ignore the President's order.

As Nick and Alice were racing across the Pacific, Eleanor and Franklin had returned across the Atlantic to New York, where they took up residence three blocks from his mother. Sara had chosen and decorated their first home. Franklin resumed his studies at Columbia Law School. He had to retake exams for two of the classes he failed in the excitement of his spring wedding. Eleanor did not resume her work with the Junior League, for Sara and cousin Susie thought she would bring dreadful tenement diseases into their home. Instead, she had luncheons and teas with her mother-in-law, attended classes in other women's homes but saw none of the vibrant artistic life she dabbled in during her previous year in New York. Under Sara's tutelage, Eleanor became an acceptable society matron, serving on the proper philanthropic boards. She sublimated her own desires in her pursuit of a secure, loving home life. Eleanor allowed Sara to plan menus, recommend servants, tell her which boards to sit on and with whom to lunch. Franklin partied with his friends while Eleanor remained the dutiful wife who managed hearth and home according to her mother-in-law's demands. Sara and Franklin benefitted immensely from Eleanor's sacrifice, but submission stunted her personal development at great emotional cost.

Though Alice and Nick had apparently worked out an understanding about their engagement, it was not until the end of November, a month after they had returned to the U.S. that Nick asked Teddy for Alice's hand. The newspapers were brimming with expectation and speculation. Alice and Nick were both undoubtedly nervous about the decision. Both would be letting go of considerable freedom, or so they expected. Nick's wild, carefree bachelor days would come to a screeching halt, as would Alice's days of frivolous pranks and gallivanting.

While Nick was downstairs speaking to the President, Alice, who had lost 20 pounds contemplating the ordeal, deliberately gave the news to her stepmother while Edith was brushing her teeth. She wanted Edith to have a moment to consider the news before speaking, aware that she disapproved of Nick's lifestyle and reputation as much as Susan Longworth disapproved of Alice. Edith, however, was pleased to see that her stepdaughter's personality had softened from being in love with Nick.

TR consented, believing Nick's maturity would tame his errant daughter. Not only were they fellow Harvard men and members of Porcellian, but Nick was a serious politician. He had good family ties back to the Mayflower, and the Longworths were a family with money.

72   Alice and Eleanor

Finally, Nick was an American, which suited TR's distaste for the current fashion of Americans marrying the titled gentry of Europe.

Alice wrote Aunt Corinne excitedly confirming that she had finally let Nick catch her. She wrote to Eleanor on December 8, 1905.

Dearest Eleanor:
I want to tell you of my engagement to Nick Longworth. I am trying not to announce it until the 17th, so don't say anything about it until then. I hope for a surprise, but I am much afraid you are not! Love to Franklin. It was so nice seeing your man for that brief moment the other day.[1]

The wedding date was set for February 17, 1906. Born eight months before Eleanor, Alice was marrying 11 months, to the day, after her cousin. When Eleanor and Franklin stood on the altar, they were upstaged by the man who had given her away. In contrast, Alice and Nick upstaged not only the President, but the start of the Panama Canal, the controversial passage between the Pacific and the Atlantic Oceans.

The news media made a bigger deal of the upcoming wedding of the country's 22-year-old "Princess" than Alice considered necessary. Alice and Nick's wedding would be the first in the White House since Grover Cleveland's in 1886. They were swamped by gawkers on a shopping trip to New York, the equivalent of today's rock or movie stars. Plunderland continued with gifts sent from foreign countries as well as government officials and admirers. The volume of gifts was so enormous, they were numbered and kept under continuous guard in a White House room. Alice was characteristically remiss about her thank you notes, continuing her aversion to the practice of social correspondence, so friends and siblings were pressed into service to help.

Alice loved her wedding loot, but it raised her father's ire. The ostentatiousness and volume of gifts offended his sensibilities. He banned all further gifts from foreign governments and would not let her accept a cash gift of $800,000 from a group of Americans.

Unlike Eleanor and Franklin, two magnets drawn down the aisle by love and shared ideals, Alice and Nick seemed reluctantly tugged towards the altar. The solemn faces in their official wedding photograph reflect their hesitancy. Alice remembered the affair with a mixture of animation and grimness. She had no bridesmaids, but Nick had eight ushers. Alice wanted to keep the event focused off her father and on herself.

Twenty-one-year-old Eleanor was pregnant with her first child and had started her confinement on Alice's wedding day. Franklin attended with his mother, the first carriage in a long line of guests awaiting entrance to the festivities. He fussed over Alice's train, arranging it before the photographer snapped her official portrait.

The day was unseasonably warm and the room was packed with wall-to-wall officials. Outside, hawkers sold souvenirs and food to the curious crowds. Edith was exasperated at Alice's final rebellion, rising late and waiting as long as possible before trading her nightgown for her wedding gown. Alice met her father at the elevator, late due to problems with her hair. It had to support her veil and train. Together, she and TR rode the elevator down from the upstairs where they were met by Nick and his ushers. They were escorted into the East Room through an aisle formed by the ushers and military officers. When asked who gave away the bride at the make-shift altar, the President silently placed Alice's hand in Nick's. He stepped back to take his place as a spectator to the marriage ceremony.

Alice used the sword of Charlie McCawley, her partner for her coming out party's first dance, to cut the cake. Then she excused herself to change while Nick and her father's Porcellian Club brothers got together. Alice gushed with praise over her wedding, but her stepmother was clearly exhausted after the ceremony. She told Alice she was glad to see her leave for she had never been anything but trouble. It was a painful message for Alice to carry away with her on her wedding night.

The newly married couple drove to Friendship, an 80-acre sumptuous estate outside of Georgetown owned by the John McLeans. They stayed for a few days before leaving on a two-week official trip to Cuba. Their traditional European honeymoon would be put off until the following June.

Alice was pleased to be back on the Caribbean Island again, but found San Juan Hill a disappointment. It was a mere slope, rather than the grand, lofty peak she had envisioned. She and Nick had their first argument, one in which Alice declared she put up a good fight and was sufficiently obnoxious. Her father had not been able to dominate her and she obviously had no intention of letting her husband do so.

From the outset, the marriage of the Princess did not follow a fairytale script. Nick was clearly Alice's husband and the President's son-in-law. They visited the scenes of TR's triumphs in Cuba, where Teddy was the hero and Alice, the celebrity.

In June of 1906 they embarked on a two-month European honeymoon during the congressional recess. The newlyweds were treated like royalty. Nick, however, was relegated to the role of gentleman-in-waiting. They were entertained by the crowned heads of England and Germany, including a formal presentation at the Court of Saint James. Nick caused a scandal because he chose to honor the English tradition of wearing breeches when presented to the King and Queen. He was accused of undermining democracy.

Their days were filled with superficial, official activities plus a crush of crowds and cameras. On their return trip, Alice was so exasperated, she threatened to have the next King she met stuffed. The pace and structure of the trip was hardly one in which the newlyweds could nurture intimacy and cultivate shared interests, in the manner that Eleanor and Franklin's explorations in the European bookshops had offered.

By the time they reached Paris to visit with Nick's relatives, contentious political rumblings could be heard, drawing Nick reluctantly into the first of many future Roosevelt/Longworth political conflicts. Nick's sister, Clara de Chambrun, disliked Teddy, as did Nick's aunt and uncle, Maria and Bellamy Storer. The Storers had been friends of Teddy's from his early days in Washington. They had even been willing to rent their home to TR's family to accommodate Alice's debut. However, Maria Storer had crossed the bounds of political correctness after Teddy had appointed her husband as Ambassador to Austria-Hungary.

To the family's horror, Maria had converted to Catholicism and had set her mind on having Archbishop Ireland of St. Paul, Minnesota elevated to cardinal. She encouraged her husband to lobby the Vatican on the Archbishop's behalf, misleading Pope Pius X that the promotion was TR's desire. Teddy angrily recalled Bellamy Storer for allowing his wife to interfere in diplomatic affairs.

The recall occurred right around the time of Nick and Alice's wedding. The air was poisoned and the Storers refused to attend the marriage. Subsequently, Maria devoted herself to besmirching TR's reputation. The conflict cast an ominous din over the family's future political alliances. All was not harmonious under the royal canopy.

Chapter Eight

"Alice!" Franklin smiled as he swept gracefully into the lobby of a Boston hotel. "What a pleasant surprise. Whatever are you doing here?"

"Meeting some friends. I've been visiting my Lee relations," Alice smiled, taking his arm. "And you? Up for a Harvard Club social?" He touched his nose, gesturing that she had guessed the reason exactly. "And where's Mrs. Roosevelt?"

"At home, rearranging the furniture, or so she says. She doesn't like these gatherings, so I come solo," he explained with a shrug.

"I'm surprised she lets such a handsome rake as you out alone," Alice teased.

Franklin tossed his head back, letting out a joyous laugh. "You always were the most horrid tease. That's what I love about you, cousin." Alice raised one eyebrow and winked, suppressing a mischievous smile. "And Nick?" he continued.

"Tied up in committee work," Alice replied flatly, "or so HE says." Her tone lightened. "Come up and have a drink with me. We'll share tales of married life..."

"And you can fill me on the latest Washington gossip," Franklin whispered naughtily as he led her towards the stairs.

An hour later, they sat perched on a trunk in an alcove near Alice's room, swinging their legs like little leprechauns. They were sipping drinks and giggling when a woman walked past. She gave the couple a disapproving glance.

"Good evening, madame," Alice provoked her. The woman tossed her nose in the air and proceeded down the stairs. "Cat's got her tongue," she chided. Franklin roared again, puffing on a cigarette. "No sense of fun."

"I think she's a friend of Eleanor's and mother's," Franklin whispered.

"Oh my, then you're in big trouble, Feather Duster."

"For heaven sakes, why?" he asked, incredulous.

"For being entertained by a married woman, dear boy."
"But you're my cousin," he retorted.
"So's your wife, but that woman doesn't know, does she?" Alice replied mischievously. "Isn't it deliciously scandalous?"[1]

Franklin threw his head back again in his characteristic laugh, then he said soberly, "Eleanor disapproves of scandals."

"But you don't, do you FD?" she prodded Franklin. "I expect you'll weather a few in your time."

"And you'll continue your scandalous behavior," teased Franklin, "unless Nick's succeeds in taming the shrew in you. I wonder if he has it in him?"

"Should anyone?" Alice shot back. "The bonds of marriage typically tie one's wings, but what if we were all unbound?" she mused, uncharacteristically contemplative. "To what heights would we reach or to what depths would we fall, each of us...you and I, Nick and Eleanor?"

Early Married Years

The seeds of discontent were planted early in both Alice's and Eleanor's marriages, but took a number of years to blossom. Their weddings became metaphors for their married lives. While Alice was the star performer on stage at the White House, outshining her father, the President, and her husband, the Congressman, Eleanor faded into the background, overwhelmed by her mother-in-law, governesses, servants and her husband. Charactcristically, Eleanor sublimated her concern, while Alice expressed hers openly.

Both young women had serious adjustments to make in their marriages. Alice was rudely awakened to the demands of domestic life, while Eleanor's notions of romance excluded the intimacies of the marriage bed. She reportedly approached her sexual relationship with Franklin as a wifely duty to be endured. She brought the same naive, prudish attitude regarding sexuality into her marriage that she showed as a 14-year-old hearing about whores from Alice.

Eleanor was not alone in her innocence for people did not discuss issues of sexuality openly in those days. Victorian mores continued to prevail. Women performed their marital duty, providing their families with progeny. Alice believed Eleanor "probably went to her wedding not knowing anything about the subject at all."

78 Alice and Eleanor

Lacking any knowledge of family planning, the pattern of Eleanor and Franklin's life was set for the next decade. "For ten years I was always just getting over having a baby or about to have one, and so my occupations were considerably restricted." Her son, Elliot, assumed that sex for his mother was never a source of joy or ecstasy. Eleanor's attitude towards sexual pleasure was an extension of her devotion to duty over pleasure. One kept "one's desires under complete subjugation." Franklin, meanwhile, was developing a lusty love of life's rich variety. Given their diametrically opposite views, it was inevitable that Eleanor and Franklin would seek satisfaction outside their relationship.

Alice, however, was ahead of her time. Margaret Sanger was openly advocating birth control, supported by such radical anarchists as Emma Goldman and her lover/publicist, Ben Reitman. Alice had a German doctor who was well versed on the subject. Most of her contemporaries, however, were too shy even to ask their doctors. The doctors were not forthcoming, perhaps in fear of irate husbands. Dr. Sophie Nordhoff-Jung provided Alice with one of "those cunning labor-saving devices," as Nick's sister called them. She would not be burdened with motherhood unless she chose it. Her sister-in-law, already the mother of three, asked Alice to send one to save her "tottering reason." Eleanor, however, never sought, nor was probably even aware of her choices.

Alice may have learned to manage birth control, but she had never learned to manage servants nor paid any attention to the practical details of life. When she and Nick returned to Washington, his mother was no longer available to run the household. Unlike Franklin's mother, who was an ever-present fixture in Eleanor's daily life, Nick's mother had returned to the family home in Cincinnati. Alice was left to fend for herself. Eleanor had run the Hall house in Manhattan when she lived there with her Aunt Pussy during her debutante years, and had learned to keep accounts from her Cousin Henry, yet she courted her mother-in-law's favor by dutifully consulting Sara and accepting her household advice. Such a role was not in Alice's makeup. She never asked Susan Longworth's advice or became the dutiful daughter-in-law.

Alice made an attempt at life as a society matron. Not surprisingly, she found the protocol involved with leaving cards at diplomats' homes tedious and afternoon teas distasteful, particularly when sightseers dropped in and walked off with her souvenirs. Her marital status precluded her from participating in the social whirl of her Newport 400 crowd.

With time on her hands, Alice gravitated back to the world she had grown up in but had rejected. The charm of her immediate family offered new appeal. Though she had pointedly avoided them during the past several years, Alice began visiting every afternoon between tea time and dinner. She gathered in Edith's bedroom with her siblings who still lived at home and discussed family matters from the trivial to the significant. Her father would invariably come in and the talk would turn to politics. Alice had avoided the subject since her baptismal foray with Uncle Joe Cannon over redecorating the White House, but politics held a renewed fascination. The topic began to passionately consume Alice.

The afternoon meetings became strategy sessions with her father. Alice became one of his most effective and trusted lobbyists. TR's former confidants, Bye and Lodge, were less available; Bye, for health reasons, and Lodge, for ideological ones. Teddy was becoming more liberal, while Lodge remained a mainstream Republican.

When Nick's 1906 re-election campaign began, Alice offered to help him win his third term. Nick was delighted to capitalize on Alice's political savvy and excellent connections. Her appearance at Nick's rallies drew huge crowds. She made politics fashionable, determined to shake as many hands as her husband. TR was particularly proud of how successfully Alice and Nick had run his son-in-law's campaign. Congressional politics, however, didn't hold the drama of national politics. Her father's political fortunes soon took precedence over Nick's.

The following year, Teddy's major preoccupation was choosing a successor for the 1908 Republican party, since he had promised not to run again. Though Elihu Root was Teddy's personal favorite, Root was too conservative for TR's progressive supporters. He settled on Alice's Far East chaperone, William Howard Taft, certain that he would carry out TR's policies. Nick came out early in support of Taft, his former law professor at the University of Cincinnati Law School. It was a courageous move since the party boss from Nick's home state of Ohio, James Cox, favored another candidate, Senator Foraker. Cox was in league with Mark Hanna, Teddy's old nemesis. Neither man had any use for seeing Roosevelt's policies continue with Taft.

80 Alice and Eleanor

As Alice became consumed with politics, Eleanor found herself consumed by the role of dutiful wife and daughter-in-law. The independence she asserted after leaving Allenswood became subsumed in the two roles. Franklin continued his law studies at Columbia, passing the New York Bar in the spring of 1907. By the time he began practicing with the firm of Carter, Ledyard and Milburn, learning his way around the municipal courts, the pattern of his early life with Eleanor had been set.

Franklin retained his self-centered and frivolous side, while Eleanor evinced self-effacement and seriousness. She kept herself under tight emotional reins. She didn't want to spoil his fun, or risk losing his love and approval, so she withdrew. She stayed home but encouraged him to go off with his friends for a spree, such as commencement festivities at Harvard or carousing with his Fly Club friends. With her first pregnancy, Eleanor had a real excuse not to accompany her husband.

On May 2, 1906, Anna Eleanor was born, a helpless bundle who wound herself around her mother's heart. The Franklin Roosevelt household now consisted of a nurse for the baby, a cook, a housemaid and a butler, all engaged by Sara. She was only too delighted to take over managing her children and grandchildren's lives.

With a grandchild living so close, Sara could hardly restrain herself from spending most of her waking hours with her son and his family. No matter how much Eleanor sought to please her mother-in-law, she was always the outsider. Sara and Franklin sat at the heads of the table at Hyde Park. Eleanor sat along the sides. Two armchairs graced the reading room, but none was added for Eleanor. She sat on the floor or on the couch.

Eleanor came to realize that nothing she could do would ever satisfy Sara. To her further distress, Franklin was not the least bit interested in their squabbles, nor was he receptive to Eleanor's suggestion that they live on their individual inheritances without Sara's involvement. The only thing Eleanor ever wanted was a home and a family of her own. Hyde Park was home to Franklin and Sara presided there, as well as over their Manhattan home.

Years later, Eleanor acknowledged that she and Franklin would undoubtedly have done better in the first years of their marriage if they had dispensed with servants and had cared for their own children. The children would have been happier and she would not have been ordered about by the nurses.

The budding flower that Madame Souvestre had nurtured to think and act independently slowly withered under the Delano influence. Eleanor capitulated her own identity for the security of a loving home life, but the result left her without an avenue to express her emotions. She sank into depressions which she called her "Griselda moods." She confessed to shutting up like a clam when her feelings were hurt or she was annoyed, a maddening habit that infuriated those around her. She would feel like a martyr and act like one in pursuit of her version of the ideal ambition—orthodox goodness. She expected Franklin to share her ideals, yet she failed to discuss her expectations with him. If he strayed from those ideals, she experienced a monumental betrayal and they became embroiled in a deep emotional trauma.

The silence that doomed Eleanor's relationship with her mother came back to threaten her marriage. The childhood tantrums, obstinacy and silent depressions were manifested in her Griselda moods. Rather than being directed at her parents, her mother-in-law and husband became her targets. As an adult, Eleanor overestimated and misjudged the people she thought needed her, which left her weak and vulnerable. When her loved ones disappointed her, she withdrew, re-experiencing the rejection she felt as a child. Later in life, Eleanor's women friends suggested that the moods gave her permission to feel sorry for herself and even allowed her a measure of enjoyment in her misery. The moods, however, did little to bridge the emotional distance between her and Franklin, or enhance their intimacy.

Alice had a similar experience of matriarchal domination during congressional recesses when she and Nick resided at the Longworth family home in Cincinnati, Ohio. Though his family fortune had once been considerable, it had dwindled significantly. Nick could not maintain a home in Washington and in his home district. As Hyde Park was home to Franklin, so, too, was Rookwood home to Nick. And like Eleanor, Alice was an uncomfortable guest in her mother-in-law's home. Rookwood would be Nick's when his mother passed away, but, until then, Susan Longworth was the head of the house. She was as devoted to Nick as Sara was to Franklin. Although Susan had other children, Nick was her only son.

82 Alice and Eleanor

Alice recognized the difficulty Susan Longworth experienced seeing Nick get married. She had expected him to remain a bachelor, and the situation was particularly difficult given her son's choice of a wife. Alice was not someone who "merged" into the family in which she married. She was an egotist and far too much a member of her own family to blend into another. The Longworth family and friends resented Alice's non-conformity and her disrespect for her mother-in-law's position. It was obvious to them all that Alice preferred to be elsewhere. Still, Alice and Susan, like Eleanor and Sara, found ways to glean happiness out of their living arrangement. Where Eleanor and Sara lunched and took classes together, Alice and Susan put together a genealogical chart which included each relative's psychosis.

Nick and Alice spent the congressional break of 1907 at Rookwood and then they returned to Hawaii, perhaps to try and recapture some of the magic from their previous Far East trip. Alice had realized soon after they returned from their honeymoon, that she had married Nick more from the need to escape her parents' control than love. Given the length of time it took them to even decide to get married, each must have been aware of the potential for disaster in their union. Their relationship had been rocky from the beginning. Minor differences like their taste in music were complicated by major ones, exemplified by Alice's public notoriety, her independence, and her passionate attachment to her father's political career.

The Longworths vacationed for ten days in Yellowstone Park, exploring on horseback, then went on to San Francisco for a few days before reaching Hawaii. They explored the volcano on Maui by horseback and led an indolent existence at a cottage in Honolulu, playing in and out of the ocean day and night.

On December 23, 1907, Eleanor gave birth to her first son, James. Alice sent the following note:

New Bedford, December 23^d, 1907

Dear Eleanor & Franklin,

Thank you most deeply for your thought to send me the joyful tidings of the birth of your blessed Baby boy! I will only take a card as the mail soon goes, to write my heartiest congratulations, and a very Merry Christmas for you

both & the two little ones. I have received also the note from Eleanor & feel I was quite right in the colour I chose, for the little jacket. I shall be at home by the 27th & hope to find you well progressed Eleanor-dear, & Baby progressing.
Cousin Alice[2]

Alice's cheerful note sharply contrasted with her cousin Eleanor's life. It had become miserable. While Franklin gallivanted off on hunting and sailing trips, she stayed with the children, servants and her mother-in-law, feeling highly anxious. She was mired in a cycle of dependence with Sara that she found onerous. She had also fashioned a role for herself as Franklin's prodder and manager, leaving him lists of things to do, a role she continued during his political career.

Franklin began staying out late, playing poker at the Knickerbocker Club, dining at the Harvard club and attending frivolous business engagements for his law firm. His behavior showed shades of Eleanor's father's errant ways. When Franklin came home near dawn, bubbling with high spirits, he found a somber, sulking, silent wife. In truth, he was bored with his existence. He was biding his time with the law, awaiting his turn to run for state office.

As Eleanor sank into the darkest period of her life, the financial crisis of 1907 sent much of the country into a panic. The Knickerbocker Trust Company of New York collapsed and TR's political foes laid the problem at his feet. Teddy was charged with the destruction of the U.S. credit system. Though Alice's income from her Lee grandparents remained safe, the Longworth family's resources were seriously compromised.

While unaffected by the financial crisis, Alice faced a medical crisis. She suffered from an appendicitis attack and submitted to surgery in the White House. Her recovery was slow, punctuated by visits from family members. During her recuperation, Teddy gave her a political task, characteristic of the esteem within which he held her as an ally. He brought Will Taft, his choice as a successor, for a visit to her sick room. The expressed purpose of the call was for Alice to find out what Taft intended to say in a major upcoming speech. TR wanted to assure himself the address would substantively advance Taft's candidacy over his rival, Senator Joseph B. Foraker. When Taft replied that he would talk about the Philippines, the President roared a protest. Alice shook with such sardonic laughter, she broke one of her stitches. Taft was bypassing an opportunity to deliver a major policy speech. Alice and TR's political antennae were raised, putting in question the wisdom of Taft's future as President.

Though Nick was running for re-election to his fourth term in 1908, Alice declined to participate in his campaign. She only appeared at specific events when asked to attend. After recovering from her appendicitis surgery, Alice spent increasing amounts of time with her father at Sagamore Hill or with Auntie Bye at Oldgate rather than on the campaign trail with her husband. She did, however, attend the Republican Convention along with Nick and their friends, Ruth and Medill McCormick. Alice found the parties and behind the scenes dealings inspiring. Secretly, she hoped that the party would renominate her father, but Taft won on the first ballot.

The Republican convention had been so exciting that the Longworths and the McCormicks decided not to miss the Democratic convention. They took a private train car to Denver, living in one car with their baggage kept in a second car. They also rented a hotel room in town where they could rotate bathing. Even the oppressive heat didn't dampen the spirit of these convention "fans," though fans of another sort would have been greatly appreciated. Living in the railroad car was like living in a sweat box. It was so hot the McCormick's butler routinely sprayed the outside of the car with a hose to cool them off. Alice said the butler was the luckiest man in town because he held the hose, luckier even than William Jennings Bryan who had won the Democratic nomination for a third time. To escape the heat, the two couples drove around in the middle of the night singing ridiculous songs and duets. Alice described herself during that period as young, silly and susceptible to laughing at the most inane things.

Alice spent election night in Cincinnati with Nick and his family. The Ohio locals celebrated Taft's victory without any reference to the man who put him in contention, Teddy Roosevelt. Alice's annoyance turned to animosity as the evening wore on with accolades for the "great Taft." The only thing great she could see about him was his girth, referring to Taft as "that lump of flesh." The stage was set on election night in Cincinnati for what Alice called the "breaking up of a beautiful friendship," not only between the Tafts and the Roosevelts but also the Longworths.

Chapter Eight 85

Bryan inspired no excitement in the electorate. The election results put Taft in office handily, as well as Nick. The results were bittersweet for Alice, who, although pleased to be returning to Washington with Nick, had to endure the transition of her family out of the White House. She would have been happy with a 99-year lease on it. Her sole consolation was that Nick was maneuvering into a powerful position on the House Ways and Means Committee.

Between the election and the inauguration, rumors began circulating that Taft was not going to continue TR's policies. The first potential conflict centered on the recall of TR's appointed ambassador to Paris, Henry White. Nellie Taft had not forgiven White for sending them tickets to the Royal Mews, the stables, on their honeymoon in London in 1886, instead of tickets to Parliament. White was on the embassy staff in London at the time. TR dispatched Alice to find out whether Taft indeed planned to recall White. The president-elect assured Alice that, "You must believe that I am big enough to forget that sort of thing." He may have been, but his wife wasn't. Taft requested White's resignation at the beginning of his first term.

Before Taft's inauguration, Teddy invited younger members of his family to the White House for a final visit. Franklin, imbued with his Uncle's ideals of public service, had already planned a political career modeled after Uncle Ted's. He had outlined a timetable to his fellow law clerks—the State Legislature, Assistant Secretary of the Navy, Governor, and then with any luck, the Presidency. He intended to run at the first opportunity.

While Franklin was laying out his political future, Alice was laying a hex on the White House. She disliked Mrs. Taft passionately. It was commonly known that Mrs. Taft pushed her husband into his political career. He wanted to be a supreme court judge, but Nellie Taft wanted to be First Lady.

She exercised a powerful hand during her husband's administration, vetoing cabinet appointments and walking in unannounced to private meetings. Mrs. Taft engendered the enmity of many, including Alice. It was no secret that Alice felt Taft had usurped her father's rightful place in the White House. Nellie further incurred Alice's anger by offering her a luncheon ticket for Inauguration Day. Alice raged that her invitation should have been assumed. After all, she had been waltzing in and out of the White House for almost eight years!

On the evening before Taft's inauguration on March 4, 1909, the Roosevelts hosted a dinner for the Tafts. The incoming President called it a "funereal." The outgoing First Lady, Edith, wore black while Nellie Taft wore triumphant white. Alice turned her sorrow into occult action. She had never given up her interest in spells and magics. After dinner, when the men retired to the study and the women to the library, Alice stole into the garden. She scooped up some dirt, took a small box from her purse, and buried it in the hole, quickly covering it with a sweep of her hand. Inside the box was a "bad little idol" which would insure bad luck for the new Chief Executive. She changed her gloves and rejoined the ladies in the library.

The weather was so miserable on Inauguration Day that the ceremony had to be held indoors for the first time since Madison became President. Seventy-mile-an-hour winds howled and the temperature plummeted. Alice reacted gleefully, crediting her ominous handiwork to the snowstorm that darkened the event.

The bleak mood of the day even changed the new President's demeanor. Taft threw himself on a sofa after his inaugural address, boasting, "I'm President now and I'm tired of being kicked around." The White House staff found their new employer snarly, scowling and curt. After getting wedged one too many times in the tub his predecessors used, the new President ordered a bathtub that could accommodate four normal-sized men.

Mrs. Taft began making changes as soon as she moved in. She hired an almost entirely new staff, including a chef. She entertained lavishly and closed most of the ground floor rooms to the public. But Alice delighted in the belief that her buried icon continued to bring ill fortune to the White House occupants. Two and a half months later, Nellie Taft suffered a devastating stroke. She had to relearn to walk and talk. Her four sisters alternated as Taft's official hostess throughout the remainder of his term.

The dark weather cast an ominous shadow over the Roosevelts, too. It seemed as if the pall had returned that hung over the family when Alice's mother and their grandmother, Mittie, died. Two weeks after Taft's inauguration, 25-year-old Eleanor bore her third child, Franklin. It was March 18, 1909, one day after her fourth wedding anniversary. She felt increasingly overwrought, overwhelmed and unhappy.

Seven and a half months later, her despair intensified. Her son,

Chapter Eight 87

little Franklin, died on November 1, 1909. Though he had been her "biggest and most beautiful" child, the infant had a heart problem. He succumbed after a bout of the flu. Eleanor could not shake her feelings of guilt. She blamed herself for baby Franklin's death and mourned him intensely.

Alice and Nick entered a dark period, too. They were drifting further apart. Alice couldn't make room for her husband to occupy the proud place her father held in her heart. Moreover, Nick could not accept his role as Alice's man-in-waiting. He bristled or exploded at being called *Mr. Alice Roosevelt* on their European trip during their second honeymoon. The words of Douglas Robinson, Corinne's husband, came back to haunt Nick. Before he and Alice were married, Douglas warned Nick that, "when you find yourself bullied and ignored or hung on the family like a tail to a kite, you will not be able to plead ignorance for you are doing this thing with your eyes open."[3]

Nick had returned to his nights out with the boys, drinking and playing poker. Rumors abounded about his renewed womanizing. To get even with him for leaving her alone while in Washington, Alice arranged Saturday nights out at other men's houses where she brought her women friends for their own poker games. Stubborn pride forced Alice to push Nick out of her life as she had her father when she felt hurt or betrayed. Friends began to whisper that Alice had married Nick for his money and now she was bitter that the Longworth millions were disappearing.

Chapter Nine

"Eleanor, whatever is the matter?" Franklin asked his wife who sat crying in front of her dressing table before dinner.

"I don't want to live in a house which is not in any way mine, one that I've had nothing to do with planning and doesn't represent how I want to live!"

"You seemed quite pleased to have mother do the planning for the house," he replied lightly.

"That's because I've been overwhelmed with the children," she sobbed.

"They have a wonderful nanny," he retorted.

"She's as awful as Madeline used to be to me. That lady terrorizes all of us," Eleanor said meekly.

"Oh, Eleanor. You're really acting quite mad. If you don't like the way things are run, discuss them with mother."

"I don't want to discuss them with her. She makes all the decisions for us," responded Eleanor, swallowing her anger.

"Naturally, because you ask her advice about everything. I've had enough of this nonsense. If you have a disagreement with mother, I don't want to be in the middle. Now, dinner is waiting," he reminded her as he brusquely left the room.

Eleanor gazed at herself in the mirror again and burst into tears. "She decides everything, what I do, who minds the children, how our adjoining townhouses were built. There's no telling when she'll appear or where. I feel like a caged animal whose trainer could appear through a sliding door at any moment on any floor!"[1]

After one more tearful explosion, she dried her swollen eyes. She listened to a cacophony of voices from her past, Grandmother Hall and her father, warning her against self-indulgent behavior. Eleanor pulled herself together, clamping her iron self-control over her emotions. She washed her face before she joined her family for dinner.

Chapter Nine 89

Shifting Political Fortunes

Alice was not only having problems with Nick, but she was unable to accept the loss of her father's powerful position. After leaving the White House in 1909, Teddy went off to Africa for a big game hunt with his son, Kermit, to shoot specimens for the Smithsonian Museum in Washington. In the year they were gone, Alice positioned herself as her father's grand defender, clawing at anyone who criticized Teddy. She refused to attend parties hosted by people who criticized him, even Nick's relative, Larz Anderson, the Ambassador to Japan.

In May 1910, Alice sailed alone to meet her father and Kermit in London. Edith and Ethel had already met them. Alice dressed in mourning clothes, for her grandfather Lee had passed away the previous March. She accompanied her family through Europe where her father was treated like a king. Her mourning clothes served a royal purpose for King Edward of England died at the beginning of May. She attended the state funeral and luncheon at Windsor Castle afterwards, watching her father walk behind the coffin as representative of the United States. Alice recalled one reporter referring to him as "the most famous of living men."

She stood next to her father on the bridge as they steamed into New York Harbor on June 18, escorted by six battleships, destroyers and hundreds of smaller crafts, all blaring their horns in welcome. Nick had met them on the boat, arriving on a Coast Guard tender. More than 2000 government officials greeted the Roosevelts that morning, plus personal friends and family. Cousin Franklin and Eleanor hovered on the fringe of the crowd. Five hundred Rough Riders escorted TR's carriage uptown on his return to New York. He received his greatest public reception ever. Tens of thousands of voices all shouted, "Teddy!" It was a rousing spectacle to behold.

During the heat of the summer, Alice read during the day, then took long walks in the late afternoon. She played hostess on the lawn at Fort Meyer, bringing a picnic basket and a half a dozen thermoses filled with iced tea and "Tom Collins," while she and her friends watched the Wright Brothers fly. It was the most fashionable attraction in D.C. that season. Her efforts as *al fresco* hostess advanced Nick's long-range political plans, for the crowd she served included Cabinet members and congressmen.

In the evening, as a reaction to the Washington tradition of "calling," the tedious, labyrinth of social guidelines for paying visits to government officials, Alice formed the Night Raiders. A group of her cronies rode out on horseback between 10 p.m. and 1 a.m., appearing in the front yards of their friends, catcalling until the door was opened and refreshments served. While initially ridiculed, a visit from the Night Raiders led by daring Alice became the highest social honor in town.

Nick and Alice attended the Ohio state Republican party convention in Columbus at the end of July, where the candidate for governor would be chosen. Nick had decided that the time was right for him to run for the office. In her autobiography, Alice claimed that he didn't want the nomination, maintaining it wasn't in line with his plans. He enjoyed his work in Congress, gaining experience and seniority with each year.

However, Nick had come through a particularly painful session of Congress. The progressives successfully limited the dictatorial power of the Speaker, Joe Cannon. Cannon had been solidifying his control over a seven-year period, appointing himself chair of every house committee, including the Rules committee. He also governed committee appointments. Nick had aligned himself with Cannon and was sent scouting for support. Even though everyone liked Nick, he couldn't save the tyrannical speaker.

A bill was pushed through the House calling for the election of committee members. Each chairman was to be chosen by the committee itself, not appointed by the Speaker. The writing was on the wall for Nick. After supporting Cannon, he would be doomed to a poor committee assignment. Consequently, he decided the time was upon him to make known his interest in becoming Governor of Ohio. Nick had informed Alice of his ambition even before they were married.

Alice was very much against Nick running for Governor, since they would be relegated to living in Columbus, Ohio. In fact, she threatened to smoke in the street to defeat his nomination. She didn't want to get stuck in another governor's mansion. Albany had been dismal when she lived there with her father, but Columbus would be worse. It was not in her plans. The town had stifling social conventions which would restrain the intrepid Alice, who was a rule onto herself.

Nick made a keynote address at the state party convention. He

Chapter Nine 91

garnered the support of a considerable number of delegates which made him a serious contender. In the end, however, he failed in his pursuit of the nomination because he was perceived as part of the old guard. Nick was only 41 years old but he was considered a lackey of the privileged rich. He had sponsored no significant legislation during his four terms in the House. With hindsight, Alice thought Nick had been wrongfully denied the nomination, particularly when the man who defeated him, Warren G. Harding, became the 29th President.

The year 1910 marked not only the clash between Alice and Nick over his political future, it also marked the beginning of Eleanor's life in politics through her husband. Franklin was approached by the district attorney of Dutchess County, John Mack, early in the year about running as the Democratic candidate from Dutchess County for New York's State Assembly. Even though the county had not elected a Democrat in 32 years, Franklin jumped at the chance. His law firm was genuinely disturbed, but Eleanor was most encouraging, listening to Franklin's plans with great interest.

Eleanor and Franklin had lunched with Uncle Ted in June when he returned from Europe and Africa where they undoubtedly discussed Franklin's plans to run for office. He was not the only family member TR had inspired to serve the public good. Cousin Ted Robinson was running on the Republican ticket for a seat in the New York Assembly from Herkimer. His sister Corinne's husband, Joe Alsop, was very involved in Republican politics in Connecticut. Franklin stuck with his father's Democratic party, in spite of Uncle Ted's Republican affiliation, and Eleanor, though raised in Republican households, followed her husband.

Eleanor spent the summer in Campobello with the children. Typically, the family summered with Sara in Hyde Park, then went up to Campobello for sailing and other water recreation. Eleanor had overcome her childhood fear of the water in order to fully participate with everyone. She conquered it with her indomitable will. The training was fortuitous for she would need all her strength to deal with future personal trials.

Meanwhile, Franklin remained in New York, attending numerous meetings with Democratic party officials. He ultimately decided not to run for the assembly seat, since the incumbent did not intend to bow out. He ran for the state senate seat instead, despite the fact that his chances of winning were estimated at one in five.

Eleanor's letters begged him to keep her informed. It was difficult to be at Campobello without him and, if he didn't write, she felt lost. She wrote that she would weep if he couldn't come up as planned. On October 6, 1910, Franklin was nominated to run for his county's state senate seat. Sara proudly listened to his acceptance speech. Eleanor, however, was at home in New York with a new baby, another son, Elliot, born on September 23, 1910.

Understandably, Eleanor was very nervous about their new baby. She hired a wet nurse so he would always be fed properly. It had been suggested that perhaps young Franklin would have survived if he had been breast-fed instead of bottle-fed, making him stronger and better able to withstand his illness.

Franklin ran a unique campaign. He hired a red Maxwell touring car, decked out with American flags. Together with the congressional candidate, Richard Conell, they travelled the length and breadth of the county, speaking on the steps of almost every small four-corners store of every village and town. Franklin aligned himself with the progressives and independents as well as his cousin, Teddy Roosevelt. He sparred with the crowd, thinking quickly and talking plainly. He was superficial, charming and enthusiastic.

At the end of the campaign, Eleanor finally heard Franklin speak at what became known as his "lucky corner," outside the Nelson House in Poughkeepsie. To Eleanor, he appeared tall, thin, high-strung and nervous at times. He spoke slowly and paused for such long periods of time, she was afraid he wouldn't start again.

The results showed the positive result of speaking to practically every farmer in the district, learning what his constituents needed and what they were thinking first hand. Franklin won his first election by 1,140 votes, an unparalleled victory. He led the state ticket.

The Democratic sweep that brought Franklin into office in the 1910 election was in part a repudiation of the Taft presidency. Alice's husband, Nick, was barely saved from defeat in his re-election bid. Alice recognized her husband's plight, but did not offer to campaign with him. Instead, she went off to visit with Auntie Bye at Oldgate for four heavenly peaceful days just before election day. She may have breathed a sigh of relief that Nick had not gotten the Governor's nod from his party when the Democratic candidate won.

Eleanor and Franklin relocated their family to Albany in

Chapter Nine 93

November. Though Sara helped them get settled in their new home, she planned to continue living in Manhattan. At the age of 26, Eleanor's independent life was about to begin.

Eleanor's narrow existence of babies, home life and society matron was poised to give way to a new life in the political arena. Politics would provide the catalyst that would save her mental health, plunging her headfirst into the dynamic waters of public service. It would not only rescue her, but it would change the entire character of her relationship with Franklin and his mother. The political arena would allow Eleanor to spread her wings as Franklin's helpmate. It was an activity she could share with her husband using her intellect and spirit, unlike his other social diversions where she felt inadequate.

Politics threw Eleanor a lifeline, giving her the opportunity to finally live in her own home, without her mother-in-law's interference. Sara would no longer have complete access to Eleanor and Franklin's home through the sliding doors that she had designed between the adjoining townhouses she had purchased and built.

As her first political event, Eleanor hosted an elaborate, catered reception for Franklin's constituents on January 1, 1911, in their new Albany home following Governor Dix's inauguration. Four hundred people made their way into the house to congratulate her husband. With remarkable efficiency, Eleanor had the family completely settled one day later. The moving boxes were put away and the pictures hung. Then she went to work meeting people in town and learning the political process. Like Alice, she began to apply the skills she observed at Auntie Byc's in order to lobby effectively and shape political opinion.

Both Alice and Eleanor found the political experience exhilarating and in it, each found a new meaning to her existence. Politics helped Eleanor regain her inner equilibrium and recapture the dreams that she and Franklin shared during their courtship. Politics offered Alice a double-edged sword. It became a vital link between her and her father, repairing the bond that had been severed during her turbulent youth. Yet that very same bond created a gulf between Alice and her husband that they never successfully bridged. Her marital tie did, however, allow Alice to retain her place within the inner circles of the powerful political elite.

Chapter Ten

"Alice, if you will only stop trying to be respectful of me, I believe you would become so,"[1] President Taft said, taking Alice's hand as a show of forgiveness.

"Then I would bore you to death as the other women do!" she replied heartily, waving to the other dinner guests at the French Embassy.

Later that evening, Archie Butt, the President's military aide and a friend of the Roosevelt family, found Alice alone on a balcony overlooking the garden.

"You may still rival the Washington monument as the greatest attraction in town, but arriving after the President is an unpardonable sin!" he chastised her lightly.

"Archie, dear, you know I never care what people say about me. Besides, you saw how Will took it. He wasn't the least bit ruffled," Alice responded, dismissing Archie's concern.

"Don't push your luck," Archie warned.

Alice leaned close to search his face. "You look terrible, Archie. The stress from your job is showing."

Archie's impeccable military bearing broke for a split second. "It's the open warfare between your father and Taft. They used to get along so splendidly."

"He's a traitor," snapped Alice. "Coddling business special interests after he promised to uphold Father's policies."

"Even if you disagree with him on policy, he is the President. He deserves your respect."

"He'll have to earn it," she said curtly. "And you have earned a good rest."

"The President has arranged for me to take a European holiday, but I'm not convinced..."

She interrupted him, laughing, "At least we agree on something. Now let's change the subject before we endanger the family friendship."

"Agreed. I've booked return passage on the *Titanic*."²

"That should be lovely. Just the thing for a hard-working man. Pampering, frolicking, and diversion—exactly what I'd recommend. When do you leave?"

"Before the election."

"Be back in time for the fireworks," she teased. "Say, do you know that my cousin Franklin is making fireworks of his own in the State House in Albany?"

"So I've heard."

"Imagine, Feather Duster, leading a pack of insurgents against Tammany Hall. I always wondered whether he had any backbone. Of course, Eleanor's got enough for the both of them," Alice mused.

"She always impressed me as a good listener with an inner strength."

"People mistake Eleanor's quiet way. When she wisens up to the ways of the world, she won't be such a ninny. There were rumblings in the family about what he saw in her, but frankly, the smart ones wondered what she saw in him! I think they outsmarted all of us. She'll prove to be a valuable political asset someday."

"What about Franklin?"

"He showed courage campaigning in that Maxwell. He kept plugging away, even after dropping off in ditches and killing a farmer's dog. The only thing I don't like are the rumors I hear about his plans to follow in Father's footsteps to the White House. Father's not finished in politics, but if anyone's to follow him, it will be Ted Jr." She smiled at Archie. "By the way, you are to be applauded for your influence in keeping Father's name alive on the president's residence."

"Executive Mansion does sound hideous. The White House is so much more tasteful."

"That's why Mother loves you—for your impeccable taste."

"Bad temper is to be tolerated, but never bad taste,"³ the Major assured her.

"Taft should have such good taste and earn such respect," she said disdainfully.

"Shall we return to the party? People will talk," he smiled.

"Let them," she teased as he offered his arm and escorted her back into the dining room.

96 Alice and Eleanor

Political Warfare

After the 1910 election, Teddy vigorously roamed the country, demanding an end to the sinister influence of special interests in the Taft administration. He advocated a new nationalism, stirring the political cauldron. By 1912, the pot was poised to boil over.

Notwithstanding her father's stumping against Taft and her own disdain, Alice found herself a frequent guest of the White House. Nick was one of Taft's cronies from Ohio and, consequently, Alice was often seated to the right of the President at White House dinners. President Taft enjoyed the company of the young Mrs. Longworth. He found her wit and repartee unorthodox but brilliant. He treated her with the same indulgence as he had on their Far East trip years before.

Alice, however, grew much more strident. She criticized Taft's policies and his wife, putting on what she called Nellie Taft's "hippopotamus face." When she committed the unpardonable sin of arriving at a state dinner later than he, Taft's tolerance diminished. It eroded precipitously after she danced like a sinuous leopard at a White House Garden Party and danced a turkey trot with a cigarette hanging from her lips at a diplomatic ball.

The Washington matrons kept waiting for Alice to be tempered by motherhood. They did not know, however, that unlike cousin Eleanor, Alice used birth control. She remained trim and wild. On the social circuit of Washington, the Longworths created a stir, staying up for all night parties and card games. Congressional partiers stopped at their house for eggs and pots of coffee to restore them before they were ferried back to the House galleries.

Alice did not consider motherhood "women's highest calling," nor did she equate a rejection of motherhood as the dishonorable equivalent of men who shirked war. Her stance was in direct opposition to her father's views on the subject. He believed that birth control was race suicide, a sentiment he expressed to a woman in Philadelphia that became known as the "Race Suicide Letter."[4] Alice claimed to have always been "a supporter of people's sexual rights as long as they don't do it in the street and frighten the horses." The unenlightened women of that era were more apt to follow the path Eleanor chose, practicing abstinence after six pregnancies.

In Albany, Franklin was making a name for himself in the Roosevelt mold of cousin Teddy. TR had stormed Albany with

Chapter Ten 97

legislative vigor in his first years as an assemblyman. Franklin began crusading against the "political manchus" who controlled the party, heaping ridicule on the Tammany bosses. He became the spokesman of a group of discontents, the anti-Tammany Hall "Insurgents," who wanted U.S. senators elected by popular vote. Until the Seventeenth Amendment to the Constitution was passed in 1913 guaranteeing their direct election, senators were chosen by their state legislatures. New York's Tammany Hall political machine supported "Blue-Eyed Billy" Sheehan, a man who symbolized city corruption, while the insurgents backed Brooklyn's mayor, Edward Shepherd.

The Roosevelt home became the insurgents' nightly meeting place. Eleanor joined the men in their discussions. With her lively intellectual curiosity and interest in people, she became an intimate of many of the insurgents. She enjoyed the atmosphere, finding the intrigues of politics as invigorating as cousin Alice did. To signal the end of these gatherings, Eleanor would serve crackers, cheese and beer, after which the men knew it was time to go home.

The press was often in attendance with the insurgents. Eleanor first met Louis Howe as a reporter in Albany. He later became Franklin's chief political strategist, the architect of his presidential aspirations and a devoted friend and confidant to both Eleanor and Franklin.

Ultimately, Tammany's candidate, Sheenan, withdrew. Franklin's insurgent group went along with the compromise candidate, Justice James O'Gorman. They were chastised for caving in to another Tammany Hall candidate and Franklin was attacked as a traitor, fop and a fool. He, however, was learning to maneuver by making deals that would insure his political survival. Party loyalty and regularity were required along with self-righteousness. Eleanor was instrumental in helping her husband smooth over his relations with the true big city reformers of Tammany Hall, men like Al Smith, Bob Wagner and "Big Tim" Sullivan, otherwise known as the "Boss of the Bowery."

Eleanor was drawn to these men for the same reasons she had worked in the tenements. She was deeply committed to reform in education, the eradication of poverty and the betterment of working conditions. She had continued her fund-raising efforts around these issues and sensitized Franklin to them. Her husband's own inclinations led him only to reform in civil service matters and insuring good government. He never took a leadership role in support of the New York

State Factory Commission that investigated the horrible fire at the Triangle Shirtwaist Company on March 25, 1911. The Manhattan sweatshop doors were locked, trapping 147 women at their sewing machines. Some jumped to their deaths. The Commission was chaired by reformers Eleanor admired and knew well, Robert Wagner and Al Smith.

Franklin did eventually come around to advocating reform through his work as chair of the Agriculture Committee and on the Forest, Fish, and Game Committee. He represented a rural district and as such, became a leading conservationist. How much he was influenced by cousin Ted in his conservation views remain speculation, however, he did come to believe that if government intervention was needed to protect and restore America's natural resources, it was also needed to protect its citizens.

Eleanor began using her spare time like cousin Alice, listening to debates in the senate gallery. Sometimes, she followed them to the assembly side to monitor a particular bill's progress. She learned the internal short-hand of political insiders and read political materials. Albany was like Washington in many ways, a small, friendly town where everyone knew everyone else and business was conducted in all locales from the marketplace to meals. Franklin came to rely on her insights and opinions, recognizing that she was a vital political asset. She found out what his colleagues and their wives really thought, as well as his constituents.

Eleanor quietly became a supporter of women's suffrage. She hadn't ever really given the matter much thought. After Franklin was lobbied by Inez Milholland, a beautiful Vassar suffragette known as "the Amazon," Eleanor decided she "probably must" favor it since her husband favored it. She wasn't an active suffragette, but she was not an anti-suffragette either. She never uttered a single public word against the vote.

Franklin's support for suffrage was conditional. He kept one eye on his wife and mother, and his other on his rural New York constituents. He thought the voters ought to express their opinion in a referendum before any legislative action was taken.

Neither Eleanor nor Alice had been moved by the arguments of the Equal Suffrage League, though in later years Alice labeled their English counterparts "glorious." One moment, she saw them as all charm and gentleness, the next, the same ladies would be throwing themselves

Chapter Ten 99

under horses and tying themselves to trees. "It was wonderful," she raved.

While suffrage was a politically hot issue, the most explosive conflict bubbling in politics was the official break between William Taft, the President and Teddy Roosevelt, his mentor. The split erupted prior to the Republican convention of 1912. Teddy felt betrayed by his hand-picked successor. Taft had failed to keep his promises regarding trust dissolutions and had caved in to special interest groups. By January of 1912, TR had decided that Taft was hopeless and that he must run against him. Seven governors drafted a letter with TR's knowledge, requesting that he accept the nomination. Teddy waited until Washington's birthday, February 25 to announce, "My hat is in the ring. The fight is on, and I am stripped to the buff."

Nick was caught in an unenviable position, solidly in Taft's wing of the party, yet son-in-law of the man who was prepared to challenge the sitting President for his own party's nomination. To the conservative wing of the Republican party, TR was committing heresy by attempting to unseat one of their own.

Alice advised her father not to undertake the fight but, once he jumped in, she supported him. Nick was left to support Taft alone. The political impact of Alice's choice carried ominous overtones. If Nick and Alice made public statements regarding their choice of candidate, the world would know that Nick's wife put her father's career above her husband's. It would be a humiliating confirmation of what was already a widely held belief—Nick could not control his wife. For Alice, however, blood was thicker than love, honor and obedience in her marriage vows. Alice came out for her father. Nick remained silent.

Nick didn't believe his father-in-law could defeat Taft for the party nomination; still, he didn't think TR would give up his fight. If he lost, Nick believed Teddy would form a third party. There would then be another candidate running against him for his congressional seat from TR's new party. Faced with such a possibility, Nick was prepared to quit his re-election campaign, rather than have to run against a candidate from his father-in-law's new party. His position was unbearable. He admired TR, was loyal to Taft, yet he had to struggle with his marital ties and his own career. Alice was sympathetic, but did not make things easy as Eleanor had, by switching parties to support her husband.

100   Alice and Eleanor

Nick's predictions were born out. While TR mounted an impressive fight in the state legislatures for direct nominations, party regulars, like TR's old cronies, Elihu Root and Henry Cabot Lodge, were appalled at the open rupture in the party. No matter how many delegates Teddy won, Taft's men controlled the National Committee. Even though TR won the all-important Ohio primary, Taft's home state, with 37 of the 40 delegates, he no longer controlled the party.

Alice was consumed by the primary process and was in open rebellion with Nick's sisters. They were avid Taft supporters. On the evening of the Massachusetts primary, Nick took his sister, Nan, to a White House party, for Alice was no longer welcome. She preferred to stick close to the telephone anyway, gathering results of the primary. Nan could barely contain her glee at Taft's victory. Alice could barely control her "bottled up savagery" at her sisters-in-law for their criticism of her father.

Alice and Nick were in a perpetual state of agitation. Nick was torn not only by his family, but also by the officials with whom he and Alice socialized, who were part of Taft's administration. To preserve the peace, all agreed to avoid open warfare by not talking about the election. Alice described herself as chronically ill during that period, suffering from a "cold and cough, indigestion, colitis, anemia, low blood pressure, and quite marked schizophrenia." Food choked her. She existed on fruit, eggs and Vichy. If she passed President Taft, they would bow ceremoniously. Though the air between them was frigid, Alice "would become hot and giddy with hate."

Alice dealt with the stress by calling Edith to "blow off steam from time to time." She would explode at her in-laws and receive "large, soothing doses of sympathy from Edith." Ironically, the open tension that existed between Alice and her stepmother while they were living together largely dissipated as they aged.

Teddy came into the Republican convention with 278 delegates but only 13 states held primaries. Eighty-two delegates were pledged to Taft. The other states were controlled by back-room political bosses who were Taft operatives. Teddy's old friend, Elihu Root, who had cried in his soup at TR's farewell White House dinner, was elected temporary convention chairman over TR's choice, Governor McGovern of Wisconsin.

Though TR arrived feeling "fit as a bull moose," good feelings did not prevail. Root routinely approved the credentials of Taft's delegates over TR's. Teddy's men walked out of the Credentials Committee in protest. It was an ironic twist of fate, for Teddy had wanted to nominate Root as his successor, not Taft. Root was considered too conservative to follow through with TR's progressive agenda, which became TR's exact complaint about Taft.

The Taft delegation from Ohio was seated, despite the fact that TR had won a decisive victory in the primary. Teddy's delegates began rubbing sandpaper together in protest, imitating the sound of a steamroller as Taft's delegates took their seats over TR's elected ones. Teddy's supporters believed the nomination had been stolen from their candidate. Alice practically lived in her father's hotel room, conferring with him over strategy. The chief topic of conversation was whether he should bolt the party and run as a third-party candidate.

Nick had not yet come out for Taft. Alice was seated next to him on the convention floor when Warren Harding offered him a deal. Harding was an avid supporter of Taft. If Nick would announce for the incumbent, Harding would support him for governor. It was a strange proposal, since Harding was the man who won the Republican party's nomination to run for Governor of Ohio in 1910 over Nick and then proceeded to lose the election. Without giving her husband a chance to respond, Alice blurted out that Nick would not accept "favors from crooks." Later, Nick pleaded with her to apologize, but Alice refused.

Before Taft's nomination was seconded, the Roosevelt family bolted the party to attend a preliminary meeting of those defeated progressives who would form Teddy's new Bull Moose Party. The Rump convention, as the meeting was labeled, thrilled TR's family. Teddy had addressed the Republican convention, declaring, "We stand at Armageddon and we battle for the Lord." After Hiram Johnson nominated Teddy as the candidate of the Progressive Party, his supporters were ready for another fight. Though the Progressives had lost to Republican party regulars, Teddy was a winner that evening. A new battle was underway.

The next day, Alice and Nick returned to Washington on a train that she saw as packed with traitors. These were men who had been on her father's team, both progressives and insurgents yet, in the end, stuck with the party regulars. Chief among them was Senator William Borah, a man who would play a significant role in her later life. Alice's spirits

102 Alice and Eleanor

were high, however, from the rush of the emotional nomination of her father the night before. When she passed Root in the train, she whispered "toot, toot," mimicking the steamroller with which he had been heckled at the convention. After a day in Washington, she left for the Democratic Convention in Baltimore. She had to see who would be her father's other opponent.

Eleanor was in Baltimore too, attending her first convention with Franklin. Alice's brother, Kermit, told them, "Pop's been praying for Clark." Senator Champ Clark of Missouri was a flag-waving, Democratic party regular but, after 46 ballots, the governor of New Jersey, Woodrow Wilson, defeated him. The Democrats knew that with their Republican opposition in disarray, they had to pick a candidate who could keep the progressive vote away from Teddy. Wilson was their man.

Alice was eagerly looking forward to attending the Bull Moose convention in August, but Nick was afraid his congressional seat might be in jeopardy if his wife were too visible at the third-party convention. He was in no mood for another loss, having just had his gubernatorial aspirations shattered by his wife's obstinacy. Nick and Teddy conferred at Sagamore and decided that Alice should not be allowed to attend the convention. She felt so sorry for herself, she entertained goading her husband into something awful that would justify her "packing my bags and hopping a train to Chicago."

While Alice stewed in her fury, Nick suffered from severe indigestion. She spent the summer in Newport, attending an extravagant ball at Cornelius Vanderbilt's, where she made headlines by leading the formal cotillion dance with Grace Vanderbilt. Alice's publicly hobnobbing with the wealthy did not play well for either her father or her husband in middle America.

Teddy tried to keep his promise to Nick not to run a Bull Moose candidate in his district, but he did not have the control to do so. TR's party operatives kept a stern watch over him to keep Teddy from making concessions, even to his son-in-law. This was Nick's first tough fight to retain his congressional seat. He feared that the Bull Moose candidate would pull enough votes away from his Republican party that the election could be thrown to his democratic opponent, Stanley Bowdle. On the national level, Wilson might come out on top of Taft and TR.

Prior to election day, however, Alice was summoned to Chicago. Her father had been shot on his way to deliver a speech in Milwaukee. He was saved when his spectacle case and a thickly folded copy of his speech deflected the bullet. TR insisted on delivering the speech, a 90-minute spellbinder, before he received care for the bullet lodged in his chest. He was treated in an emergency room, then put on a train to Chicago.

Alice cared for her father and attended speeches made by his running mate, Hiram Johnson, in between stints at the hospital. She infuriated every one of her in-laws but, most of all, her husband. He had specifically asked her not to go to Johnson's speech because it would look bad for him. Friends said it was as if Alice were saying to the Longworths, "I'm going back to my family. Screw you."

The Longworth women were working tirelessly for Taft. Alice was a traitor staying in their midst. The tension was unbearable. She enjoyed antagonizing Nick's mother and sisters, even contemplating becoming an active suffragette just to spite Susan Longworth, whom she knew opposed women's suffrage. The Bull Moose platform contained a suffrage plank but, like Eleanor, Alice supported the vote but didn't work for it.

Nick and Alice had a bitter fight on the Sunday before Election Day. She told her family she wanted a divorce. Enormous family pressure forced Alice to reconsider. Her father's stand on the sanctity of marriage was well known.

The problems between the Longworths and the Roosevelts were not the only family rift that occurred during the 1912 election. Cousin Franklin came out strongly in support of the Democratic candidate, Woodrow Wilson. He headed up Wilson's campaign in New York. Franklin's progressives allies in the New York state legislature saw their political future riding with Wilson against the Tammany bosses. He and William Church Osborne tried to drum up support for Wilson at the state convention, but failed. Even so, they decided to convene a New York State Wilson Conference. Franklin accepted the chairmanship.

While Eleanor was devoted to Uncle Ted, her duty was at her husband's side. She had lunched with her uncle and Auntie Bye in March as Teddy eagerly prepared his assault on Taft. When Eleanor and Franklin visited their friends the Fergusons, they found them wrapped up in Teddy's campaign, along with other young progressives who were hitching themselves to Teddy's star. Franklin's law partners supported Teddy and even Sara, Franklin's mother, wasn't certain for whom she would vote. Nonetheless, Franklin and Eleanor supported Wilson.

The Republican voters were split, giving the national election to Wilson. Teddy came in second and Taft was repudiated with a dismal third. Nick lost too, by 101 votes. A recount showed the same results. While the magnitude of his defeat was considerably less than Taft's, the painful realization of it was no less severe. Nick's mother and sisters blamed Alice for the loss. Just by sitting on the stage with Johnson, Alice figured she had pulled more than the hundred votes from her husband. What she had not figured on with Nick's defeat was being banished to Cincinnati. The dark days of Alice's life were beginning just as Eleanor's began to sparkle.

Eleanor found the Democratic convention hot and boring. She decided to leave for Campobello. Franklin was not a delegate, but he worked the crowd, making important contacts for his future. He telegraphed her that Wilson had won. While Eleanor publicly supported her husband's position, privately she wrote to Bob Ferguson and his wife, Isabella, hoping Uncle Ted would win. Her heart was with the progressives. "Uncle Ted's progressive ideas have fired so many of the young men to real work in this state that even if he doesn't win this time, I feel a big work will have been accomplished."[5]

Franklin returned to New York to work on his re-election campaign for his state senate seat. He also established himself as an ardent Wilson supporter. Franklin won his re-election even though both he and Eleanor were bed-ridden with typhoid fever. He engaged Louis Howe, the political reporter and strategist who attended the insurgents' meetings at their home. Though he "looked like a troll out of a Catskill cave," Howe was witty, artistic and became an invaluable cog in Franklin's political career.

Franklin was rewarded for his support of Wilson. He was offered a position in the new administration as either Assistant Secretary of the Treasury or collector of the Port of New York. The position he longed for, however, was cousin Teddy's former post, Assistant Secretary of the Navy. While he was weighing his other offers, Josephus Daniels, the newly appointed Secretary of the Navy, offered Franklin the position he coveted. He accepted immediately, borrowing TR's verbiage: "I'd like it bully well." Daniels noted in his journal, "His distinguished cousin TR went from that place to the Presidency. May history repeat itself." As a congratulatory gift on his political appointment, Alice gave cousin Franklin a long cigarette holder, which became a trademark of his image.

Alice and Eleanor witnessed a raucous suffrage parade along with 500,000 other spectators during Wilson's inauguration. The suffragettes received more notoriety for their scanty dress in the freezing weather than their cause. Their progress was halted numerous times as the crowd surged forward. The rest of the parade stopped while the suffragettes own mounted escort pushed the crowd back along with the police. The *New York Times* devoted a full page to the parade, led by Inez Milholland on horseback and accompanied by floats. Five thousand women marched to the steps of the Treasury building where the event culminated in an elaborate, allegorical performance.

Eleanor wrote to the Fergusons that the parade was "too funny and nice fat ladies with bare legs and feet posed in tableaux on the Treasury steps." Alice recalled seeing the parade from a lunch wagon on Pennsylvania Avenue beside the line of march. She had started out on foot with some friends, but soon lost them and circulated by herself.

After the inauguration, Eleanor paid a visit to Auntie Bye at Oldgate, determined to learn the social customs of becoming a successful political partner in Washington. Bye instructed her on the card-calling tradition that Alice had mocked with her Night Raiders. Eleanor's family rented Bye's Washington home, much to Alice's disdain. Whenever she visited, the place was overrun with children.

Meanwhile, Alice headed by train to Cincinnati. The torrential rains that soaked the city were a portent for the emotional misery that Alice would suffer living at Rookwood with her mother-in-law and her philandering husband.

106   Alice and Eleanor   **Early Childhood**

Eleanor Roosevelt, May 1989. Photograph courtesy the Franklin D. Roosevelt Library.

Early Childhood Photographs 107

Alice, age 3, with Auntie Bye. Photograph courtesy Houghton Library, Harvard University. Reprinted courtesy Theodore Roosevelt Collection, Harvard College Library.

Alice and Eleanor on ice. Courtesy the Franklin D. Roosevelt Library.

Alice Roosevelt. Courtesy the Library of Congress.

Eleanor Roosevelt at 15. Photograph courtesty Franklin D. Roosevelt Library.

Alice Roosevelt soon after her debut. Reprinted with the permission of the Theodore Roosevelt Collection, Harvard College Library.

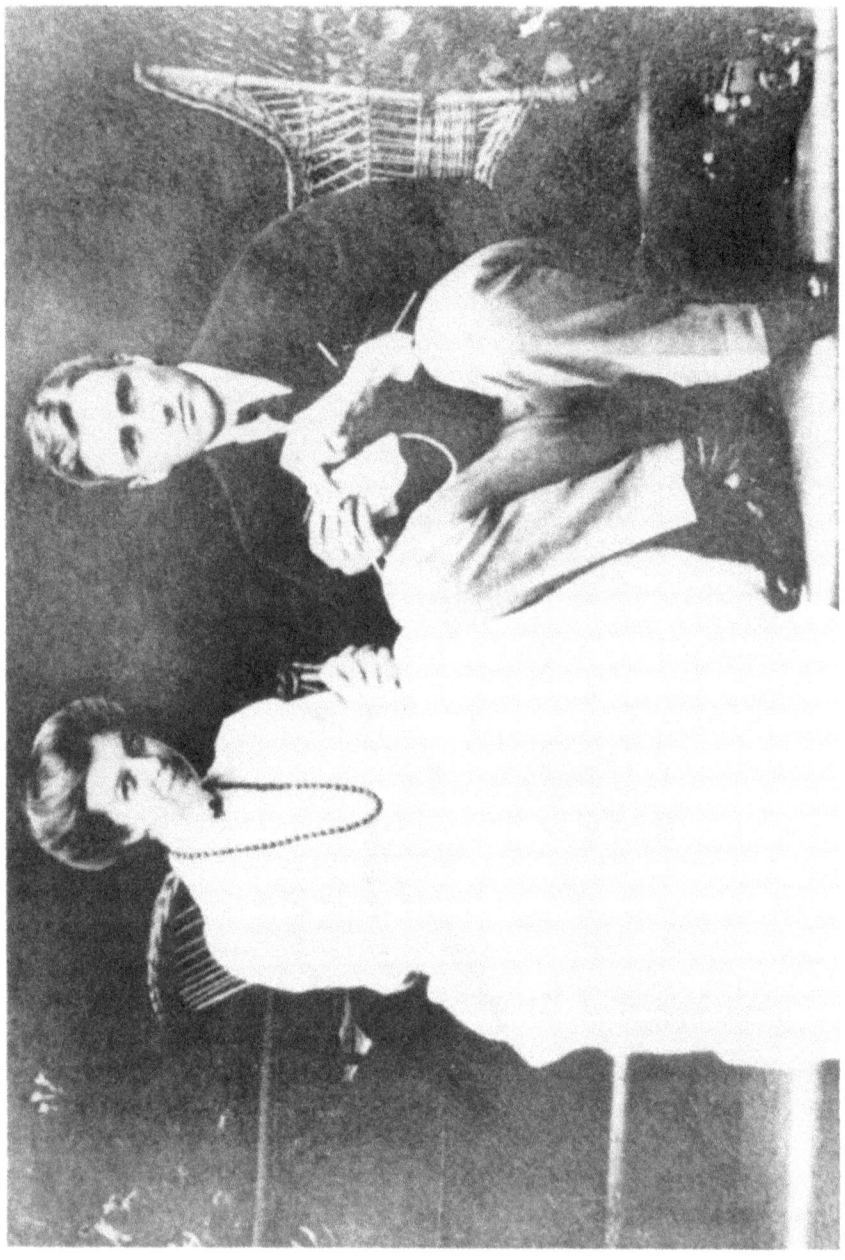

Eleanor and Franklin on the steps at Hyde Park. Their first child, Anna, was born in May 1906. Photograph courtesy Franklin D. Roosevelt Library.

Early Married Years

Alice and Nick Longworth. Courtesy the Library of Congress.

From 1906 until 1916, ER felt forever with child. For ten years, she wrote, she was either pregnant or recovering from pregnancy. "My family filled my life." This family portrait was taken in Washington, c. June 1918, before "the bottom dropped out" of ER's world. Seated left to right: Franklin, Jr., FDR, Eleanor, John, and Elliott; standing: Anna and James. Photograph courtesy Franklin D. Roosevelt Library.

Family Life   Photographs 115

Alice, Nick and Paulina Longworth. Courtesy the Library of Congress.

Holding her crowning achievement—The U.N. Universal Declaration of Human Rights. Photograph courtesy Franklin D. Roosevelt Library.

Beloved humanitarian, Eleanor is shown in 1948 at the United Nations with Dr. Charles Malik and several children.

Alice showing cousin Eleanor's toothy grin. Courtesy Michael Teague.

Fourth lady from left, Alice. Second lady from right, Eleanor. Lash, *Eleanor and Franklin*. Bridesmaids at cousins Theodore and Helen Roosevelt's wedding. Photograph courtesy Franklin D. Roosevelt Library.

Chapter Eleven

"What a thoughtful gift, Auntie Bye. Thank you so much, for everything. Franklin and I are very grateful for your advice. We want to do things right when we move to Washington," Eleanor gushed with excitement.

"You're most welcome, dear. *The Green Book* is the most valuable guide for calling. Let me briefly go over some of it with you, then you can study it. Tuesdays are reserved for calling on the wives of Representatives in the House and Wednesdays are for cabinet members. If you are calling on a man with his wife and a daughter who is under 21, you leave two cards of your husband's, one of your own, and two of your daughter's. When calling on a man and his wife, you leave two cards of your husband's and one of your own, or you can leave one double card—saying Mr. and Mrs. Franklin D. Roosevelt—plus a card of your husband's. On certain occasions..."

Eleanor's eyes glazed over as her aunt went on. She began reading through the book, sighing and shaking her head in bewilderment. "I shall never master this protocol."

"Of course you will. And if you need help, hire a social secretary. You'll find it an immense aid, given that you will still be running your own household and taking care of your children."

"I couldn't possibly do that. What will Franklin think?" she argued. "I've managed on my own in Albany."

"Washington isn't Albany, and no one will begrudge you some help. You are a splendid manager, but you needn't be a martyr. This town can consume you," Bye warned.

"It didn't consume Alice."

"That's because Alice makes her own rules. Washington society blacklists matrons who don't make and receive calls...all, that is, except your cousin."

"How did she manage...?" Eleanor wondered aloud.

"...to avoid the tedious, time consuming task?" Bye interrupted. Eleanor nodded. "It's her unique gift to mock tradition, and still be invited to participate." Bye watched her niece staring at her clasped hands in her lap.

"You're wondering why Alice is the way she is," Bye observed. Eleanor looked up, signalling yes with her gentle, searching eyes. "To be noticed. It's difficult to be your Uncle Ted's daughter. He demands a lot of attention. Alice has always fought against existing social order and expectations. She shapes her own. She possesses the wit and charm to mock the customs without offending most people. But even she pushed too far with Taft," noted Bye sadly, "and now she's paying the price. My best advice, Eleanor, is to build bridges on both sides of the aisle. And if you need help, ask for it."

Insiders to Exiles

The 1912 campaign didn't permanently damage the Roosevelt family's relationship. Franklin received a note from Uncle Ted dated March 18, 1913, expressing pleasure at seeing him in another of TR's old positions. "I am sure you will enjoy yourself to the full..., and that you will do capital." He went on to encourage Eleanor to be particularly nice to the naval officers' wives, who had to make do with little and still keep up their position.

Eleanor settled her family into Bye's home on N Street with typical efficiency. She had become accustomed to moving her children, assorted household help and luggage between Albany, Manhattan and Campobello with an ease that amazed those who knew her. As she had in Albany, she began building bridges for Franklin.

Franklin's ties to the Wilson democrats, plus the Roosevelt family ties to the old Washington network, served their family well. Washington society consisted of three groups in those days—"The Aborigines" or the "cave dwellers," who were the old Washington families, the top-ranking officials on the social register and, finally, the diplomats. Eleanor and Franklin were put on all three lists. They were soon socializing as a part of Washington's inner circle, attending balls and dinners.

Those close to Uncle Ted opened doors for them to the centers of political power. They, in turn, charmed Washington as a devoted, hard working, loving team. The stress and strain of their early years under Sara's domination had vanished. Eleanor had blossomed into an efficient manager with remarkable social standing who Franklin had come to respect, appreciate and value as his ally.

Chapter Eleven 121

Part of their successful transition to life in Washington was due to Eleanor's devoted effort at "calling." She embarked on it with zeal almost every afternoon, calling on ten to 30 wives a day. She never spent more than six minutes at any home. It was exhausting, but Auntie Bye had advised her to make the calls and Eleanor did what was expected of her. Though marginally useful, she met everybody from the wives of members of the House and Senate to the Supreme Court. She recorded all her visits and reported back to Franklin. In the process, she served tea for political allies and friends.

Their evenings were filled with formal dinners and dances. At 28, Eleanor was tall, slender and radiant. Her hair curled softly, framing her sensitive eyes. Franklin, now 30, was debonair and fun loving. Two Sunday evenings a month, the Roosevelts hosted intimate dinners with eight to ten long-time friends. The group called themselves "The Club," engaging in serious conversation over salad and eggs which Eleanor scrambled at the table.

While Eleanor and Franklin were charming Washington, Nick Longworth was back in Cincinnati charming young women. His narrow defeat in the 1912 Ohio election race hit hard and Nick took out his disappointment on Alice. He began getting drunk during the day and not showing up for dinner. He didn't try to hide his womanizing either. He openly and belligerently flaunted his flirtations.

The thick skin Alice developed as a child served her well in the alien environment of Cincinnati. The raging hostility she felt for Nick's family and Nick himself was obliquely covered with a veneer of indifference and cordiality. She endured living with a resentful mother-in-law and antagonistic sisters-in-law who also blamed her for Nick's loss. The Longworth family's mood blackened further when they learned that Taft had been ready to appoint Nick as ambassador to China, but Mrs. Taft vetoed the idea.

Nick filled his time playing golf and his beloved violin. He renewed a boyhood pleasure, picnicking on the hill overlooking the junction of the Ohio and the Little Miami Rivers where his grandfather had planted his vineyards. Alice was relegated to cooking chops on the hill while Nick held hands or lay in the grass with his arm around various young women.

Alice bided her time, learning to tolerate chamber music in the evenings. Nick often played first violin from after dinner until the early morning. He was accompanied by conservatory students on the concert grand piano, a viola and cello. He sang, cracked jokes and performed parlor stunts for his guests too. Those guests who had a proclivity to talk were shunted into the dining room during the performances.

Alice found Nick's mother's behavior reprehensible in regard to a libel suit TR brought against a small paper published in Ishpeming, Michigan. The editor spread the rumor that "Roosevelt lies and curses in a most disgusting way, he gets drunk, too, and that not infrequently." Teddy testified in court and won the action for the nominal damages he requested, six cents. Alice wrote to Auntie Bye that her mother-in-law never congratulated her for TR's victory or said one friendly word. Alice pledged not to forgive or forget.

When Alice visited Sagamore Hill for her sister Ethel's wedding in the spring, Edith noted her step daughter looked "horribly ill and worn and has a dreadful time with Nick." Nick refused to attend the wedding, claiming that floods in Cincinnati kept him away. He didn't even send a congratulatory telegram. The stress continued to build, taking a further toll. By the time Alice visited her family at Oyster Bay five months later, Edith complained that her behavior had turned "spiteful with everybody."

Alice used any excuse to get out of Cincinnati. She could always escape to Auntie Bye's for a few days. But her outlook didn't change until returning to Washington looked possible. Nick worked diligently in his district over the two years between the 1912 and 1914 elections to regain the political upper hand. By the time of the 1914 election, he was ready to confront Bowdle again.

Alice had returned to Washington for a visit only once during the the congressional term in which Nick did not serve. She was invited to a White House party, but her behavior incurred the wrath of many, insuring that she would not be invited again while Wilson was President. For most of the evening, Alice sat in the East Room whispering unflattering remarks about the current administration to those who gathered around her, principally her father's sympathizers.

Though initially enamored by the protocols of Washington, Eleanor became overwhelmed with the constant barrage of "calling" and other social engagements. Though others, like cousin Alice, thought she did her job "a little better than anyone else," Eleanor felt she needed help.

During the winter season of 1913-14, she hired Lucy Page Mercer three mornings a week to respond to social correspondence.

Lucy was young and attractive, always cheerful, and eager to do everything asked of her without regard for the clock. Her father had fallen on hard times and died poor, but he had been one of the founders of Washington's exclusive Chevy Chase Club and a pillar of the Metropolitan Club. After her parent's marriage broke up, Lucy's hardworking mother trained her daughter to be self-sufficient as a social secretary, a profession for young ladies with impeccable social standing and slim purses.

With her warmth and charm, Lucy was able to fill the role of an extra woman at dinner parties. The Roosevelt children adored her and Eleanor considered her a reliable friend. Sara approved of Lucy for she came from an irreproachably patrician background. Men fell in love with her dark velvet voice, her admirable beauty and her efficient organizational skills. Franklin found her ability to bolster a man's ego without challenging him irresistible and refreshingly different from his wife.

Though Eleanor and Franklin were considered an ideal working couple, the diversions they sought were distinctly dissimilar. Franklin loved to drink and he was always the life of any party. He was a high-spirited, handsome man beginning to feel his strength and power. The flirtatious behavior of his youth re-emerged. Eleanor treated it lightly while she felt secure in his love. However, she couldn't bear to confront the women he flirted with, so she would absent herself from such situations.

Franklin's behavior was painfully reminiscent of her father's. Eleanor had learned to repress her feelings of jealousy early in life. When her father was exiled from the family, he had written glowingly about entertaining the children of his friends in Abington. She employed the same techniques with Franklin believing that, if companionship and love were not freely offered, they were not worth having. She didn't want to freeze her husband out of her heart the way she believed her mother had done to her father. She chose, instead, to look the other way and tried to be gallant.

Just as she had encouraged him to go off to Boston or sailing and riding with his friends early in their marriage, Eleanor chose not to interfere with Franklin's endless social engagements. However, she didn't want to participate and, privately, she wanted him to decline. She considered many of his pursuits frivolous, boring, even annoying and she disapproved of companions like Harvard classmate Livy Davis. Livy drank all day and partied all night. As early as 1909, Eleanor and Franklin had reached an agreement. He could do as he pleased as long as she didn't have to be with him.

The pattern intensified in Washington. Franklin stayed later and later at parties while Eleanor's departures became increasingly early. Between his memberships in the Metropolitan and Chevy Chase country clubs, plus golf, poker, stag dinners, his Harvard pals and the diplomatic functions, there was no lack of entertainment for a gaiety seeker like Franklin.

Eleanor was not a total recluse. She did enjoy some social occasions in Washington much more than in Albany, particularly the diplomatic balls. She liked the entertainment and dancing and the fact that deals, liaisons and work were often done at these affairs.

After the disastrous election of 1912, Alice's father and her brother, Kermit, embarked on an expedition to explore the uncharted Amazon River basin with a Brazilian army unit and other naturalists. They left at Christmas, 1913, and were not heard from until four months later. In the interim, the family feared for their lives. Two members of the expedition died. One drowned while another was killed by his sergeant after having gone mad from the arduous life in the rain forest. The expedition saw no other humans for 48 days. They subsisted on what they could hunt or fish. They were continually soaked by rain. TR's leg was crushed trying to save a runaway canoe, the same leg that had been injured previously and had never healed properly. He had to be carried in a litter and he also contracted jungle fever. Teddy's temperature shot up to 105 degrees and he couldn't be moved for days.

"I had to go," TR exclaimed when he finally saw Alice in the next spring. "It was my last chance to be a boy." Though the voyage had been a success in charting the Amazon basin, it had drained much of the life out of Teddy. He lost 75 pounds and never regained his former vigor. The expedition discovered and mapped 1500 miles of the River of Doubt. In TR's honor, it was renamed *Rio Teodoro*. He received another hero's welcome in New York upon his return.

Shortly after TR's return, Alice seized an oportunity to leave Cincinnati. She sailed with her father to Spain to attend Kermit's wedding to the daughter of the country's U.S. Ambassador. With a recent inheritance of over $10,000 a year from Grandmother Lee's estate, feisty and now financially independent, 30-year-old Alice extended her trip while Nick stayed at home to work on regaining his seat in Congress. She stopped in Paris for a night and then went on to London.

Alice was fascinated by the English and made the rounds of their aristocratic homes. Many men were delighted to squire her about, particularly F.E. Smith, soon to become Lord Birkenhead and a conservative cabinet minister, along with Neil Primrose, a member of parliament. Alice was once again the belle of the ball, circulating with stylish, attentive, carefree companions. When she crossed the English Channel with a group spending a weekend in Paris, Primrose escorted her to the mansions of his Rothchild relatives. They drove to Longchamps to watch the running of the Grand Prix on June 28, 1914.

During the race, word reached the crowd that the Archduke Ferdinand, heir to the Austro-Hungarian throne, had been killed by a Serbian student in protest over the seizure of his country by the Austrian Emperor Franz Joseph. Nobody seemed very concerned, though they agreed it was tragic. "None of the people there who talked about it gave any sign of realizing that it was the match that touched off the fuse," Alice wrote. The race continued and afterwards, Alice and Neil returned to Jimmy Rothschild's, where they drank Napoleon brandy-and-sodas. From there they danced until the early morning hours at Maurice de Rothschild's.

She made the crossing back to London the next morning, and continued her intense party pace for another week. Alice finally decided to return home but, the night before she left, she played bridge all evening with Neil Primrose, Jimmy Rothschild and F.E. Smith. Then she hurried to bathe and eat breakfast before catching the boat train from Waterloo Station to Southampton and back to the United States. Two weeks after her return, the war to end all wars began.

Though Teddy initially supported Wilson's neutrality pledge, once Germany overran Belgium, he wrote a series of articles denouncing the "Belgian tragedy." Americans of German descent raged. When German U-boats torpedoed the British mailship *Lusitania*, killing 114 Americans, TR demanded a clampdown on trade with Germany. Even though it was known that the ship carried armaments, Alice supported her father's position, pitting her once again against her husband. Nick was courting the German Americans in his district while Teddy was rattling his saber.

Franklin made an unsuccessful bid for the Democratic senate nomination in New York during the summer of 1914. Eleanor had taken the children to Campobello and was awaiting the birth of her fifth child. Though the baby wasn't expected until August 26, he arrived early on August 17, the second Franklin, Jr. The birth kept her far from her husband's primary fight, but she encouraged him in her letters. With his loss to the Tammany Hall candidate, James W. Gerard, Franklin returned to his post in the Navy Department.

Nick won back his congressional seat in the 1914 election. With TR's progressive party weakened, Nick defeated his Democratic opponent, Bowdle, by over 7000 votes. Alice returned to Washington with her husband, released from exile in Cincinnati. She reopened their house at 1736 M Street, promptly turning it into a kind of chancellery where the best and brightest people in town gathered. She became an ambassador in the service of her father, cultivating inside information with the passion of traders on Wall Street. Information was the political currency of Washington and Alice became a master at extracting her pounds of flesh.

Concurrently, she developed an acrid dislike for the current resident of the White House, Woodrow Wilson, and his pacifist followers. Alice continued her fascination with "magics," having a doll with Wilson's visage carved out of wood. She stuck pins into it and hurled it onto the White House lawn.

The United States had declared its neutrality in the European war. Franklin's sympathies were allied with Uncle Ted's, urging preparation for war, which included building more battleships, artillery and training more men in uniform. His superior, the Secretary of the Navy, Joseph Daniels, noted that Franklin's strong views on preparedness brought him close to insubordination. Eleanor publicly sided with her husband. Privately, however, she favored Wilson's peace plank.

In Washington, the contrast between Alice and Eleanor in style and purpose sharpened. Alice could tolerate Franklin's company, but she had difficulty with Eleanor. Her first cousin represented all the righteousness that Alice disdained. Sunday dinners were a showpiece of their distinctive styles. While Eleanor and Franklin's friends in the "The Club" thought the Sunday evenings scintillating, Alice found them dreadfully boring. She described the meals as "rather fine and solemn little Sunday evenings where one was usually regaled with crown roast, very indifferent wine, and a good deal of knitting." Eleanor knit through most of the evening. Edith teased Alice that she seemed to swell up when she was bored. Her eyes receded and her face became fat. At one particularly staid evening, Edith told Alice she thought her eyes would disappear completely.

As the political situation heated up over the war in Europe, so too did suspicions of infidelity in both the Longworth and Roosevelt households. The Washington party lifestyle that intrigued Franklin also recaptured Nick. His public indiscretions continued. Like Eleanor, Alice looked the other way. Occasionally, she was confronted with harsh directness. When Cissy Patterson, her former partner in crime with Maggie Cassini, returned to Washington as a flamboyant divorcee, Nick began to squire her around town. Alice discovered them making love on her bathroom floor with the door unlocked. Cissy had divorced her Polish husband, Count Josef Gizycka, an abusive man who beat her.

An adventuress, Cissy was known as one of the most outrageous women in wicked Washington. Her wild ways remained untempered and she retained her reputation for stirring up trouble where she could. She would spend several months hunting and living in Wyoming but return to Washington in the winter. As heir to the family who founded the *Chicago Tribune* newspaper, Cissy didn't apply her considerable intelligence, energy and resources to the newspaper business until later years when she worked with William Randolph Hearst editing and publishing the Washington *Times-Herald*. During the days shortly after Alice and Nick returned to Washington in 1914, however, Cissy merely created havoc.

Alice created some havoc of her own in the press. She wore flesh-colored stockings rather than the black that proper ladies wore. She even began wearing pants in public, encouraging other women to wear them because they were comfortable, economical and saved considerable cloth. She only expressed displeasure at her own publicity on one occasion. Alice came down with the mumps as a guest of Mrs. Cornelius Vanderbilt in New York. When the *New York Times* called to verify the story, Alice told the reporter, "I am thirty-two years old and do not wish to have my mumps in the newspaper."

128 Alice and Eleanor

Some have accused Alice of maliciously taking out the difficulties in her marriage on her cousin Eleanor by encouraging Franklin's romance with Lucy Mercer. When Alice would see him driving with Lucy, she would tease him about having his hands on the wheel but his eyes on Lucy. Alice's own account suggests that like all her other exploits, no viciousness was intended. She was out to have a little fun, and Franklin should be allowed his, too, since Eleanor couldn't loosen up to do so. She wished Eleanor had "learned to enjoy herself a little more. She had so little enjoyment, so little amusement." Her view of Franklin and Lucy's relationship was "very much a lonely-boy-meets-girl thing. The rose behind the ear, the snipped-off lock of hair. That kind of thing."

Though courted in the 1916 election by his former party, TR declined to pursue the nomination of the Republicans. He campaigned vigorously for the Republican candidate, Charles Evans Hughes, an associate justice of the Supreme Court, not so much in support of Hughes but in fury against Wilson. Nick ran for re-election again and won easily.

Alice's ongoing feud with Nick's family continued in spite of her husband's victory. Once again it was over national politics. On election night in Cincinnati, even though she despised Wilson, Alice stayed up all night to gather election returns. With Nick's election secured, the Longworth family went to bed believing that their candidate, the Republican Hughes, had won. Alice, however, waited up until the returns came in from California. She took malicious delight the next morning in informing the Longworths that their man had lost. Wilson had squeaked out a victory with 277 electoral votes to Hughes' 254. Wilson had outpolled his opponent by 2000 votes in California to take the state and the election.

Though the country narrowly supported Wilson's non-interventionist plank, the President's own cabinet reflected the strong sentiments aroused over U.S. policy in the war. His Secretary of State, the ardent pacifist William Jennings Bryan, quit his post after the sinking of the *Lusitania* to head a country-wide peace campaign. Years later, Eleanor admitted that Bryan's pacifism appealed to her. She did not join those who laughed in official Washington at the miniature plowshares Bryan had made out of old swords.

Chapter Eleven 129

Like Alice, Eleanor spent the election night of 1916 with her mother-in-law. It was a gloomy evening for the Democrats. Eleanor was shocked when she heard another relative praise Uncle Ted for returning to the Republican party to support their candidate against Wilson. She did not believe party loyalty made Teddy a bigger and finer man than before. To Eleanor, Uncle Ted had abandoned the progressive ideals that the Bull Moosers had supported at precisely the time when Wilson was pushing his progressive agenda through Congress. Unlike TR, most progressives and socialists had swung their support to Wilson.

Issues of principle were paramount in Eleanor's mind over party affiliation, setting her at odds with the practicalities of party politics. The conflict she felt over TR's choice would reappear over political decisions made by her husband.

Chapter Twelve

"You are quite the little devil, Franklin, stealing Lucy right out from under your wife's nose." Franklin blushed, taking a long drag on his cigarette. "But, you deserve a good time, F.D.," Alice said, patting his hand "because you are, after all, married to Eleanor.[1] You must bring Lucy around to dinner some night. It must be terribly lonely for you with your wife and the chicks[2] up in Campobello," she observed suggestively.

"What a capital idea," he agreed, winking at her naughtily. Franklin shook his long cigarette holder at Alice, chastising her. "Hadn't we better get on with our work?"

A male voice crackled over the wire. "May, darling..." The voice was followed by kissing sounds.

Alice and Franklin leaned closer to the ear piece from their hidden spy headquarters in May Ladenburg's converted horse stall. They elbowed one another to keep from giggling, like children spying on adolescent lovers.

"Is that Baruch?" a gruff military aide whispered. Alice and Franklin nodded simultaneously, eager to overhear the conversation.

"Bernard, please...(throaty laughter). Be patient (more kissing and laughter). How many locomotives are being sent to Romania?" The response was muffled, covered by heavy breathing.

Some time later.

"Eleanor, how good to see you," Alice bubbled as she nearly collided with her cousin on the steps of Capitol Hill later that summer. "I thought you were in Campobello with the children?"

"Franklin's been ill. I came down to nurse him," she replied evasively.

"It's a shame you had to interrupt your vacation. Wasn't there anyone else who could tend to him? Say, Lucy, or his mother? I'm sure either woman would be pleased to minister to him," she said mischievously.

"It's a wife's duty," replied Eleanor curtly, "but then you wouldn't understand. You'd never think to interrupt your vacation to help your husband."

"Why should I? Nick is quite capable of taking care of himself," Alice replied acidly.

"You didn't understood before you were married, and you certainly don't now. I'm afraid you never will," sighed Eleanor.

"I understand plenty, sweet Eleanor. By the way, I wonder if Franklin has told you the most delightfully scandalous secret..."[3]

Eleanor interrupted Alice before she could complete her sentence. "He hasn't and I don't want to hear anything that my husband doesn't feel fit to tell me himself." She immediately turned and walked down the steps, leaving Alice quite alone, ready to explode with her secret. When Eleanor paused to look back, Alice skittered down the stairs to meet her.

"I didn't think you'd really leave without knowing," she said cunningly. "Women need to be as well armed as men in the battle of the sexes."

"The only reason I stopped was to tell you that I think this spying business you and Franklin are engaged is positively vile. It's most unjust to poor May Ladenburg."

"I admit it's a disgraceful thing to do, but it's for the war effort. Besides, it's sheer rapture.[4] Unlike you, Franklin understands this kind of fun."

"If you want to do real war work, come down to the Red Cross canteen and pass out yarn," suggested Eleanor firmly.

"Perhaps I will." As she turned to go, Alice called, "Eleanor, if curiosity gets the best of you, ring me up."

War and Infidelity

Eleanor delivered her last child, John Aspinwall, on March 13, 1916. Society had changed since her first confinement during Alice and Nick's wedding. Eleanor dined out almost every night and hosted huge Navy receptions in her last month. Not only had she become the mother of five of Franklin's children as well as his organizational manager, she had taken on the role of mitigating his brash ego-centrism. She reminded him when he was being patronizing. She prompted him to respond to letters immediately that he would otherwise have ignored. She passed on praise she heard, while tempering it with chastisements about the heavy

132 Alice and Eleanor

responsibility that other people's trust engendered. Where adulation intoxicated Franklin, it bothered Eleanor. She felt it was important to earn the public's trust to justify their blandishment.

Perhaps Franklin flirted with other women because they fed the very nature that Eleanor modulated, his frivolousness. Alice was cut from the same mold. Both she and Franklin had self-indulgent streaks which characterized the social elite of the early 1900s. Each thrived on carefree escapism. Neither was in direct contact with the upheaval in American society as it struggled to transform itself from an agrarian into an industrialized nation. And only on brief occasions was either confronted with the issues of poverty, or social and racial discrimination.

On the homefront, the eight-hour work day became law as part of the progressive plank that Wilson championed. Pancho Villa led invading troops into New Mexico, prompting Wilson to send U.S. troops into Mexico. At the 1915 international Women's Congress meeting in The Hague, Jane Addams outlined a peace platform which became the forerunner of Wilson's Fourteen Points plan for peace. She had supported TR's 1912 presidential bid, even though he was not a supporter of women's suffrage. Margaret Sanger, who had been indicted for sending birth control information through the mail, was on hand at the 1916 opening of the nation's first birth control clinic. The first woman was elected to the U.S. Congress in the 1916 election, Republican Jeannette Rankin from Montana. And the National Park Service, so dear to TR's heart, was established under the Department of the Interior. Though these dramatic changes significantly altered America, it was the Great War that permanently changed the foundations of the world of privilege from which the Roosevelts came.

A month after Wilson was inaugurated for a second term on his peace plank, the President was forced to the brink of war. On January 17, 1917, the German ambassador, Count van Bernstorff, effectively limited the supply line from the U.S. to Britain and France by restricting the number and route of ships through prescribed sea lanes. He declared that U-boat warfare would rage unrestricted in the Atlantic. Even Wilson could not ignore the belligerence of the German act for our allies relied heavily on the supply ships.

Though most Americans supported Wilson's neutrality doctrine, emotionally they sympathized with the Allied forces of the British and

Chapter Twelve 133

French. They disdained Germany's militarism, its refusal to submit the Serbian question to arbitration, and the invasion of Belgium.

Franklin and Eleanor's social circle were fervent Allied supporters. When Franklin lunched with Sir Cecil Spring-Rice at the Metropolitan Club, he told Eleanor that Count van Bernstorff was seated at the next table, "trying to hear what we were talking about. I just *know* that I shall do some unneutral thing before I get through."

On January 22, several days after the German Ambassador's announcement, Alice went to Capitol Hill to hear Wilson call for a negotiated settlement, a "peace without victory." The Germans' only response was a resumption of unrestricted submarine warfare. On February 3, Wilson broke relations with Germany and Ambassador von Bernstorff resigned. Franklin had been sent to Santo Domingo to inspect the Marine operations and evaluate the security of approaches to the Panama Canal. When Wilson broke relations with Germany, Franklin was called home.

A month later, with U-boats destroying American shipping, the President asked Congress for the right to arm American merchant and other ships. The British intercepted a German offer to Mexico of several American states: Texas, New Mexico and Arizona, if Mexico entered the war with them. Then three American vessels were torpedoed. Wilson's cabinet finally unified in a single voice and on March 20 they recommended that the President ask Congress for a declaration of war.

In Alice's opinion, the chief executive was a mollycoddle who would never go far enough; but, on April 2, 1917, almost two years after the sinking of the *Lusitania*, Wilson finally went to Congress with his request.

Eleanor listened breathlessly as the President solemnly addressed the members of Congress. There was no alternative to war for "the world must be made safe for democracy...It is a fearful thing to lead this great peaceful people into the most terrible and disastrous of all wars, civilization itself seeming to be in the balance.... we shall fight for the things which we have always carried nearest out hearts." Eleanor "returned home still half-dazed by the sense of impending change."

On April 6, the President signed the declaration putting the United States at war with Germany. Teddy wanted a personal meeting with Wilson to ask for permission to recruit a reconstituted fighting division of 200,000 Rough Riders. Though he had to swallow his pride in order

134 Alice and Eleanor

to meet with the man whom he had publicly criticized for several years, TR's sense of duty called louder than his ego. Arousing the nation to a worthy fight was of paramount importance now. Cousin Franklin helped set up the appointment by appealing to the Secretary of War, Newton D. Baker.

TR stayed with Alice at her home on M Street, awaiting his meeting with Wilson. He visited Eleanor and Franklin, grabbing Franklin, Jr. and John, one under each arm and roaring, "Oh, ho, ho, these two little piggies are going to market." They protested happily as he charged down the stairs. But a charge led by Teddy was not what Wilson had in mind for the American troops.

Alice drove her father to the White House where TR asked Wilson to let him take his men to France. The new Rough Riders would be drawn from a private military training camp that had been set up in Plattsburg, New York, near the Canadian border. TR would have his men fighting in France before any division of draftees was ready. Alice recalled her father telling Wilson, "Anything that has gone before will be as dust in a windy street, Mr. President, if you will let me have this division."

Wilson did not say no immediately, falsely raising TR's hopes. Teddy's friends in Congress passed an amendment to the Selective Draft bill being deliberated which would allow the President to authorize his Rough Rider divisions. Clemenceau of France wrote to Wilson requesting that he send Roosevelt to "gladden their hearts." However, neither the Secretary of War, nor the Commander-in-Chief, would countenance such a move. "He and many of the men with him are too old to render effective service," Wilson noted, adding that, "He as well as others have shown intolerance of discipline." Not only was the War Department concerned that TR's division would drain off the best officers, but they wanted a professional, disciplined, organized assault, not a gallant charge up the French equivalent of San Juan Hill.

The blow was direct and blunt, a repudiation and outright rejection of Teddy's politics. Though Eleanor felt her uncle's kindness towards her family, he was preoccupied by the war. She hated to see him disappointed by Wilson's rebuff, yet she was loyal to the President. A year later, however, she got angry with Uncle Ted for urging her to convince Franklin to resign his position and enlist. She would have supported such a move, but she felt it was her husband's decision to make alone. Franklin was itching to do just that, however, his superiors were uniformly against it.

Alice accompanied her father to bid farewell to her brothers, Ted and Archie, who were on the first troop ships that left New York on June 20. Though they exchanged casual goodbyes, the grim reality of death or injury was present. Watching her father at his sons' departure, Alice recalled an Old Testament reading from the prophet Job: "The old lion perisheth for lack of prey, and the stout lion's whelps are scattered abroad."

Ten days later, Quentin, only 19, also departed for duty as a combat aviator. Eleanor's brother, Hall, enlisted with Quentin and according to his sister, both must have memorized the eye chart, for neither could have passed the test otherwise. Hall had slipped away from his work at General Electric to enlist. Since he was responsible for the production of war materials, he was technically prohibited from signing up in anything except aviation. Hall felt compelled to join the other Roosevelt boys, even though he was leaving his wife and young children. Grandma Hall wanted to know why her grandson didn't hire a substitute as they had in the Civil War. Eleanor furiously defended Hall, declaring that gentlemen owed the same duty to their country as other citizens. It was unthinkable to pay someone else to risk his life instead.

During the first few weeks after the declaration of war, Alice and Eleanor busily entertained the allied missions that came to Washington. They attended some luncheons together, like the sobering one in which French Marshal Joffre described the large numbers of troops needed to help in the fight. Joffre quickly dispelled any notions that American involvement would be limited to sending money and foodstuffs or escorting war materials to Europe. Twenty-five thousand troops were required immediately, and 25,000 more after that, and on and on.

In his late 40s, Nick was too old for the draft. Rather than volunteer, he put his seniority as a congressman to work on tax questions, searching for ways to raise the $7 billion needed for the war. He followed the order of the day with the other Washington visitors, partying as hard at night as he worked during the day. He danced or played poker all night, then bathed and shaved, ready to greet the new day. Nick rarely slept, drank endlessly, though he never became objectionably drunk. In addition, he made it a point to defend German-Americans from attack by his colleagues.

Eleanor rallied to the war effort with a sense of duty. She instituted a food-saving program in her house that was reported in the *New York Times*. She was mortified by the publicity, especially when the story became a joke about model programs for large, wealthy households. Franklin teased her and she vowed never again to be caught having her words twisted by the press.

However, Eleanor's war efforts were genuinely appreciated at the Red Cross Canteen where she worked. She volunteered for two or three shifts a week in the railroad yards. Washington was a major railroad junction which saw as many as ten troop trains a day sitting in the yard. The canteen served soup, coffee and sandwiches to the waiting soldiers. The food was prepared in tin shacks.

During the winter, Eleanor took day shifts to be home with her children at bedtime and to entertain dinner guests. She rose at five to get to the canteen and did any work that was necessary, including mopping floors. Among her other volunteer tasks, Eleanor worked out the canteen's accounting system. In addition, she persuaded Franklin to set up a special unit to handle the massive number of postcards which the volunteers furnished for the men.

Once a week she visited the naval hospital, taking flowers and cigarettes as gifts for the men who had returned from overseas. These visits led Eleanor to start putting her political influence to use for humanitarian efforts. After a particularly distressing visit to St. Elizabeth's, the only federal hospital in the country for the insane, she left overwhelmed by the neglected condition of the patients, many of them shell-shocked veterans. She proceeded to lobby Secretary Lane of the Department of the Interior, under whose jurisdiction the hospital fell, for an investigation. Subsequently, Congress appropriated increased funding to make the hospital a model for the country.

In addition, she raised $500 from the Colonial Dames to build a recreation room at the hospital so the patients could start occupational therapy. After a short time, the men were able to sell what they produced. With growing confidence in her management and organizational ability, Eleanor took over the distribution of free wool to volunteer knitters for the Navy's Red Cross. In addition, she organized the Saturday collection of finished articles. She was in charge of more than 40 units, each of whose captains reported to Eleanor.

Chapter Twelve 137

Happy and unhappy news from the front reached the family. Alice's brother Archie returned, an invalid paralyzed in one arm by a shrapnel wound. Though TR was filled with pride that Kermit had been awarded the British Military Cross and Archie received the French *Croix de Guerre*, Ted, Jr. was nursing wounds in a Paris hospital.

The most devastating report informed the family that Quentin, TR's youngest son, had been shot down behind German lines on July 14 in a battle with Richthofen's "flying circus." He was buried at Cambrai, France, overlooking the Marne River. Eleanor wrote to Franklin, "Think if it were our John. He would still seem a baby to us." She grieved for Aunt Edith and Uncle Ted.

Alice spent the summer travelling back and forth between Washington and Sagamore Hill, but Eleanor was reluctant to leave Washington for Campobello that summer. Intuition cautioned her about Franklin's attachment to Lucy Mercer, though she had no direct proof of an affair. Lucy had started working in the Navy Department as a third class yeoman in June. When she finally did decide to go to the family summer retreat, Eleanor arranged for Lucy and Mary Munn to take charge of the Saturday collection of knitted wool articles, leaving instructions for how the women should be paid. Their work was to be strictly business, not a favor to Mrs. Roosevelt, Lucy's former employer.

Eleanor and Franklin's letters during the summer professed missing one another, but also contained rebukes of one kind or another. Eleanor complained that her husband never read her letters for he never answered her questions and the things she requested didn't appear. Franklin complained of being busier and busier, so he couldn't get away, yet he wrote of jolly days spent dining, playing cards, or sailing with friends. They included Livy Davis, Nigel Law, a friend who worked at the British Embassy, and Lucy Mercer. The Washington gossip paper, *Town Topics*, which had regaled the town with tales of Alice's exploits, frequently reported Nigel squiring Lucy about town, but rarely reported Franklin being with them. An official purpose was always attached to their excursions, like the trip down the James River to Richmond for an inspection of the naval fleet. For propriety's sake, Nigel and Livy accompanied Franklin and Lucy, serving as covers for their affair.

At the end of July, Franklin came down with a serious throat infection. Eleanor rushed to Washington to nurse him. When she left in mid-August to return to Campobello, she reportedly cautioned him to eat

138 Alice and Eleanor

well, sleep well, and go to the doctor twice a week. She professed how she hated to leave him, but warned that her "threat was no idle one." The actual content of Eleanor's threat was never disclosed.

Alice and Franklin's relationship intensified during the summer of 1917. While Eleanor was in Campobello, they were asked to participate in a spying scheme on a mutual friend. Colonel Marborough Churchill, head of the Army Secret Service unit called G-2, wanted Alice's help bugging May Ladenburg's house and attached studio, a converted horse stall. May was a friend of the Roosevelts and daughter of the senior partner in a German-American banking house. May was having an affair with Bernard Baruch, a wealthy financier who was Wilson's appointed Chairman of the War Industries Board. May was suspected of passing information from Baruch to her uncle in Bucharest.

Alice knew May's home well, for it was a social center in Washington. She told the secret service where to plant the listening devices and, along with Franklin, listened in on the romance from a command post in the studio. Franklin provided false documents that a friend of Alice's planted inside the house which contained information regarding the destination of a navy ship.

The offer gave Alice a chance to serve her country at a time when she was being criticized for doing nothing more serious for the war effort than dishing out ice cream, washing dishes, and slicing apple pies in the canteens for soldiers who came through Washington. Alice considered first-aid classes a waste of time, posed uncomfortably in a Girl Scout uniform for publicity photographs and sold Liberty bonds in front of one of the hotels. Of course, the Colonel's request wasn't very serious either. "All I was being asked to do was to look over transoms and peep through keyholes. Could anything be more delightful than that?" The surveillance revealed nothing and charges were never filed. The exercise merely provided Alice and Franklin, two adults in their mid-30s, with an opportunity for a delightful bit of sanctioned pranksterism.

Alice never developed a serious interest in war work like Eleanor. In fact, when she ran into Eleanor at a party where she was amusing guests by turning back somersaults, she asked her cousin about volunteering at the canteen. Eleanor agreed to take Alice with her, but she was dubious about her cousin's usefulness. "I doubt if she does much and they told me they were almost afraid to take her on!"

Eleanor's concerns were well-founded. Alice decided "she did not like scrubbing and ironing." She announced having conveniently contracted a rare and untreatable malady which she dubbed "canteen elbow."

However, the war work Alice truly enjoyed was entertaining the Allied missions who came to town to lobby for necessary materials and supplies. Such entertainment had a recognized part in "winning the war" and was far more pleasant than the kind of work Eleanor had undertaken, though it could not be considered nearly as noble.

In the autumn of 1917, Eleanor and Franklin moved their family into a larger home on R Street in Washington. The wool distribution and collection were moved to the Navy Department. Lucy was released from her navy duty in October. Eleanor still employed her as a social secretary and invited Lucy to parties when an extra woman was needed. But she also began writing almost daily to her mother-in-law. She may have needed the comfort of Sara's well-defined position on a husband's responsibilities to his wife and family. If Eleanor saw disaster looming, she was seeking shelter under Sara's protective wing.

One evening, Eleanor left a party at ten because Lucy was there. According to cousin Alice, Franklin couldn't bear to be away from Lucy's side. He returned home at four in the morning in high spirits, only to be greeted by the wan apparition of his wife rising from a mat in the vestibule, "looking like a string bean that had been raised in a cellar." She told him she had forgotten her key. When Franklin asked why she hadn't phoned for help, Eleanor replied, "I've always understood onc should try and be considerate of other people." She didn't want to disturb the servants, nor did she return to the Club because she knew they were having such a glorious time and she didn't want to spoil the fun.

Whether this episode drew her back to the time her father abandoned her in front of the Knickerbocker Club, no one will ever know; however, such self-destructive behavior was typical of Eleanor's "Griselda" moods. The incident typified the strain that had grown between her and Franklin. She had previously tolerated his innocent flirtations; but, as her suspicions about Franklin's feelings for Lucy grew, her own insecurities and feelings of abandonment returned. Eleanor retreated to her familiar pattern of silence and martyrdom. Both she and Franklin had become unreasonable and touchy. They argued but

140 Alice and Eleanor

did not confront their suspicions directly. Franklin's tales of mirth seemed like lies to Eleanor. They barely saw one another during the winter and spring of 1917-18. Franklin, however, was frequently seen with Lucy.

In May of 1918, the Red Cross asked Eleanor to go to England to organize a canteen there. She refused, feeling her primary responsibility was to stay with the children. She also knew her family would not approve. During that summer, Eleanor decided to stay in Washington to continue her war work and, perhaps, to keep an eye on her errant husband. She sent the children to Hyde Park to be with their grandmother. During long, sweltering days in the tin shack, she toiled from ten in the morning, often until one a.m.

Uncle Ted had established a permanent Industrial Peace Committee in Washington with part of his monetary award from the Nobel Peace Prize. During the Great War, he directed that money be dispersed to those he thought were best aiding the war effort. Teddy was so proud of Eleanor's work, he allocated one of the largest sums, $5000, to his niece.

Franklin sailed to Europe to inspect the American fleet on July 9, 1918. The trip was timed partly to avoid the New York Democratic State Convention because Louis Howe was trying to appease Tammany Hall for Franklin. Howe reasoned that if his man were out of the country, he would avoid the conflict between Tammany Hall and the anti-Tammany candidates that Franklin supported for state office.

On September 12, Eleanor received a telegram at Hyde Park to meet Franklin's ship in New York with an ambulance and a physician. He was suffering from double pneumonia and influenza, along with most of the men on the ship. The deadliness of that flu epidemic, which put Eleanor's entire household in bed within a week, was less noxious than the blow she received while unpacking Franklin's bags. Among his papers, she discovered a thick packet of letters from Lucy Mercer. They were the smoking gun that confirmed their affair, the cruelest betrayal in Eleanor's life. She was tortured by the thought that after having borne Franklin six children, she was being discarded for a younger, gayer, prettier woman.

Eleanor did not refer to the incident in her writing or confide in her closest friends. She did, however, offer Franklin "his freedom." After thinking over what the consequences might be for the children, if he still wanted to end their marriage, she would give him a divorce. She found that solution preferable to being in a home where she was not loved. Eleanor had lived in too many places like that. She insisted, however, that if Franklin chose to stay but did not break off with Lucy, she would insist on a divorce.

Sara, however, would not hear of divorce. Not only would Franklin's political career be ruined, but she promised to cut him off financially. Her son would not abandon his wife and five children with her blessings. Another complicating factor was Lucy's religion. As a practicing Catholic, it wasn't clear whether she could marry a divorced man. Franklin had to choose.

He had succumbed to the temptations of Washington as his new power and independence soared. He had indulged the frivolous, flirtatious side of his nature, the side his wife was well aware she didn't fulfill. Yet, he loved and cared for Eleanor. He also recognized that they had much to accomplish together. Louis Howe helped convince Franklin that his political dreams would be over if he divorced Eleanor. He not only needed her as his wife, but he needed her special skills. Louis also convinced Eleanor that Franklin could not go on successfully without her. She had no intention of destroying her husband's career, if he wanted her.

Franklin opted for the life he knew, agreeing never to see Lucy. Publicly, Eleanor and Franklin were committed to try again, protecting and defending one another. Franklin, however, told Lucy that Eleanor would not give him a divorce when, in fact, she had offered him one. He didn't keep his promise to Eleanor either. Numerous secret liaisons have been documented between Franklin and Lucy over the years until his death. He saw Lucy every time she visited her mother in Washington. He arranged to have her at his first inauguration and visited her at her estate in Aiken, South Carolina. Ironically, these visits were arranged by Bernard Baruch, the man Franklin and Alice had spied on during his affair with May Ladenburg. There are stories about Franklin's railroad car being taken off near a siding at Allamuchy in New Jersey to meet Lucy, as well as social evenings in the White House when Eleanor was away. Lucy was with Franklin at Warm Springs, Georgia, when he died.

The only written communication by Eleanor regarding Lucy after the affair was in a postscript to her mother-in-law on February 14, 1920. "Did you know Lucy Mercer married Mr. Wintie Rutherfurd two days ago?" Franklin apparently heard the news at a party and was stunned.

142 Alice and Eleanor

Eleanor suffered not only from Franklin's private betrayal, but his public humiliation of her. He had appeared all over Washington with Lucy and the two even dined together at cousin Alice's, while Eleanor was in Hyde Park or Campobello with the children. In one swift blow, the confidence Eleanor had rebuilt during her years in Albany and Washington out of her mother-in-law's sphere of influence was extinguished.

The affair initiated a period of intense introspection. At age 34, Eleanor was determined not to abandon her husband in the cold manner Uncle Ted had urged her mother to withdraw from her father. Eleanor concluded that their marital crisis required the soothing balm of a tender, loving heart.

Alice, meanwhile, took another course of action. She responded to her husband's flagrant indiscretions with bared claws.

Chapter Thirteen

"Aurora Borah Alice," Cissy teased. "What a lovely ring that has, so...poetic." She sauntered past Alice in the crowded parlor of the Lodge home. "Leave it to *Town Topics* to continue to highlight your flagrant antics."

"It does roll right off your tongue, doesn't it?" Alice smiled acidly. She spoke in a low whisper to avoid being overheard, maintaining a pleasant smile to disguise her anger. "One can't do much with a cowardly name like Cissy, can one? Are you trying to defy your name by your scandalous actions? No, I think your behavior is a poorly aimed reaction to that abusive, former husband of yours. I believe you're trying to get back at him by striking out at everyone in your wake. But for all your brilliance, Cissy, dear, you haven't learned that Washington is a town of *secret* scandals. Mums the word. Men of power, while they may be seduced, do not want the seductress babbling aloud. It's bad manners and, for all its faults, Washington still likes to keep up its front of decorum and respectability."

"Jealousy is unbecoming to you, Princess. I did appreciate your sending back my hairpins, though," Cissy added, viperously. "Bill's reputation befits him, 'the stallion of Idaho.' It's no wonder his wife left town. If you've ever seen her, you know there's no way she could harness his appetites."

"I imagine a fine horsewoman like yourself knows just how to rein him in," Alice sizzled.

"Oh, no. It's much better to give a horse his head," Cissy jested seductively. "You know what I mean. You ride, Alice, don't you? You should take a few lessons from your cousin. Eleanor knows how to give her man his head. She left town so he could enjoy himself."

Alice smirked to herself. "Yes, Franklin did have some fun, with a little help from his friends."

"The same, I dare say, of your husband, who can be as self-centered as Franklin. They both demand immediate satisfaction, just like children. Nick and Franklin are so alike in that way—charming, impetuous rakes, obviously spoiled by their mothers."

"Eleanor may have treated her husband that way, but I assure you, not I," Alice retorted coldly.

"That's why Nick looks elsewhere for comfort, darling. Men need their egos massaged as much as their more base natures. But your ego dwarfs most mortals. You will tolerate no competition."

"How wrong you are, Cissy. There are men of great stature to whom I am willing to join forces. Nick, however, is not one, either physically or financially. You might benefit in your career if you understood how powerful men operate. They want more than a breed mare. They want a passionate partner who shares their ideology. They also expect privacy. A lady ought never divulge the details of her conquests. If you learned that, you might still be in Bill's good graces. The true test of a woman's power is her ability to be a trusted ally *behind* the scenes. By gloating and chattering indiscriminately in your column, you have doomed yourself to adolescent dalliances on bathroom floors with Nick or library couches with Bill, but no true access to power. And that, dear friend, is what living in this town is about," Alice smiled haughtily. "Otherwise, you might just as well spend the entire year hunting in Wyoming."

"Power is in my hand, sweetheart. It's just you don't recognize how powerful your husband has become. Oh...and by the way, my hairpins aren't all your maid will find in the library from my dalliance with Bill. He tossed my panties up and they got caught in the chandelier. I should be dreadfully embarrassed, but you know me...I thrive on earthy scandals. Do check, and of course, you'll be so good as to return them, too."[1]

"If we find them, we'll toss them where they belong, as a reminder of what becomes of those who pursue trash. Need I remind you that you were seduced by a man of title and paid with a body of physical and emotional bruises," Alice rebuked her.

Cissy retained her condescending air, staring at Alice with sweet innocence. Her gaze was met by steel coldness. "Poor Alice. I believe I hurt you. You and Nick haven't been together for how long now? You loved him once and now that love is lost. There's nothing more painful to a woman than the realization that love she's given freely has been scorned."

Cissy took a long drag on her cigarette. When she spoke after a reflective exhale, her vindictive tone had softened. "We could both learn something from Eleanor. She is the wisest of the three. I never thought I'd see something in common between us, but our situations are the same—love given, love scorned. She among us is selfless. Our egos are too big to admit defeat. We never give in, not to love or to tenderness. Look at her. She gave her heart and was betrayed by fickle Franklin. Yet, rather than striking out, she offered tenderness and he stayed with her."

"For the sake of a political career. Franklin's no fool, Cissy. He knows what he married. She's his best political asset, and Louis Howe knows it."

"She has nobility, Alice. We had best recognize it. You want revenge over every occupant who displaced your family from the White House and I'm just a plain old vindictive shanty Irish bitch.[2] But Eleanor is a beacon of strength. She's the noblest woman I have ever known."[3]

"She's still a 'ninny'," Alice squeaked, imitating Eleanor's high-pitched voice while she drew her face into a bucked tooth grin.[4]

Cissy couldn't resist dissolving into laughter at Alice's precise imitation. "You haven't lost your touch," she said devilishly, grabbing the elbow of a passing friend. "So nice to chat, Aurora, dear."

"We Roosevelts give good show," Alice replied, then whispered in Cissy's departing ear. "You can do what you will with that drunken gambler husband of mine. He's not worth your time, I assure you, but the less I see of him, the better." They smiled deceptively at one another for the benefit of the surrounding guests.

Family Conflict Amidst Worldwide Chaos

Alice spent Thanksgiving of 1917 with her family at Sagamore Hill. She saw frustration and uselessness eroding her father's giant spirit. With his sons fighting in Europe, the former Rough Rider sat at home wasting his considerable political talents. He was overwhelmed with his own futility, signing some of his weekly letters to his sons, "The Slacker *Malgre Lui*"—the slacker in spite of himself. He mourned the death of his old friend, the British Ambassador to the U.S., Cecil Spring-Rice, who had unceremoniously been recalled when America entered the war.

Though TR wrote to occupy his time, including articles for *The Kansas City Star* in which he took issue with the way Wilson was conducting the war, Alice was convinced that her father needed a new challenge. With her energies directed thoroughly towards politics, she had a long talk with him. She felt that "he alone could steer and eventually lead the party." Alice encouraged TR to come to Washington to begin positioning himself as the 1920 Republican candidate.

On January 8, 1918, Wilson outlined his peace proposal to Congress. In the speech, he proposed his Fourteen Points, the basis of a master plan to "end war." It was a "peace without victory" and, consequently, TR was against the plan. His daughter joined the opposition. Wilson's long-standing vision of a "league of peace," which evolved into the League of Nations, emerged as a vital part of Wilson's peace doctrine. Freedom of the seas and a passage to the Baltic Sea through the Polish Corridor were other elements in the proposal. The seminal and the most controversial element of the League was a commitment of U.S. economic and military forces to solving issues of world concern prior to any independent consideration of America's self-interest in a particular conflict. In addition, the public was dubious about decisions in which their partners included the Germans. The United States was emerging as a world power while the colonial nations were in decline, and the isolationists' voice rang loudly.

The President returned from Europe to confront his "enemies in the Senate." He stayed for just ten days, denouncing Congress' obstructive action. In a speech before he sailed back to the continent, Wilson warned that he was going to "tell the people on the other side of the water that an overwhelming majority of the American people were in favor of the League of Nations." The President misread the public's sentiment on the League, which caused him a stunning political defeat later in the year.

Teddy and Edith arrived at Alice's home on M Street for a four-day Washington visit on January 22, 1918. The Longworth house became the rallying point for Republicans and Democrats alike who were displeased with the President's conduct of the war. TR was besieged by visitors. He consorted and consulted with politicians downstairs while family and friends congregated in the upstairs library during his stay. Alice noted that she "leaned over the banisters and counted thirty-three newspaper correspondents, fairly stacked in the small house."

During his stay, TR wrote a response to Wilson's Fourteen Points. He opposed the plan because it was a "peace without victory." He feared that an international peace-keeping body would lull the U.S. into complacency, no longer preparing for its own defense. He could not abide American dependence on such proposed League members as

Russia and Germany for its protection. He told Lodge that the plan was not "the unconditional surrender of Germany but the conditional surrender of the United States" to the overriding sovereignty of the league. He didn't put "much faith in the League of Nations or any corresponding universal cure-all." Teddy's proposal for "rapid victory and peace with honor" became part of the Republican platform.

He delivered a speech at the Press Club, dined at a men's dinner at Senator Lodge's, breakfasted with the New York delegation in Congress and met with foreign ambassadors, as well as Supreme Court justices back at Alice's home. On the last night of the Roosevelt's stay, Nick and TR went to another political dinner while Alice and Edith dined with Eleanor and Franklin.

Alice used her time during her father's visit to lobby for the appointment of a progressive admirer of Teddy's, Will Hays of Indiana, to be the Republican national chairman. Campaign funds were pledged and TR seemed ready to fight, but he became extremely ill shortly after he returned to Sagamore Hill. He was suffering from one abscess in his right leg and two in his left ear. TR was admitted to New York City's Roosevelt Hospital for surgery in early February.

Alice was summoned to his side at the hospital. She rarely left him. From her father's hospital room, Alice kept reporters informed of his progress and simultaneously lambasted Wilson's League plan. TR recovered slowly but the succeeding months were difficult. He had to learn to walk again after the surgery on his right leg. The abscess in his left ear left him deaf on that side. He suffered from sciatic rheumatism and a boxing blow from his Harvard days was slowly robbing the sight from his left eye.

With the end of the war in sight, Teddy was preparing a speech to be delivered at Carnegie Hall on October 28. Wilson issued an appeal to the country to re-elect him with a Democratic Congress if they approved of his conduct of the war. A Republican majority in either house would be interpreted by the European community as a repudiation of his leadership.

TR threw away the speech he intended to give and drafted one in response to Wilson's appeal. He denounced the President, his conduct of the war and his peace proposals. As he prepared each page, he passed it to Alice for her comments. The speech was received with extraordinary enthusiasm. Alice envisioned it as the beginning of her father's

148 Alice and Eleanor

triumphant return to the White House.

Alice and her cadre of supporters for "war to a finish" were strong opponents of Wilson's peace proposals. They agreed with TR that unconditional surrender should be insisted upon, not a negotiated peace. They met often, dining together, finding flaw with each renegotiation of the peace terms. They were suspicious, furious and ingenious in their criticism, Alice recalled in her autobiography. They were opposed to the notion of U.S. resources being pledged to resolve problems out of the country's scope, interest or control.

When the armistice was signed on November 11, 1918, to end the war, Alice walked along the Grandin Road in Cincinnati listening to every whistle within five miles blowing full blast in the early morning hours. She wanted to "feel that the morning stars were singing together and the sons of God shouting for joy." Though the whistles were extraordinary, the sound was not ineffable. At first they seemed "all dissonance, and then one would catch what seemed to be a wailing melody, or a crescendo of harsh harmonies."

The Peace Conference in Paris which convened after the signing of the armistice commanded the world's attention. Wilson attended specifically to bring back a League of Nations, but a backlash grew over the secrecy with which the President was conducting his plans. TR, Senator Lodge and others spoke out, concerned that Wilson was committing the U.S. to agreements that Congress was not prepared to authorize. During December, a group of dissidents began mapping out their strategy to fight the trend towards internationalism which they felt menaced the very existence of America as an independent nation.

Eleanor and Franklin sailed to Europe in January 1919 aboard the U.S.S. George Washington with President Wilson. Franklin had convinced his boss, Josephus Daniels, to let Eleanor accompany him as he presided over the liquidation of America's vast military stores. While the voyage was of monumental political importance for the President's league, it also held great personal significance for the couple. It was serving as a second honeymoon, in part, a reconciliation for their troubled marriage.

On the surface, friends and relatives observed how gay Eleanor and Franklin had become. They were each trying to become the partner the other had hoped for when they married. Franklin understood how deeply he had hurt Eleanor and sought to do things that would please her. He spent more time with the children and she made an effort to be frivolous. At the same time, however, they began evolving more independent lifestyles which would more fully meet their personal needs. The process, however, was not easy and they struggled continually from 1918 to 1920.

Prior to the opening of the Peace Conference, Alice was dealt a shocking blow. Her father died quietly in his sleep at the age of 60 on January 6, 1919. He had worked on an article and read during the day. Edith played solitaire close by. "I wonder if you will ever know how I love Sagamore Hill," he told his wife as they gazed out on the wintry water of Long Island Sound from his bedroom. TR retired earlier than usual. His wife kissed him goodnight and he suffered a stroke during his sleep. Archie cabled his brothers, Kermit and Ted, informing them, "The old lion is dead."

Eleanor and Franklin learned of Uncle Ted's death on board the ship. "Another great figure off the stage...I fear the last years were for him full of disappointment," she wrote. She grieved for the country and for Aunt Edith who would be very much alone.

Alice was profoundly affected by her father's death. Sadness from the personal loss engulfed her, along with the realization that she would never witness Teddy's triumph return to the White House. Fate had snatched that possibility from her, a bitter and devastating disappointment in her life. Meanwhile, Eleanor and Franklin observed another form of devastation as they toured hospitals and battlefields in Europe—the firsthand realities of war. Eleanor became a confirmed supporter of Wilson's postwar vision. She dedicated herself to the fight for the League of Nations.

"What hopes we had that this League would really prove the instrument for the prevention of future wars," Eleanor wrote, "and how eagerly we read through it [the League charter]." She described Wilson as a savior to the people of France and saw his position in America as impregnable. "No organized opposition had as yet developed." Little did Eleanor know what was brewing inside her cousin.

Alice sat through her father's funeral, her lips drawn tight and her eyes cold while some 400 personal friends paid their respects. The burial was without military honors, eulogy or music. TR was laid to rest in a plain oak casket on a plot near Sagamore Hill.

As the winter turned to spring, Alice's grief became determination

150 Alice and Eleanor

to win her father's final fight. The historic senate debates on the League of Nations began while Wilson was still at the Paris Peace Conference. Alice spent most of her waking hours in attendance, often staying in the Senate gallery until three a.m. She was consumed by the battle against the League. It took on monumental proportions to her as the embodiment of her father's legacy. She sat with her friend, Ruth McCormick, whose husband, Medill, was a senator and one of the senate "irreconcilables." Senator William Borah, the second speaker against the League, captured Alice's complete attention.

Borah was the same man Alice had reported seeing on the train when she and Nick returned to Washington after the controversial 1912 Republican Convention. Though she had been unable to get Borah to switch his support from Taft to her father, she described him being "progressive in his policies" and a man who "had long been one of the insurgent group in Congress, and had ardently supported Father up to the 'split'." Throughout the 1912 campaign, Bill Borah denounced Taft's "theft" of the nomination by controlling the seating of the delegates.

Borah was a bull of a man, much like Alice's father, with a complicated personality. He was an eloquent spokesman who had a reputation for being able to bring senators to their feet in spontaneous applause. He was also opinionated, powerful and insufferable.

Politics consumed him, as it did Alice. With the same tireless energy Eleanor displayed working at the canteens during the war, Alice devoted herself to the defeat of Wilson's international body. While Eleanor struggled to restructure her relationship with her husband, Alice embarked on an ongoing liaison with Borah. Gossip mongers in Washington had given her a new nickname, Aurora Borah Alice.

Borah was as aloof and contrary as Alice had been branded long ago. He was an unsociable recluse, the antithesis of Nick who was the House team player, good-old-boy and jolly entertainer. Where Nick was beloved by his colleagues, Borah was described by Hiram Johnson as being about as responsive as cold marble. He was selfish, secretive and anything but popular. Still, Borah held great power, serving in the Senate into his 70s. He became head of the Senate Foreign Relations Committee in 1924.

Alice and Nick were married in name only by this time, as reported in the era's best-seller, *Washington Merry-Go-Round*.[5] Even her relatives gossiped about Alice's relationship with Bill Borah. When a cousin asked her about the affair with him, Alice responded by giggling. On another occasion when she was visiting her parents without Nick for an extended period, her sister-in-law unpacked her bags because the maid wasn't available. She was shocked when to her horror, she found a diaphragm in Alice's bag, a clear indication that she was having an affair.

Bill Borah's reputation as the "Lion of Idaho" became cynically known as the "Stallion of Idaho." Rather than staying home in the evening with his wife, Mary, he was out with adoring women. Apparently the stallion's pattern was set early in life. He was born in Illinois and educated in Kansas. At age 25, he had been planning to move to Seattle or Portland to practice law, but he was forced to leave town for allegedly impregnating a young woman. He left in such haste he had only enough money to make it to Idaho.

The son of Borah's closest political adviser, Harry Shellworth, Jr., reported that, "Borah got off the train completely broke and slept in my grandfather's coal bin. The following morning my grandfather asked him, 'Why don't you take a look at Idaho? It's got a great future'."

Borah's reputation as a skirt chaser was reiterated by Harry Shellworth, Sr. When he was working as a newsboy in Boise, Harry sold the Idaho *Statesman* from three in the morning until sunrise outside of the city's 28 "sporting houses," which provided women and liquor. "Borah spent *every* night in a cathouse. Newsboys would know where to find him. Borah's philosophy: 'Better to pay for it before than afterwards'."

Marian (Mame) McConnell, the daughter of the former Governor of Idaho, Bill McConnell, confirmed similar rumors about Borah's marriage. "...the rumors...were that it was a shotgun wedding, that he got her pregnant and she had an abortion. I tried to drag this out of the man who was her physician at the time...I asked him the question point blank, 'Did Mary Borah have an abortion before she married him?' He wouldn't answer me. I have ever since been convinced that the reason he wouldn't was because...in those days if the abortion was performed in a certain way it meant that the woman could never have children. Her father was furious and made Borah marry her."

The Borahs' never had children. Mary surrounded herself with canaries. She was called "the flightiest numbbrain there ever was. She knew absolutely nothing about politics and wasn't even interested."

152 Alice and Eleanor

Mary Borah was clearly no match for Alice's wit and political instincts, so akin to Bill's own.

Like his wife, Nick had his own favorite companion. Though he had relations with many women, including Alice's former friend and rival for Borah's attention, Cissy Patterson, Nick had a special relationship with another Alice. Alice Dows was a passionate devotee of music, like himself. A grand dame from an old Hudson River family with close ties to Franklin and his mother, Alice Dows helped start the National Orchestra. Men described her as "so beautiful...extremely regal in her bearing," though women found her comically buxom and flirtatious.

Pearson and Allen kept on top of Washington gossip, labelling Alice Dows as one of Nick's girls in the *Washington Merry-Go-Round* with the same prurient interest in which they reported that Nick and his wife Alice had gone their separate ways.

In a replay of their younger days, when Alice, Cissy Patterson and Maggie Cassini were squired around town by Nick and others, Alice and Cissy again found themselves competing for the affections of the same man. Their rivalry was veiled in public until Cissy, still officially Countess Gizycka, went after Bill Borah. Though he initially responded to her pursuit, he was soured quickly by her public display of affection. In an article for the Hearst paper, the *Chicago Herald Examiner*, during the 1920 Republican convention, she wrote a piece entitled, "Borah is Countess Gizycka's Hero." Her affection was blatantly apparent. Borah warned Cissy to keep her passion to herself. Subsequently, her family paper, the *Chicago Tribune*, ran a critical editorial about Borah. Bill was certain Cissy had put her brother up to the deed as a reprimand for his criticism.

Cissy didn't play the role of the gracious lost love. Instead, she wrote a thinly disguised novel, entitled *Glass Houses*, in which the main characters were clearly Alice, Cissy and Bill. Cissy's character got her revenge by killing the burly Western senator with whom she was having an affair. Alice's character, who jealously lusted after the senator, was left with her vicious and vindictive venom.

In life, Alice triumphed in solidifying Borah's attention for she was not only discreet, but a powerful political ally. She described Borah as "a great friend...a great speaker. He had a great leonine head and was a fascinating conversationalist. He could hold one spellbound for hours

Chapter Thirteen   153

with tales of labor disputes in Illinois at the turn of the century. Unusual subjects like that. But there was a withdrawn, rather secretive quality about him which seemed to hold him back. He was a most intriguing person...[he] alternated between being very stimulating or very taciturn. ...*never* boring. Humor was the great bond between us." Though Borah was nearly 20 years her senior, they shared a similar attitude towards life. "I will travel with the devil," he claimed, "if he is going in my direction."

What began as a partnership of ideology, had clearly become one of passion as the fight against Wilson's League of Nations intensified. Alice and Eleanor were on opposite sides of the battle and each described the country's response to Wilson from their personal vantage point. When Eleanor and Franklin returned with Wilson from Europe in 1919, Eleanor recalled the cheering crowds that greeted Wilson at every station. Alice described the gatherings as scanty.

Throughout the spring of 1920, Alice waged war on the League. She became known as "the Colonel of Death," leading her colleagues in the Senate in their "Battalion of Death." The group became known as the "irreconcilables." Alice plotted strategy with Borah, dispatched notes to the Senate floor for Lodge and threatened senators who wobbled in support of the cause. The senators muddied the League plan with so many amendments that, by the time it came to a vote, the League's demands on the U.S. were rendered impotent. In addition, the battalion took their cause to the people, crisscrossing the nation to stir up mass rallies against the League. Alice's efforts with the irreconcilables were similar to those of Franklin's group of insurgents in Albany who had fought for the direct election of state senators against Tammany Hall's control of New York State politics.

Alice not only fought against the League to complete her father's final charge, she also fought to save his reputation. League supporters publicized that Teddy would have supported the League, based on his Nobel Prize acceptance speech, called for a "League of Peace." Alice furiously denounced their claim. Her father's concept, Alice argued, contained the strong proviso that America had to remain militarily prepared to defend herself.

On March 19, 1920, the vote was taken in the Senate rendering the League effectively dead. The senators roused 39 votes against Wilson's international body with 49 in favor. Supporters lacked the two-thirds

154 Alice and Eleanor

needed to pass the measure. In an uncharacteristic display of affection, Alice raced down from the gallery and embraced an exhausted Senator Lodge, despite their differences during the debate. At one point, Alice began to tease Lodge, addressing him as "Mr. Wobbly," when she was uncertain whether his stance against the League was firm.

Alice boasted of having broken Wilson's spirit and his heart, as he had done to her father. Rather than breaking the "heart of the world," as Wilson said America's rejection of his League of Nation would do, her battalion had broken him. The irreconcilables held a victory party at the Colonel's house, with Warren G. Harding's wife, Flo, scrambling the eggs.

Late in life, Alice denied that her group was irreconcilable. "We were against the League in that form," she explained, but Wilson could have had his League any time had he been willing to compromise with the Senate. "All he had to do was to take the reservations."

A shrewd, insightful Washington observer, Alice denied having any political influence because to have claimed any political power would have been undignified and unwise. Alice knew all too well that such a declaration would diminish any real power she wielded. "All that nonsense about my killing the League with a bunch of diehard cronies is ridiculous," she said. "It is true that I took a great interest in the debates but I don't think I influenced matters one way or another."

She did, however, admit to the personal nature of her hatred for Wilson. "We were against the League because we hated Wilson, who was a Family Horror. He couldn't do any good in our eyes because he had beaten Father." She also contradicted her own autobiography in which she argued that her father would not have supported the League. "We felt that my father had advocated the idea of the League of Nations in his Nobel prize acceptance speech. And then Taft had come up with his League to Enforce Peace and we had squabbled about that. We didn't like other people's Leagues muscling in on our own. It was entirely personal politics designed purely to annoy. As far as I was concerned anyway."

By the time Wilson returned from Paris after his second trip to discuss the League of Nations in July, Alice went to Washington's Union Station to gloat over the sparse crowd that greeted him. Public sentiment had turned against the President due in large part to the battalion's efforts. Alice got out of her car to watch Wilson's party pass. As they did, she crossed her fingers, making the sign of the evil eye, "A murrain on him, a murrain on him!" she cried, to the embarrassment of her unnamed companion. She was invoking an arcane call to Satan to strike her foe with pestilence.

Just as Alice believed her "magics" contributed to the dismal weather at Taft's inauguration, so, too, did she believe they affected Wilson. Several months after his return from Europe, the President took his fight for the League to the people. He collapsed from fatigue and nervous tension during a speaking tour, which forced him to retreat to the White House. On October 3, he was paralyzed by a stroke and remained a bedridden invalid for six months. His second wife, Edith, met with the Cabinet and guided his hand while he signed official documents. The battalion did not let up even though Wilson was incapacitated.

Though she was consumed by the fight against the League, Alice still carved out time to visit her crippled Auntie Bye. Bye's arthritis left her confined to Oldgate, no longer able to move or even feed herself. She used an ear trumpet for all conversations because her hearing was so poor. "She was still the most interested, and interesting, person that you could talk to," Alice remembered. She continued to draw inspiration from her aunt, despite the fact that her home had replaced the salon Auntie Bye's had been during Teddy's Washington days. Bye bore her physical pain nobly with stoic courage, never letting it interfere with people visiting her. Inspired by her Aunt's condition, Alice took up yoga in her later years to keep her body supple. She would sit in the lotus position for hours.

The battle over prohibition had been raging during the war years, inflaming men and women across the country in passionate debate. The issue came to a vote in Congress on January 16, 1919, as the Eighteenth Amendment. In the reformist ardor of the times, the amendment passed. Nick was bitterly opposed to the plan because his family had been in the wine business. When he waged his first fight for Speaker of the House at the beginning of the congressional session, his stance on prohibition undermined his campaign and Nick lost.

He began defiantly making bootleg beer in his cellar. He instructed the Longworth butler on how to make gin from oranges in a small still and used his inherited knowledge to turn grapes into his great grandfather's forgotten Catawba and Isabella wines. Guests were

156 Alice and Eleanor

delighted with dinner invitations to the Longworth home on which the initials B.Y.O. (Bring Your Own) did not appear. Nick scorned those who proclaimed to be "dry." Alice began her tradition of wearing broad-brimmed hats and carrying enormous purses which concealed, among other things, flasks of bourbon or rye. In her autobiography, she recalled, "I sometimes think I may have been one of the first bootleggers."

During the spring of 1920, Congress finally passed the Nineteenth Amendment to the Constitution. Women had won the right to vote. Alice Wadsworth, chair of the National Association Opposed to Woman Suffrage, lunched with Eleanor on the train between New York and Washington just prior to the vote. She tried to "persuade me to come out against ratification. I was very noncommittal," wrote Eleanor. She urged her mother-in-law to avoid endorsing Wadsworth's position. Nick voted for the amendment, one of the few times he and Alice were publicly on the same side of a political issue.

The passage of Women's Suffrage offered a bright spot in an otherwise repressive period of social upheaval. Alice remembered returning from a party near midnight on June 2, and being informed by a policeman on the beat of an explosion at the house of Attorney-General Mitchell Palmer. He lived on R Street across from Franklin and Eleanor's home.

Alice, Nick and the policeman proceeded immediately to her cousins'. The fact that they were on opposite sides of the League fight did not preclude the families from dining together. When Eleanor invited Sir Edward Grey, an old friend of TR's and Britain's former foreign secretary to dinner, Alice and Nick came too. Grey was in Washington to persuade Wilson to accept the amendments to protect U.S. sovereignty which Lodge attached to the League.

Alice described the scene of crossing R Street after the blast with remarkable detachment. She claimed it was "curiously without horror," even though as they walked across, "it was difficult to avoid stepping on bloody chunks of human being." The Palmers escaped injury, having retired earlier. Mitchell Palmer's sitting room was blown to bits, as was the man who had thrown the bomb. The roof of Eleanor and Franklin's sun parlor and their front windows on the lower floor were blown out. Their front curtains and shades were down on all three floors, with plaster down inside and out. Only their son James was home at the time and, while he was oblivious to the explosion at the time, according to

Eleanor, "James glories in every new bone found. I only hope the victim was not a poor passerby instead of the anarchist."

Palmer was an appropriate target for a revolutionist's bomb attack because he led the repressive crusade that greeted the country's outcry for reform. Armed with the Espionage Act of 1917 and the Sedition Act of 1918, his agents portrayed the individuals fighting for social justice as America's enemies. Communists, anarchists, trade unionists and others who demanded better working and living conditions were relentlessly pursued. Palmer's men had the power to arrest anyone who gave aid or comfort to the enemy, seemed disloyal, opposed the draft or criticized the President. Even Teddy Roosevelt was suspect for the newspaper articles he wrote criticizing President Wilson.

Racism and xenophobia raged through Palmer's writings. "Out of the sly and crafty eyes of many of them leap cupidity, cruelty, insanity and crime; from their lopsided faces, sloping brows and misshapen features may be recognized the unmistakable criminal type." Reds had to be guarded against, for, "Like a prairie-fire, the blaze of revolution...was eating its way into the home of the American workman, its sharp tongues of revolutionary heat were licking the altars of churches, leaping into the belfry of the school bells, crawling into the sacred corners of American homes, seeking to replace marriage vows with libertine laws, burning up the foundations of society."

Alice's brother, Ted, Jr. was serving in the New York State Assembly when five elected socialists from New York City were refused their seats. He protested, arguing for a free, representative government and against the disenfranchisement of the constituents of the disputed elected officials. In response, the Assembly Speaker Thaddeus C. Sweet read a passage TR had written on Americanism and then derisively denounced Ted, Jr. as "painfully un-American."

Secret agents infiltrated meetings, keeping notes that formed the basis of J. Edgar Hoover's subsequent index file on revolutionary Reds. Suspects were aggressively rounded up and incarcerated on Ellis Island. Ironically, this same island had been the symbol of hope to many of these same immigrants when they came to America. The first deportation of activists occurred on December 21, 1919, carrying Emma Goldman and Sasha Berkman among its passengers. These anarchists were persecuted for exercising their right of freedom of speech. Their deportation made a mockery of America's boast of liberty and human rights.

158 Alice and Eleanor

As Alice and Nick left Eleanor and Franklin's in the early morning hours after the Palmer explosion, Alice coldly noted that "a large number of pieces (of the body) had been assembled on a piece of newspaper...(they) seemed no more than so much carrion." The severed body parts served as a metaphor not only for the international devastation Eleanor and Franklin had witnessed in the aftermath of the world and the personal trauma in both Alice and Eleanor's marriages, but it also symbolized the chaos of the times.

World politics was undergoing massive changes. The map was redrawn, dividing up former colonial empires. The Russian revolution struck joy and horror in people's hearts. Strikes by workers of the world were rampant. They were demanding education, economic security, political equality and dignity. Minorities were advocating an end to repression. Race riots raged in 26 cities around the United States, including Washington, during the summer of 1919. The titled nobility of Europe had lost their prestige and even though The Treaty of Versailles had been signed as a peace document, its punitive provisions sowed the seeds for another world war.

Chapter Fourteen

"Hello, dear. It's so nice of you to join us. Have you heard the latest antic invented by those uppity relatives of ours from up the river?" Alice asked a guest as she guided him into the crowded parlor.

"You mean the steam teapot business?" a smartly dressed fellow replied.

Alice nodded, scrunching her face up so that her teeth protruded like Eleanor's. In a high-pitched voice, she mocked her cousin's facial expression. "Anyone for tea? No? Then how about a teapot dome!"

"Personally, I'd rather have a drink. Any of Nick's brew upstairs? I haven't come to a dry house, have I?"

"That's a contradiction in terms," Alice smiled mischievously. "Nick and dry. Never. Thread your way through." She pointed him into the overstuffed living room. "I'll find you later. I must attend to a few other guests. Then we'll sit in a corner and tell scandalous tales."

She made her way across the room to greet her other guests. Nick intercepted Alice, taking her elbow and steering her into a quiet corner.

"To what do I owe the honor of your undivided attention when so many young lovelies are in the crowd," she teased sharply.

"I noticed Bill brooding by himself in the corner, Aurora," Nick shot back. "Listen, I saw the seating list for dinner. We'll be lucky to get through the meal without a row on our hands," he warned. He looked across the room, glaring. "They'll hate each other."

"I know. Isn't it marvelous!" she replied, eyes twinkling as she clapped her hands.

"He's a bigoted Southerner and she raises money for black universities! It's positively malevolent to seat two people who have diametrically opposite views next to one another," he lectured her.

"I'm afraid I'm rather that way about people. You have to have a bit of malice to be a good hostess.' That's why people love to come here. Spirits and spirited conversation," Alice reminded him.

Nick bristled, forcing a smile to his face as he nodded towards a colleague. Alice patted his arm, adjusting the lapel on one of his infamous waistcoats. "You have a reputation to maintain, dear." He fidgeted like a little boy being fussed over by his mother while Alice continued. "Now, don't worry about dinner. I'll try and do better next week. I know the perfect pair to invite—cousin Eleanor and my brother Ted. That'll set the sparks flying."

"You're incorrigible," Nick sighed with exasperation, straightening his own coat.

"Do you think she'll accept, for the sake of the family?" Alice asked, feigning innocence. "Louis Howe has turned her into quite the political front runner for poor Franklin."

"Your mother said she might turn into a swan. I'll see you later."

"You'll be too drunk to 'see' anything later," she uttered under her breath as they amicably parted company.

Their interaction took place under the watchful eye of three young, fresh-faced federal employees huddled together in the Longworth parlor.

"She's getting rather thick around the middle," whispered Elizabeth, a young woman with shoulder-length brunette hair.

"Even a princess isn't immune to middle age," remarked Annette, a young, blond clerical aide in a hushed tone.

"I still think she's regal and radiant," added their male admirer, Eddie. "She defies tradition," he said, gazing approvingly at their hostess.

"You've heard the rumors, haven't you?" Elizabeth asked mischievously. "She's pregnant and the 'Stallion' is the father."

Annette gasped innocently. Her companions tossed a knowing glance at one another.

"You'll get used to such gossip once you've been here for a while," Elizabeth assured her.

"*Town Topics* says she and Nick haven't slept together for years. Eighteen years of marriage and no children, then suddenly, she's in the family way," Eddie laughed. "I'd say it's Borah, all right. Just look at the two of them plotting in the corner." He shifted his glance across the crowded parlor where drinks and hors d'oeuvres were being served.

Alice spoke with animated conviction to the brooding Senator Borah, who listened attentively, eyebrows furrowed. The young man nudged his two companions, nodding in the direction of the dapper Nick

Longworth. He was joking with a buxom, regal older woman, evincing the same self-styled charm that earned him a reputation as one of Washington's favorite entertainers.

"Another Alice," Elizabeth offered. "*Grande dame,* Alice Dows."

"How do you know?" Annette wondered in astonishment.

"Washington's a town for secrets," Elizabeth informed her. "If you keep your ears open but your mouth sealed, you'll find out lots of fascinating tidbits."

"Shhh, here he comes," Eddie warned, straightening up. "Good evening, Mr. Speaker," he said, extending his hand to his boss. "Thank you for inviting us. Annette and Elizabeth, may I present the Honorable Nicholas Longworth. They work in the Justice Department, Mr. Speaker."

"You can dispense with the formalities, Eddie. It's a pleasure to have you and your lovely guests. Have a drink. Do you play poker? There's a game upstairs." While he addressed both women, his eyes never left Annette, disarming the newly transplanted resident. She glanced away uncomfortably. "I hope to see you again."

"Thank you, Mr. Speaker. It would be my pleasure," Annette replied, glancing awkwardly at Eddie.

"Only in town for a month and already you've caught his eye. What will your family back home in Indiana say if they find out you've become one of 'Nick's girls'?" her friend teased.

"You've been here too long, Elizabeth. You expect the worst of everyone. Some of us were brought up with morals. He's a married man, for heavens sake!" Annette huffed.

"They don't call Washington the wickedest city for nothing," Eddie reminded her.

"I thought that reputation was reserved for San Francisco." Annette retorted, glaring at her two friends. "You twist everything around to make it appear scandalous. How do you know Mrs. Longworth is pregnant? And even if she is, no one has a right to snoop around in other people's bedrooms! Maybe they have an arrangement," she offered tentatively, eyeing the Speaker across the room. He caught her eye and winked. "You said this was a town of secrets. Can you keep one?"

Unconventional Challenges

The 1920 Republican presidential nomination was an open fight. Had Teddy Roosevelt been alive, he would have handily been awarded the nomination. Though two men in Alice's life, Nick and Bill, were long-shot contenders, the fact that her father should have been the nominee was a bitter pill for Alice to swallow. Warren G. Harding, with his call for a return to "Normalcy," got the party's nod. Calvin Coolidge, a successful businessman, was nominated as his running mate.

Alice had no particular affection for Harding, even though he had been one of the irreconcilables in the fight against the League of Nations. He was her husband's drinking and poker crony, but she was appalled by his affairs. He conducted them in closets while his wife pounded on the door. "My God," Alice later remarked, "we have a president...who doesn't even know beds were invented—and his campaign slogan was 'Back to Normalcy'!"

Alice delighted in entertaining her guests by reading unpublished copies of Harding's love letters to one of his paramours, Carrie Phillips. They had been sent to Alice by a friend at McGraw Hill Publishers. The letters were supposed to be included in a biography of Harding entitled, *Shadow of Blooming Grove* by Francis Russell, but were left out because of a lawsuit brought by Harding's nephew. In protest, the author left blank spaces in the text where the letters were to have appeared.

Despite her distaste for Harding, Alice struck a deal with the Republican nominee. In exchange for her support, Alice extracted a promise that Harding would back her brother, Ted, Jr., for New York Governor in 1924. Her calculated move was ironic in light of how she had rebuffed Harding's offer to support Nick for Governor of Ohio at the 1912 Republican convention in exchange for Nick's support for Taft over her father.

Alice was annoyed when the Democrats picked her cousin Franklin as their vice-presidential nominee. Alice wanted the next Roosevelt who occupied the White House to be her brother, not a usurping cousin. Even Eleanor had not expected Franklin to be chosen for the vice-presidential spot. When he left for the Democratic convention in San Francisco, Franklin had not decided whether to run for Senator from New York or Governor. He delivered a rousing nomination speech for the unsuccessful progressive candidate, New York's Governor, Al Smith. The party had been in disarray after 44 exhausting ballots. Finally, James

Cox, Governor of Ohio, was chosen as a compromise candidate with Franklin as his running mate.

When Eleanor heard about her husband's nomination from his boss, Secretary of the Navy Daniels, she told her mother-in-law, "I really think F. had a better chance of winning for the Senatorship but the Democrats may win, one cannot tell and at least it should be a good fight." Her instincts were correct. However, no matter what the outcome of the election, Franklin was positioning himself as a presidential candidate in 1924.

The Democratic ticket of Cox and Roosevelt tied their campaign to support for Wilson's League of Nations. The Republican platform contained TR's position against it. Many felt Franklin had been picked for the ticket to take advantage of his Roosevelt name. Republican strategists were most concerned about Franklin's claim that the conservatives in their party who opposed TR's progressive view now opposed the League. If people believed the claim, Bull Moosers might vote for the Democrats. As a result, Alice's family went out in force to campaign for Harding.

The rift in family relations strained and finally burst at the seams as the 1920 campaign progressed. Family loyalty evaporated. Franklin was frequently mistaken for TR himself or his son, Ted, Jr. He capitalized on the confusion, invoking Teddy's name in the western towns where his cousin had hunted. He even borrowed Teddy's gestures and sprinkled his speeches with "bully," "pussyfooting" and "square deal."

To counter the confusion and clarify in the voters' minds what Franklin represented and what TR advocated, Ted, Jr. was assigned the distasteful task of tailing Franklin's campaign. He was to dispel the myth that Franklin was Teddy Roosevelt's legitimate political heir. Eleanor wrote her husband, "Did you see that Alice is to go on the stump for Harding and that Auntie Corinne is to speak for him in Portland, Maine on September 8th, starting his campaign there. Ted also speaks in Maine."

Ted, Jr. not only spoke in Maine, but all around the country. He reminded crowds that Franklin didn't wear "the brand of our family." Even Nick got into the fray, calling Franklin a "denatured Roosevelt." Sara went wild when she heard the remark, claiming that the Oyster Bay Roosevelts were antagonistic because her side of the family had "all the looks!"

Eleanor was hurt but Franklin was infuriated, especially when the *Chicago Tribune* called him "the one-half of one percent Roosevelt," and said, "Franklin is as much like Theodore as a clam is like a bearcat." Then, Teddy's widow, Edith, labeled him "nine-tenths mush and one-tenth Eleanor." Franklin fired back that in the 1912 campaign Senator Harding had called Teddy Roosevelt "first a Benedict Arnold and then an Aaron Burr...This is one thing, at least some members of the Roosevelt family will not forget."

Eleanor was drawn into the election, too, but her purpose was not to add to the family diatribes. Franklin invited her to join his campaign train as a record keeper, but her real purpose was to capitalize on the new women's vote. Eleanor served a minimally strategic, largely decorative function. Franklin was seeking the women's vote and having Eleanor at his side made a strong political statement. She smiled graciously while her husband made appearances from town to town across America. She was frequently called upon to tug hard at his coattails in order to curtail his long, enthusiastic speeches. Eleanor was bored much of the time and often retreated to her room to knit.

The most positive outcome of the campaign train trip was the alliance that evolved between Franklin's political advisor, Louis Howe, and Eleanor. She had been critical of Louis before, but he involved her actively in the campaign. Howe recognized her value to Franklin's political career and continually told her so. He discussed drafts of Franklin's speeches with Eleanor on the train trip, in addition to the issues of the campaign and the politics of the towns through which they travelled. He helped Eleanor develop into the political helpmate her husband needed, a role she truly desired.

A former newspaperman, Louis also taught Eleanor a valuable lesson on how to develop a friendly relationship with the press. The skills she learned served her well during her years as First Lady and helped erase the memory of the ridicule she endured after the press published her meal-saving plan for large households during the war.

Her only other press experience had come in an interview with a reporter from the Poughkeepsie *Eagle News*. The reporter had been dispatched to find out more about the vice-presidential candidate's wife. Franklin was a newcomer on the national political scene and so was Eleanor. She succeeded in charming the reporter by admitting her interest in politics, and strongly endorsing American's entry into the League of Nations. "If we don't adopt it, it will be useless," she told him.

The 1920 election culminated in a Republican avalanche. Harding and Coolidge defeated Cox and Roosevelt. Alice's brother, Ted, Jr., was rewarded for his campaign work against cousin Franklin. He was appointed Assistant Secretary of the Navy, Franklin and his father's former post. Nick subsequently captured the leadership role of the House as Speaker, a position he relished. Eleanor and Franklin took the loss philosophically, though as she wrote, "We all feel very badly over the result of the elections." The loss gave Eleanor time to resolve several issues about her own life after the Lucy Mercer affair.

Though publicly, Eleanor and Franklin had committed to a reconciliation and seemed to have revitalized their relationship during the period between 1918 and 1920, privately Eleanor had been struggling to regain her equilibrium. She reproached herself harshly over Franklin's involvement with Lucy, convinced that she had failed as a woman and was responsible for his straying. She suffered headaches, was tired, looked depressed in photos, lost her appetite and often lost the meals she ate. A modern diagnosis would probably have been anorexia.

Redefining their relationship was difficult. They spent more time together, but there was more tension. They argued over politics, food, money, social attitudes and clothing styles. Eleanor spoke when she was displeased, no longer brushing aside her hurts. When Franklin flirted, she interceded and they left social events together. She no longer indulged in her sulking behavior of the past.

Their tension extended to Sara and her Aunt Susie. Eleanor found their views intolerable, self-indulgent and reactionary. Early in her marriage, she thought the Delano women personified generosity and familial love. Now, however, they made her "want to squirm and turn Bolshevik" at their "serene assurance and absolute judgments on people and affairs going on in the world."

Eleanor slowly came to the realization that she could not live her life through someone else. "You can never really live anyone else's life, not even your child's. The influence you exert is through your own life and what you become yourself," she wrote.

She had wanted her marriage to be like Beatrice Webb's description, "apart we each of us live only half a life, together we each of us have a double life." But Eleanor recognized that this was her husband's career, not hers. She viewed Franklin's nomination as if she were gazing from behind a glass partition. She felt she was an outsider, much like long ago when she watched her mother from the doorway. Eleanor's mother had to beckon her "Granny" inside, and Franklin needed to do the same. "I was glad for my husband," she admitted, "but it never occurred to me to be much excited."

Eleanor had discovered a place of solace for herself in a quiet holly grove in Washington where she could give vent to her emotions. Before a statue entitled *Grief*, she contemplated the purpose of her life. The women she knew who created new lives after personal traumas, like Auntie Bye and Madame Souvestre, were in distinct contrast to the unhappy lives of her mother and her grandmother. Eleanor was determined to rebuild, not waste her life.

She felt a deep connection to Clover Adams, in whose memory the statue *Grief* was erected by her husband, Henry Adams. Though Clover was a skilled translator and researcher who contributed significantly to her husband's work, Henry never acknowledged his wife's contribution. In fact, he discredited her and prohibited her from continuing her own work as a highly regarded portrait photographer. Henry's infatuation with a woman named Elizabeth Cameron caused Clover to take her own life.

Eleanor and Clover Adams had a similar quest. Though they had been trifled with and humiliated and lived during a time when women were without place or honor, they sought to live generous lives. Each was determined to give of their talents and vision, to do significant work, and to find meaningful activity.

When Eleanor's Red Cross work ceased after the war, she began distancing herself from the confines of her past. Many of her gestures were symbolic, like firing all the white servants that her mother-in-law had insisted upon and replacing them with an entirely black staff. At the time, Eleanor was still bound by her class and culture. Her action was tied to racial stereotypes of the old South where blacks were devoted, loving servants, not altruistic aims.

Eleanor offered her services as a translator at the first International Congress of Working Women. It was her first contact with organizations interested in improving working conditions for women. Despite living across the street from Attorney General Palmer, Eleanor joined with activist labor women at the conference and befriended many of the leaders who were pursued by Palmer's Red Scare agents.

The Working Women's conference was financed and organized by Margaret Dreier Robins, who along with her husband, Raymond, was an old friend of Uncle Ted's. They were active participants in the Progressive Party, and Robins had joined Borah and the other irreconcilables in opposition to the League of Nations. Margaret was one of the women responsible for swaying Harding to adopt the plank of the newly formed League of Women Voters. This league grew out of the National American Suffrage Association, a nonpartisan organization dedicated to the election of reform candidates. Harding received most of the progressive women's votes in the 1920 election, the first in which women could exercise their newly won right, and a direct result of his support for suffrage.

After the election, Louis Howe stayed on Franklin's payroll with Eleanor as his chief advocate. The rest of his organization dispersed when the family moved back to New York. Eleanor and Franklin each had serious, but individual, plans for the future. Franklin formed a new law firm with Grenville Emmet and Langdon Marvin. Emmet, Marvin and Roosevelt specialized in estates and wills. Franklin also became a vice president of the third largest surety bonding house in the country, Van Lear Black's Fidelity and Deposit Company of Maryland. He was paid a substantial salary of $25,000 a year to run the bonding house's New York office, which delighted the family. His earnings from all his years in government service had been under $5,000 per year. In addition, Franklin became a Harvard overseer to supervise students, and he agreed to head the Navy Club and the Greater New York Boy Scout Council.

Eleanor's plans were modest by contrast. She was no longer satisfied with Sara's ideal of a woman's role in her social position, an ornamental woman whose name appeared on the letterhead of charity boards. She wanted real work with real people. Initially, Eleanor wanted to learn how to cook, type and take shorthand. She found a housewife who had been a cook and went to her apartment twice a week to prepare an entire meal. Eleanor left the meal for the family to critique. She also enrolled in a business course where she attended typing and shorthand class each day she was in New York. These skills built her confidence, removing her feeling of dependence on others and proved extremely useful in the future.

168 Alice and Eleanor

Concurrently, Eleanor became involved in championing the 1920-21 progressive agenda of the League of Women Voters. Their proposals called for national health insurance, federal aid to education and the participation of women at every level of national life. Seventy-two years later, the 1992 campaign was still advocating some of their reforms and criticism of the agenda had an eerie, reverberating echo at the Republican convention. The U.S. Attorney General, Palmer, denounced the 1920-21 progressive platform of the League of Women Voters with the same arguments used by Patrick Buchanan in 1992. Both charged that the progressive agenda was weakening America by destroying the family.

Eleanor was invited to join the board of the League of Women Voters to monitor their legislative program. Uncertain that she was up to the task, Eleanor hesitated, but when she was offered the help of an attorney, Elizabeth F. Read, she accepted. One morning each week, she went to Elizabeth's law office where they went through the Albany calendar and the Congressional Record to determine which bills were of interest to the league. Eleanor decided which bills she wanted to be briefed on more fully. She also met Esther Lape, a prominent English professor, journalist, researcher and publicist. Elizabeth shared Esther's home on East 11th St. in Greenwich Village. The two women had been activists for women's suffrage and co-edited the weekly legislative review issued by the League, *City-State-Nation*. Esther and Elizabeth became Eleanor's close personal friends, the core of her female support network. Through them she reconnected with the vigor of her Allenswood days. Esther and Elizabeth's circle of friends reminded Eleanor of Madame's Souvestre's circle—cultured, stylish, political, activist and intelligent.

A Roosevelt family reunion took place in June of 1921 for the wedding of Auntie Bye's son, Sheffield Cowles. It was the first meeting of the family since the onerous 1920 campaign and it did not repair the damage between the Oyster Bay and Hyde Park branches. In fact, it proved humiliating for Eleanor. Franklin, who had begun drinking and partying frivolously after the vice-presidential defeat, became loud, drunk and silly, prompting comparisons of "poor Eleanor's" husband with her father. The Oyster Bay relatives were surprised at Franklin's earthy, "uproarious" behavior, calling it, "the Roosevelt spirits." Such descriptions irritated his mother, Sara, who thought of her son as a Delano more than a Roosevelt.

Chapter Fourteen 169

After the election, Alice found herself back in favor at the White House as Nick's wife, who was from Ohio like the new President and loved to play poker. She was among a group of influential Republicans who called on Harding before his inauguration to discuss his cabinet choices and policy issues. She was very concerned about the appointment of Harry Daughtery as Attorney General. Daughtery had been a shrewd political manager, but his reputation for greed and lack of scruples had preceded him to Washington. Alice argued against his appointment.

Though she found her renewed access to the White House pleasurable, the company within was not. She sometimes yearned for the days when she was an "out" rather than being a critical "in." President Harding's behavior accosted her sensibilities. The contempt and condescension that saturated their conversations did not escape the President's wife. Flo Harding kept a little red book in which she wrote the names of people who snubbed her. Alice's name appeared regularly, for although Flo and her husband had frequented the Longworth house at Nick's infamous poker games, Alice refused to go to their home until after Harding became President.

Neither moral consistency nor conviction were attributes of Warren G. Harding's character. Alice was appalled that the President complied with Prohibition on the bottom floors of the White House during official functions yet, in the private rooms upstairs, a barroom atmosphere flourished. Whether Harding agreed with the laws or not, Alice believed he had an obligation to uphold them as President. At least Nick had always been staunchly opposed to Prohibition in the home, though he supported a community's right to vote to close their saloons.

In addition, Harding smoked cigars in public, but chewed tobacco in private. Harding insisted on having toothpicks at his table, put his feet on his desk when officials called and entertained his cronies with his jacket off and his waistcoat open. He passed out so many favors, his own father once told Harding, "If you were a girl, you'd be in the family way all the time. You can't say No."

The President, in fact, had gotten at least one woman pregnant out of wedlock. Nan Britton wrote a book entitled *The President's Daughter*, alleging that he had fathered her child. Stories abounded about the "Ohio Gang" fixing poker games so the President could win at a little green house on K Street. Wild, wanton, even naked women were alleged to

170 Alice and Eleanor

frequent the house. Alice didn't believe Harding was a bad man. "He was just a slob," she said.

To Alice's distress, Harding's moral lassitude, pork-barrel politics and political advisors like Daughtery, endangered the political career of her brother, Ted, Jr. and also her brother Archie. The Teapot Dome scandal, which erupted during Harding's first term, outraged the nation and became the most flagrant abuse of a political office until the Watergate affair. In one of his first acts as President, Harding had turned over navy-owned lands at the Teapot Dome oil reserve in Wyoming to the Department of the Interior chief, Albert Fall.

As Assistant Secretary of the Navy, Ted, Jr. was uncomfortable about Harding turning the land over to the Interior Department. He had the order modified to stipulate that "no general policy as to drilling... shall be changed or adopted except upon consultation and in cooperation with," his boss, Edwin Denby, or in Denby's absence, Ted, himself. He was concerned about exploitation of the drilling rights and his doubts proved prescient.

After Fall leased the reserves to the oil magnate, Harry Sinclair, the Senate began an investigation looking for evidence of a conspiracy. When the scandal hit, Ted, Jr. thought his political career was finished. Prior to entering public life, he was involved in a partnership with some Philadelphia investment bankers. Sinclair Oil was one of the clients the company helped finance. Ted served as a director on the oil company's board until after the war. Subsequently, he arranged for his disabled brother, Archie, to work for Sinclair Oil.

Archie had been informed by Sinclair's secretary that when the lease was signed, Albert Fall was sent a check for $68,000. It definitely looked like a payoff. Archie didn't know what to do, so he asked for advice from Ted, Jr., Nick, Bill Borah and others. They all told him the same thing—resign from the oil company and volunteer the information to the senate investigating committee immediately.

The senate demanded the resignation of the Secretary of the Navy, Edwin Denby. South Carolina's representative, William Stevenson, called for Ted's resignation also. Stevenson thought Ted's wife owned Sinclair stock and, as Assistant Secretary of the Navy, he was part of the conspiracy that would benefit from Sinclair Oil's exploitation of the lease. Gratefully, however, Ted discovered his wife had sold their Sinclair stock the previous December, though she neglected to tell him.

Nick used his new position as Speaker of the House to defend his brother-in-law on the floor of Congress and Alice talked Ted out of beating up Stevenson with her straightforward humor.

"Ted? I hear you're going to beat up Stevenson.... Yes, of course he deserves it.... I know he's a rat.... By the way, he's a little elderly man and wears glasses.... Remember to have him take them off before you hit him," she warned.

Harding was spared the exposure his cronies suffered. He died 29 months into his term of office in August 1923. Archie Roosevelt became the prosecution's key witness. Both he and Ted, Jr. were absolved of any complicity and were credited with helping to crack the case. Fall went to jail for taking a bribe. Daughtery was never convicted of graft but some of his associates served time. Another committed suicide and one fled the country.

The residual effect of the Teapot Dome scandal brought Alice and Eleanor's families into a nasty confrontation during the 1924 election. Between the 1920 and 1924 elections, however, Eleanor began dipping her toes into the political pool. She found, as Alice had, the baptism immensely to her liking.

Through her work monitoring legislation with the League of Women Voters, Eleanor became a delegate from Dutchess County to the New York State Convention. It was her first experience as an active participant in the political process, rather than as an observer. She was called upon to draft a bill requiring political parties to give equal representation to men and women at all committee and staff levels and then to gather bipartisan support for the bill.

Franklin encouraged Eleanor's work and enjoyed tutoring her on political tactics, but he worried that her pronouncements might tarnish him. Eleanor, too, worried whether she had the right to engage in controversy if her husband might be adversely affected. Though such thoughts may have crossed cousin Alice's mind, they never deterred her from pursuing a political course that put Nick in a compromising position.

Though the women Eleanor befriended through the League were militant feminists and advocates for equal rights, she found their stridency irritating. She was not like the women Louis Howe and Franklin sarcastically called "she-males." In spirit, however, Eleanor had become a social feminist, committed to emancipation and social reform. She was not the flapper, speakeasy type of "New Woman" who sported short hair and skirts, drank, smoked and was promiscuous. Rather, Eleanor was serious and reform-minded.

She joined the ranks of those she believed would continue the progressive struggle. As her involvement in the League expanded, so, too, did her exposure to activist women outside her privileged social class. These women, who crossed political parties and who differed on the focus of their reform political agendas, were vigorous supporters of political change and lived emancipated lives, which included sexual freedom.

Sexual freedom was at the bottom of a naval scandal that haunted Franklin's family in a front page headline of the *New York Times* on July 23, 1921. Franklin was charged with sanctioning the entrapment of homosexuals at the Newport Training Station during the time he served as Assistant Secretary of the Navy. Though Franklin authorized the drive against homosexuality in a secret operation on June 11, 1919, he later denied any involvement. During the summer of 1921 when the program came to light, Franklin was forced to defend himself against a Senate committee's investigation that he immorally abused his office.

By the time he met his family in Campobello for vacation at the end of the summer, Franklin was exhausted from the stress of the proceedings and constant entertainment. Still, he kept up a schedule of endless recreation—sailing, fishing and swimming. He came down with a fever in August. Eleanor had weathered many storms in her life, but Franklin's illness would confront her with her most permanent and serious challenge.

The chill turned to pain in his back and legs which became paralysis of his legs. On the remote island, Louis found a doctor on vacation who diagnosed a blood clot, but Franklin's condition worsened. His hands and arms became paralyzed, then he lost control of his vital functions. His eyesight became impaired. He was in constant pain, alternating between delirium from the fever and sleepless nights.

Finally, his diagnosis was changed to infantile paralysis, commonly known as polio. Louis provided Eleanor with immeasurable support during the early weeks of Franklin's illness. Not only did he describe the symptoms to Uncle Fred, who consulted with doctors in New York to obtain the correct diagnosis of poliomyelitis, he helped Eleanor move Franklin, bath him and turn him over regularly.

Chapter Fourteen 173

Eleanor nursed her husband for two weeks, day and night with devotion and loving intensity. She brushed his teeth and shaved him, as well as administering enemas and massages. She slept on a couch in his room until a private nurse came from New York. The sight of her large, helpless husband reminded Eleanor of Michelangelo's *Pieta*, the mother grieving over the broken body of her son. The statue had moved her to tears when she saw it, for it symbolized universal woman grieving over man.

Franklin showed incredible fortitude, tolerating the agony of intense pain whenever he was moved. His leg muscles froze in a jackknifed position and had to be put in plaster casts to stretch the tendons. The acute pain he experienced rekindled Eleanor's childhood memory of her father's agony when he had to have his leg reset after a riding accident.

Franklin was ultimately transferred to Presbyterian Hospital in New York on a private train car where he was put under the care of Dr. Draper. Louis orchestrated the transfer in the utmost privacy and secrecy to keep the news out of the papers. Both he and Eleanor were dedicated to insuring Franklin's recovery. Dr. Draper felt the key to his patient's improvement lay in Franklin's desire to resume an active life.

Eleanor concurred. She argued with Sara that "if you place a patient in a doctor's care you must at least follow out his suggestions and treatment." The doctor felt that any suggestion of permanent retirement, which Franklin's mother advocated, would diminish his patient's ability to recuperate. No one knew at the time whether Franklin would recover the use of his legs or be permanently disabled. Through the ordeal, Eleanor became fully emancipated from Sara's domination, for it was she, not her mother-in-law, who stood in firm concert with her husband over his care and his future. The path, however, was not a smooth one.

Faced with the united resolve of Eleanor and Franklin that her son intended to continue his business life and ultimately return to politics, Sara fomented rebellion among the children. The strain reached crisis proportions when Franklin was moved back to their 65th Street home in New York at the end of October. Louis moved in with the family and was given Anna's room. The house was so overcrowded, Eleanor slept on a cot in her youngest boy's room and dressed in Franklin's bathroom.

174 Alice and Eleanor

Sara poured out her resentment on Louis, whom she disliked intensely. She referred to him as "that ugly, dirty little man." She encouraged Anna into open revolt, claiming that her mother cared more about Louis than about her. Fifteen-year-old Anna was too young to realize the sacrifices both Louis and her mother were making for her father's recovery.

Though Eleanor functioned with remarkable composure and effectiveness, one day the strain exploded. She burst out in a fit of sobbing while she was reading to Franklin, Jr. and John. No one could console her, including Louis. She cried for hours, unable to stop. Finally, she retreated to a room in Sara's house to compose herself. It was the only time in her life she recalled going to pieces during "the most trying winter of my entire life."

She was bitterly disappointed the next summer when Sara took her oldest children to Europe for their first visit. Eleanor had looked forward to such a journey, knowing what a splendid experience her first trip had been with Madame Souvestre. However, she could not afford the expense or the time. Franklin had begun his therapeutic trips south for the winter. Initially, he rented a houseboat, but later settled in Warm Springs, Georgia for its medicinal waters.

Eleanor realized that although Franklin had regained the use of his arms and was learning to walk with crutches, if the boys were to have an active parental companion for hiking, camping, swimming and other outdoor exploits, she would have to participate. She did with vigor during the summer of 1922.

As their new life evolved incorporating Franklin's disability, Louis encouraged Eleanor to increase her involvement in partisan politics. He wanted her to keep Franklin's interest in the party alive, as well as the party's interest in him. He offered her succinct advice for public speaking, chastising her nervous laugh and telling her to be prepared. She should know what she wanted to say, say it and sit down.

Consequently, when Nan Cook called to ask her to preside at a fundraising luncheon for the Women's Division of the State Democratic Committee in 1922, Eleanor accepted. Both Nan and her longtime companion, Marion Dickerson, had been active in the suffrage movement. Eleanor had met Marion on several different occasions that spring through their mutual interest in working conditions for women. Nan and Marion became intimate friends of Eleanor's, along with

Caroline O'Day, Nan's boss and head of the Women's Division, and Elinor Morgenthau.

Eleanor also befriended Rose Schneiderman, director of the Women's Trade Union League in New York through her membership in the Union League. Though her other close friends were of old American stock, Rose was a Polish/Russian emigre from the lower East Side of New York. Sara disliked most of Eleanor's friends; but, of all her close associates, Rose was the only one never invited to visit Hyde Park, which was still her mother-in-law's domain.

Alice and Eleanor were positioned on opposite sides of the senate chamber once again in 1923. Eleanor was asked to work with her friend Esther Lape on the Bok Peace Award. Edward Bok, the former publisher of the *Ladies Home Journal*, was offering a $100,000 award to the individual who developed the best practical plan for the United States to achieve and preserve world peace. The winner was selected from 22,000 entries, including one from Franklin. The prize plan called for America's entry into the World Court and her conditional support of the League of Nations, without becoming a member.

In a vitriolic response, several of the senate irreconcilables branded the award a sinister, propaganda exercise for the League of Nations. They launched an investigation. Lape was called to testify. Eleanor went along to "hold her hand," according to Franklin. Alice had a privileged seat on a leather sofa at the back of the committee room to watch the proceedings.

By the election year of 1924, Eleanor had an office at the Democratic State Committee. She had become a visible political activist. As chair of the Finance Committee, she organized women in the state, particularly rural counties, and pushed the women's agenda. For six years, she, Marion, Nan, Caroline and Elinor travelled throughout New York "Trooping for Democracy" in the blue roadster they collectively bought. The more Eleanor achieved, the more she reassured her husband that she was doing it all for him.

At the Democratic national convention, she worked tirelessly for a child-labor amendment in the party platform. She lost but was determined that the State platform would include the amendment. In this task she succeeded.

Eleanor had become so active in democratic politics, she had no qualms about campaigning. She even supported a few dirty tricks which she felt were part of the political game. "In the thick of political fights one always feels that all methods of campaigning that are honest are fair." When her cousin, Alice's brother, Ted, Jr., ran for Governor of New York in the 1924 election against the Democratic candidate, Al Smith, she supported a plan to set a frame resembling a teapot which spouted steam on top of the automobile that led the procession around the state following Ted, Jr.'s campaign. Though Eleanor admitted her cousin had nothing to do with the Teapot Dome scandal that sank Harding's administration, she viewed the antic as a fair response to the war of words leveled against Franklin in the 1920 presidential campaign.

Auntie Bye was less than pleased with Eleanor's political activities. "Alas and lackaday!" she exclaimed when her niece drove the teapot automobile to Connecticut to show it off. She was dismayed by Eleanor's unseemly display of political muscle. "Since politics have become her choicest interest all her charm has disappeared." Bye's displeasure extended to Eleanor's companions—"...and the fact is emphasized by the companions she chooses to bring with her..."

Ted, Jr. narrowly lost the 1924 election to Eleanor and Franklin's candidate, Al Smith. Alice blamed Eleanor for the loss in the same manner her in-laws had blamed her for Nick's 1912 election loss. "Like the Republican elephant I am," Alice vowed, "I never forget." She had other upcoming events to occupy her mind and her time, however.

Though Alice disapproved of Harding, she approved of his successor, vice president Calvin Coolidge. She had developed a special bond with the taciturn new President, "Silent Cal." She appreciated his dry wit and his tight-lipped presence at dinner parties, taking him into her confidence. She once sat next to him during dinner observing that he did not exchange one word with the woman next to him who droned on and on. At the end of the dinner, the woman pleaded with him to say something, since she had bet a friend of hers that she could get the President to say more than three words. In his inimitable manner, Coolidge turned to the woman and said, "You lose."

While Eleanor adjusted to the physical demands of her husband's new life and the new demands it placed on her, Alice took on an unlikely physical and emotional challenge of her own. Though almost 41 years old, Alice continued to stoke the fires of Washington's rumor mill during the 1924 campaign. Her news, however, did not concern the election, but

rather, was of a more personal nature. When a United Press journalist phoned to asked her to confirm the rumor that she was pregnant, Alice answered, "Hell, yes. Isn't it wonderful?"
Edith was most surprised. "Alice's news was rather a blow..."
Calvin Coolidge was one of the few people who knew. When Grace Coolidge told her husband that Alice had confirmed her pregnancy, he replied, "Yes, I knew that. Alice told me a couple of months ago." His wife was flabbergasted. "Imagine," she told some friends, "a man having a bit of gossip as choice as that and keeping it a secret!" Coolidge's taciturnity was precisely why Alice confided in him.

Alice had her child at the Chicago Lying-In Hospital on Valentine's Day, 1925, the 41st anniversary of her mother Alice Lee's death. She wanted the best hospital and obstetrician she could find, to avoid the disaster of her own home birth. In her typical piercing style Alice described the birth experience as "trying to push a grand piano through a transom."

To rumors that Nick couldn't possibly be the father, she replied wantonly that the child "really looks very much like Uncle Joe Cannon." Relatives speculated that Nick was a drunk, incapable of having a child. Some said Alice had barred him from her bed. Others speculated that Borah was the father and there was even talk that Alice had been artificially inseminated. Whether Nick was the biological father or not, he accepted fatherhood lovingly, doting on his tiny daughter.

The child went unnamed for several days, referred to as "the Valentine's baby" in the press. Nick reportedly vetoed Alice's suggestion of the biblical name Deborah. "With all gossip going around, why would you want to name her De-Borah?" he asked. "Don't you think that will raise too many eyebrows."

Alice settled on Paulina, a variation on the name of her favorite apostle. In her typical mocking style, Alice picked a controversial, yet ironic image, for Paul preached the virtues of self-denial. She let it be known that, had the child been a boy, he would have been named Paul. Were the child actually Nick's, undoubtedly he would have insisted on another Nicholas Longworth.

The 1920s were a time for Eleanor to spread her political wings, achieving self-confidence, independence and a new circle of friends with a new purpose to her life separate from being wife and mother. Cousin

178 Alice and Eleanor

Alice had never relinquished her independent life for the role of wife and mother. She was accepting the mantle of motherhood as her exclusive identity and purpose, at precisely the time Eleanor was shedding that veil.

Chapter Fifteen

"Good morning, Mrs. L," a passerby smiled as Alice wheeled Paulina's perambulator around her block of Massachusetts Avenue.

"A lovely day, isn't it," Alice replied, smiling proudly. The woman paused to admire the babbling baby, sitting contentedly in her carriage. She cooed at the teddy bear tucked in beside her.

"She must give you great pleasure," the woman said.

"At my age, she's a complete joy," Alice laughed.

"And I'll bet her father adores her," commented the woman.

"He's crazy about her," Alice confirmed, "as she is about him." She looked up to see several photographers gathering. "No pictures, please."

"But it's her birthday," one photographer cried.

"Our one time a year to shoot her," another shouted.

"You'll have your chance when Nick and I agree on the time and place," Alice commented firmly, but politely. "Good day, gentlemen." She excused herself and stepped up her pace, nodding and smiling to other mothers walking their infants.

"Many happy returns of the day to you both, Mrs. Longworth," shouted a young photographer, tipping his hat.

"Thank you, young man. Do enjoy this sunny day. There are so few in February."

Returning home, she was delighted to find Waldie arranging her favorite long-stemmed yellow roses in a vase next to the stacks of presents piled high for Paulina.

"And this just arrived," Waldie beamed, showing Alice a package.

"Red satin hearts filled with creamy chocolates," Alice laughed. "Perfect for a Valentine's baby. I'm sure they'll become a favorite of hers. What child did you ever know who didn't like chocolates?"[1]

"Why on earth you would prefer to spend time with those ladies, and I use the term very loosely, rather than with your own children is quite beyond me, Eleanor," huffed Sara. Eleanor listened silently, her jaw muscles twitching from the tension of her clenched teeth. "You should be with your husband at Warm Springs or with the children, here with me."

"I am available for my children at a moment's notice and Missy is taking care of everything Franklin needs," Eleanor responded stiffly.

"I don't understand these modern relationships—women working, earning their own money, building their own vacation houses while their husbands build separate ones. And the children, neglected by both of you. Why if I weren't here..."

"I've heard quite enough, Mama," Eleanor burst aloud. "What Franklin and I agree works within our family..."

"Such independence may have worked for the likes of cousin Alice, but even she's fallen into line. Did you see that picture of her in the paper, a devoted mother pushing Paulina around the block in her carriage," Sara carried on.

"I thought you'd criticize Alice for pushing it by herself, instead of ordering Waldie to do it," Eleanor said sarcastically. "I should have taken a few lessons on independence from Alice years ago. I'm finally discovering my own voice. Alice has had hers for years."

"You've swung too far, Eleanor. You're constantly travelling, or writing, or lecturing for every liberal cause, and now this ridiculous idea of your teaching...The children are lucky to have me! I am really their mother. You merely bore them." Her statement stung sharply.

"The Cottage won't be done soon enough for my taste," Eleanor fumed, storming out of the room.

Later that evening she wrote to Franklin,

Mother and I had another row today over Val-Kill and my other pursuits. I hate being at such cross-purposes with her, but she can be so infuriating. She disapproves of everything I am doing, from writing to my new teaching responsibilities, but what hurts deeply is her criticism of how we are raising the children. I fear that had I stood up to her years ago, I would not feel such guilt about them, for I believe I should have spent more of my own time caring for them, rather than listening to her advice and turning over the childrearing to the nurses. Can you imagine? She even complimented Alice today, for her motherly devotion! Alice—of all people, who she has blatantly criticized over the years for her wild, defiant antisocial manners. Perhaps we would all have been better off had we adopted some defiance of our own long ago.

Lately I have been thinking and will probably even write an article on the benefits of letting our children go for a change. Just because we live in the same house, does not mean we have an inner understanding of them. We should help them in the way they wish to be helped and not in the way we think they should be helped. That is precisely how your mother views childrearing. "Do as I wish and I will help you in every possible way, but otherwise, oh, no!"² I think we'd do better if we didn't offer advice unless asked. I have yet to see when telling our children an unpleasant truth out of our own feeling of duty has really helped in a difficult situation, other than relieving our own minds. I hope we do better with our grandchildren.

I close this evening thrilled about Anna's progress and the baby's.³ She weighs seven and a half pounds, her eyes are blue, hair black, mouth large, and ears very flat. Anna is sleeping a lot. We certainly missed you being here for the great event.

Much love dear, E

Changing Roles

Alice guarded her new daughter from the press throughout her infancy. She refused to let Paulina be photographed by the press when she emerged from seclusion after a two-week stay in the hospital. She shook hands with the hospital's superintendent and a host of new mothers greeting her in the lobby. Paulina was carried by her nurse, Waldie, a World War I Red Cross nurse who worked at the hospital.

The family's return to Washington caused such a stir that troops had to be called out to control the well-wishing crowd lining the streets from Union Station to their home. The new mother and child continually made headlines, with their reception linked to royalty. Paulina was doted on as "America's most famous baby" in magazine articles and the press dubbed her a "Princess," like her mother.

Within her first month, Paulina was seen in a basket balanced on her mother's knee driving past the White House with her uncle Kermit. Alice told reporters briskly, "It's only an ordinary market basket and it cost sixty-five cents, including the ribbons and the paint." Paulina arrived for her first visit to the White House to see Grace Coolidge in the same basket.

Paulina was allowed to be photographed by the press once a year on her birthday. In many subsequent photos, she posed with an aloof, rigid stare, standing beside Nick, who was outfitted in his high stiff collar and his legendary gold watchchain and diamond stickpin.

Alice described herself as "a shy, embarrassed, rather furtive creature who likes her baby." As an older mother, she "had no desire to escape from my responsibilities. Had she been born when I was a great deal younger, I might have welcomed distractions that would have taken me away from her." Paulina had abundant dresses and pets, including two Scotties and a pony like the one Alice had as a child at Sagamore Hill. Later she acquired a horse and a Bethlehem donkey. Alice expanded her repertoire of imitations to include animals, particularly a melancholy mother monkey who hopped on chairs and uttered primal shrieks.

Nick, who quite easily could have ignored this child, fell in love with her instead. The affection was mutual. He had his own nickname for Paulina, "Kitz," by which she was known in her intimate circle. By the time she could walk, Nick was ordering special nursery lunches for Kitz once a week in the Speaker's private dining room. He was terribly indulgent of this child. Normally a fastidious dresser, Waldie once observed Nick with Paulina in his study. The little girl was making sugar cakes on top of her father's bald head by moistening powder sugar with spit and patting the mixture flat with a teaspoon.

The Longworths moved to a bigger home on Massachusetts Avenue to accommodate their larger family. Alice decorated the house in Empire style and hung some of her father's animals skins on the wall beside the stairs. Servants reported that Mrs. Longworth was a pleasant and kind employer, even though Alice continually told people how mean she was.

Her relationship with Nick had evolved into mutual tolerance of one another's eccentricities, as well as poking fun at one another in the vein of their frivolous past. Alice was forever taunting Nick. Once she tried to trip him at a charity ball as he walked arm in arm with President Coolidge. On other occasions, she chased him around the house, spraying him with her perfume. Nick retaliated in his own way. When asked how far his fingers could stretch over a piano keyboard, Nick clasped both hands possessively across his wife's bottom and announced, "Two octaves."

Gambling and drinking filled Nick's off-business hours. After Harding's death, his partner in merrymaking became the Democratic minority whip, "Cactus Jack" Garner from Texas. Nick picked Garner up each morning on the way to the Capitol. They reviled one another on the floor of the House, then, each night at five, Garner would signal for Nick to break off debate. They would retire to their fictitious "Board of Education" to engage in continuous rounds of booze.

Nick's reputation as a fun-loving, witty womanizer continued as he aged. He climbed out the back window of his house to visit an ambassador's daughter whose roof adjoined the Longworths'. With his ability to think quickly and cleverly, he could extract himself from potentially embarrassing situations with grace and humor. When a brash congressman compared Nick's bald head to his own wife's behind, taking the liberty of feeling the Speaker's head for comparison's sake, rather than exploding, which is what the congressman had hoped, Nick ran his hand across his own head and replied thoughtfully, "So it does." Another man took a cigarette from a box on Nick's desk, only to find out before he lit up that it was a condom disguised as a cigarette.

While Alice adjusted to full-time motherhood, Eleanor was busy being both father and mother to her growing brood. In 1925, Franklin and Eleanor's children ranged in age from John who was nine to Anna at 19. Franklin spent the winters between 1923-27 in Florida, searching for warm, healing waters and the summers in Marion, Massachusetts, where he worked with a neurologist named Dr. William McDonald. McDonald had designed exercises specifically for polio victims.

Franklin purchased a run-down resort at Warm Springs, Georgia, in 1926. He spent longer and longer periods of time in rehabilitation there. He rebuilt the facilities into a first-rate therapeutic environment. The resort flourished under the supervision of Dr. LeRoy W. Hubbard, an orthopedic surgeon, and Helena T. Mahoney, a physiotherapist. It eventually earned approval by the American Orthopaedic Association.

Louis Howe continued living in the Roosevelt home on 65th Street during the week, returning to his family in Fall River on the weekends. He provided a strong emotional anchor for Eleanor, who took the brunt of the battles with Sara. Her mother-in-law undermined the discipline Eleanor and Franklin tried to instill in their family. She referred to her grandchildren as her own. Franklin, Jr. recalled his granny telling them that she was their real mother. Eleanor had only given birth to them. Sara manipulated the children when she felt neglected, constantly threatening to leave one or another out of her will.

184 Alice and Eleanor

Eleanor was experiencing the type of tension between herself and Anna that Alice had experienced with her parents. Anna didn't want to go to college because young men would be intimidated by her. Her parents persuaded Anna to attend a "short-horn agricultural course" at Cornell because she had a talent with animals and liked outdoor life. She married a stockbroker named Curtis Dall at age 20, in order to "get out." Meanwhile, her brothers were meeting with varying levels of academic success at Harvard, Groton and the Buckley School.

As Eleanor struggled to manage her disparate flock alone in New York, she deepened her association with her women friends, Marion Dickerman, Nancy Cook and Caroline O'Day. They formed a partnership called "Val-Kill" which ultimately encompassed several enterprises: the Todhunter School in New York City which the women bought in 1926, the Val-Kill furniture factory, which opened in 1927 under the supervision of Nancy Cook, and the *Women's Democratic News*, begun in May 1925 and edited by Eleanor.

Val-Kill was a stream at the eastern end of Franklin's property at Hyde Park in Duchess County, New York. While he was busy building his Warm Springs resort, he also facilitated the building of a stone cottage for "the girls" at Val-Kill and the creation of an old-fashioned swimming hole in the stream. He donated the property and sent numerous presents.

Sara detested the enterprise as well as Eleanor's independent friends and her children's lifestyle. Franklin had his own conflicts with his mother but it was Eleanor who could no longer tolerate living in Sara's Hyde Park home, the Big House as it was called, when Franklin or the children were gone. She needed a place of her own, away from the critical eye of her mother-in-law. The cottage offered her the retreat she needed for herself and for her friends.

The Val-Kill factory produced replicas of hand-made, Early American furniture. Franklin's interest in the enterprise was to develop an industry, offering employment in rural communities for young men who might otherwise leave the area. While it was never a financial success, the furniture manufactured at Val-Kill populated the Warm Springs Resort as well as Eleanor's cottage. When the factory was closed during the Depression, she converted it to her private, "if somewhat odd" home, with an apartment for her secretary, Malvina Thompson, and a guest cottage. During Franklin's years as President, it was in frequent use, and the old swimming hole abandoned for a fine swimming pool.

Marion Dickerman had been assistant principal and then principal of the progressive Todhunter School. When Miss Todhunter decided to return to her English homeland, she offered to sell the school to Marion. Eleanor suggested that they buy the private girls school together, recalling her years with Madame Souvestre. With her children away at boarding school, she was looking for a professional outlet and an escape from Sara. Eleanor lamented the fact that she had no real talent, experience or training in anything, but she found the idea of teaching older girls particularly appealing.

At the Todhunter School, Eleanor taught courses in literature, drama and American history. She took her students on field trips to the New York City courts and even visits to the Lower East Side tenements. According to her partner, Marion, "teaching gave her [Eleanor] some of the happiest moments in her life...She loved it. The girls worshipped her. She was a very inspiring person."

Along with her newfound personal independence, Eleanor became financially independent. She wrote for popular magazines like *McCalls* and *Redbook*, reaching a wide, popular audience on issues surrounding women in politics. She wrote on topics such as "What I Want Most Out of Life," encouraging women to have interests of their own apart from their families. With radio coming into its own, Eleanor was often asked to present the woman's viewpoint.

She became an effective and sought-after lecturer. She cared about her audiences and understood the importance of eye contact and connecting directly with the entire room. She found joy in athletic pursuits that she had always feared, like mountain climbing and swimming, and she became an incomparable walker. Though she wanted to become a pilot and took preliminary lessons from Amelia Earhart, she didn't follow through because Franklin persuaded her that he had enough to worry about without his wife soaring above the clouds. She did promote flying as a hobby for the thrill of the adventure.

As 1928 neared, Eleanor's activities for the women's division of the Democratic State Committee increased. Louis Howe taught her the nuts and bolts of newspaper design and layout for the *Democratic News*. She took on the job of advertising manager in addition to being editor.

186   Alice and Eleanor

She lobbied Albany legislators on behalf of legislation for women and children, battling fiercely for the 48-hour work week.

Though Louis Howe and Eleanor had agreed long ago, that she should keep Franklin's name before the public and the politicians, Eleanor did not attend the 1928 Democratic convention. Franklin and her friends Elinor Morgenthau and Caroline O'Day did, however, with Marion Dickerman as an alternate. Franklin heroically leaned on his son Elliot's arm, dispensing with his crutches to totter across the stage with a cane to deliver the triumphant presidential nominating speech for New York's Governor, Al Smith.

After the convention, Eleanor was drafted by the Democratic National Committee to be director of the Bureau of Women's Activities, along with Mrs. Nellie Taylor Ross, Wyoming's first woman governor. She worked at the headquarters for Al Smith's campaign for President, setting up committees for special interest groups of independent voters, professional women and working women.

At campaign headquarters, Eleanor successfully fought for equality of space and comfort for women political organizers. Her rooms were "identical in size and location" to those of the Democratic national chairman, John J. Raskob. She held the most powerful position ever occupied by a woman in party politics. However, she soon realized that equal space did not guarantee equal power. "Women Must Learn to Play the Game as Men Do," she wrote in an article for *Redbook*. They needed to become their own "women bosses" within their parties in order to achieve real power.

Eleanor's success in politics set the stage for Franklin's nomination by acclamation to be the Democratic candidate for Governor at the 1928 New York State Convention. She encouraged him to run, against his initial wish. Louis was against Franklin running, too, fearing that if Smith lost nationally, his man wouldn't carry the state. Louis was looking to the future and wanted Franklin to run in four or possibly eight years. Franklin thought he needed two more years of exercise to regain the strength of his legs, but Eleanor knew his progress had ceased. He could walk with great effort using braces, a cane and the strong arms of his sons, but his legs had no real strength.

Franklin accepted the nomination and was energized by his nonstop campaign. He continued to believe that if he had another six months of rehabilitation, he would be able to throw away his cane.

Eleanor devoted her political energies entirely to Smith's campaign, not Franklin's, but the country was not yet prepared to elect a president with a New York accent and image, one who sported a derby hat, smoked cigars, promised to repeal Prohibition and was a Roman Catholic. Eleanor carried a letter that Uncle Teddy had written while he was President, in which he expressed the belief that someday the United States would fulfill its democratic mandate by electing a Catholic or a Jew to the country's highest office. Smith lost in a landslide to Herbert Hoover, 444 electoral votes to 87. Everyone in the family was convinced that Franklin had lost too, except his mother. Sara stayed at campaign headquarters until the early hours of the morning to await the final vote count. Franklin beat his opponent, the popular state attorney general, Albert Ottinger, by slightly more than 25,000 votes.

Eleanor took Smith's loss hard, commenting with uncharacteristic coldness on her husband's victorious return to politics. "If the rest of the ticket didn't get in, what does it matter?" She was not excited about her husband's victory, wondering in retrospect whether she had really wanted him to run. She resigned from the Democratic National Committee and the *Women's Democratic News*, for she didn't believe she should continue being identified with partisan politics.

Eleanor returned to Albany, her first political home 18 years before, not as an eager neophyte, but as a seasoned political veteran, a teacher, a grandmother, a writer, a lecturer and a radio personality. Eleanor intended to continue her teaching schedule three days a week, as well as her writing. She would manage the Governor's mansion, making it a home that ran smoothly for her husband, as well as being available at any moment for her four sons away at school. She became New York's part-time First Lady, speeding down to New York City on the Sunday night train to teach Monday through Wednesday, then dashing back up to Albany to resume her role as Mistress of the mansion Thursday through Sunday.

As Eleanor settled in the Governor's mansion and continued her independent career as a teacher and political activist, Alice luxuriated in her new roles as the wife of the Speaker of the House and mother. Paulina's nurse, Waldie, took full-time charge of her child when Alice resumed her role pulling strings and pushing buttons in Washington. The Republican heyday of the 1920s were a time, as she described them, "when the golden calf gave triple cream."

188 Alice and Eleanor

At the height of the diplomatic season of 1926, when Eleanor was immersed in her Val-Kill projects and Democratic work, Alice attended a state dinner honoring Queen Marie of Romania at the White House. According to protocol, no one could leave until the Queen rose from her seat. Mrs. Coolidge had arranged to be seated on a sofa with the Queen after dinner. When she rose, the Queen would rise and the evening would end. However, after the President's wife stood up mid-evening, the Queen beckoned for Alice to sit beside her. Protocol went out the window. No one was able to leave for Alice entertained her majesty into the wee hours of the morning.

On August 3, 1927, President Coolidge announced, "I do not choose to run," leaving the 1928 Republican convention wide open. Nick set his presidential wheels spinning. He courted support discreetly at formal dinners in his honor, by delivering commencement addresses and receiving honorary degrees. He hoped to be chosen as a compromise candidate. Rather than taking his traditional European vacation, Nick toured the United States during the summer.

By the following February, however, an engineer serving as Coolidge's Secretary of Commerce, Herbert Hoover, was the clear Republican front runner. Even though he had never been elected to any office, backers claimed Hoover was an economic genius who promised Americans "two chickens in every pot and a car in every garage."

The newspapers speculated with headlines that read, "Will Princess Alice Return to the White House?" but by the time the Republican convention convened in Kansas City on June 12, 1928, Nick's name was not even put into nomination. Hoover had the candidacy sewn up. As Alice left the convention hall, she started to open her umbrella. A friend cautioned her that it would bring bad luck. "If that is the case," Alice replied, "there must be an open umbrella over all of Kansas City!"

Nick was not the only man in Alice's life who left the convention unrewarded. Bill Borah was passed over for the vice-president's position even though Coolidge had supported him. Bill was quoted to have said, "I'd rather be right than President."

Alice, like Eleanor, campaigned during the 1928 election, but not for her husband. While Eleanor worked tirelessly for Al Smith, Alice stumped with Mrs. Hoover in support of the Republican Presidential nominee. She also counselled her dearest friend, Ruth McCormick, who

Chapter Fifteen 189

ran for and won a congressional seat. Hoover was victorious, and appointed Alice's brother, Ted, Jr., to the post of Governor of Puerto Rico. On Inauguration Day, Paulina was given a special place in the stands where she heard the new President announce, "I have no fears about the future of our country...It is bright with hope."

The Longworths became frequent dinner guests at the refurbished White House. With Hoover's self-made millions, his wife, Lou, replaced the former farmhouse atmosphere of the Coolidge days with extravagant furnishings. She also established a precedent, placing the Speaker of the House firmly behind the Vice-President in protocol.

Before Hoover's term was a year old, however, his optimistic inaugural predictions came crashing down with the collapse of the stockmarket on Black Thursday, October 24, 1929. Though the President toiled seven days a week to stem the country's economic collapse, the "Crash" deepened into the "Depression." Millions of men and women were out of work as businesses went under. People lost their life savings as banks failed. Hoover bore the blame, though Alice told a journalist, "Blaming Hoover for the Depression is like blaming the people of San Francisco for the earthquake of 1906." She compared the press lynching of Hoover to "primitive" religions which held the High Priest responsible for the success or failure of crops. If they failed, the leader was killed.

Though Alice's trust funds and other investments remained safe, Nick took a beating on his stocks. The Longworths were besieged by free-lance photographers desperately trying to make ends meet by catching a candid shot of Paulina at the circus or skipping rope in the park. In order to bring back a feeling of prosperous bygone days, Alice threw a party for her and Nick's 25th wedding anniversary. Guests were to wear something from 1906, or shirtwaists, skirts and sailor hats. She wore an elegant, gold satin gown preserved in her trousseau, topped off with a diamond tiara in her 1906 pompadour hairstyle.

The party was in sharp contrast to the sinking fortunes of the country. The Washington Monument became a campground for grim, hungry men who erected tents out of cardboard and tin, sarcastically named "Hoovervilles." Riots broke out in front of the White House. The angry crowds were sprayed with tear gas by the U.S. Army, under the command of General Douglas MacArthur. He assigned the task of clearing the area to a major named Eisenhower.

As the depression deepened, a Democratic majority took control of Congress in the 1930 election. Though Nick retained his congressional seat by a margin of only 3,500 votes, he lost his position as Speaker to his "Board of Education" drinking buddy, former minority leader, Cactus Jack Garner.

Paulina was on hand when her father adjourned the Seventy-first Congress on March 4, 1931. A rousing tribute followed, with the members standing, beating their hands in his honor. Several rebel yells were offered from the Democratic side of the aisle. Nick grew redder and redder with pleasure and gratification, waiting for the noise to subside so he could make his final address. After his speech, in which he offered, "whatever providence may decree I am abundantly satisfied," a wild party began with a marching band, a men's chorus, and a radio orchestra playing. Cactus Jack acknowledged, "There are a lot of Republicans we could do without, but you are not one of them, Nick."

The 1930 election renewed a conflict between three former lovers, friends and rivals. Cissy Patterson, the *Washington Herald*'s new editor-in-chief, lambasted Alice in her column for her role as an advisor to Ruth McCormick in her race for her late husband's senate seat. Cissy reported that Alice would not campaign for her friend since she couldn't "utter in public. Her assistance will, therefore, resolve itself, as usual, into posing for photographs." William Borah accused Ruth of trying to buy the election when she spent $300,000 of her own money on the race. He threatened to unseat her if she won because of her excess. Ruth lost in the Democratic sweep throughout the country.

Franklin was re-elected as Governor with the largest vote cast for any Democrat up to that time in a gubernatorial election. The results, as Eleanor noted, made her husband, "strong in the state and strong as a potential candidate for the Presidency." The prospect did not interest her, particularly, she noted, but it did interest his political supporters.

The fortunes of the two branches of the Roosevelt family paralleled the political vicissitudes of the country. Theodore Roosevelt's progressive message had been drowned out by the conservative business interests of the Republican party. His banner was picked up by the Democrats, now led by the Hyde Park Roosevelts. As America's fortunes plummeted, the progressive Democrats became the voice of the people. Alice and Nick remained loyal to the Republican Party, rather than TR's agenda. Political power and influence shifted out of the hands of the Oyster Bay branch and into the hands of their upstream relations.

Chapter Sixteen

"What do you mean, you won't let us in?" asked Alice, indignantly. "I'll have you know, young man, I used to live here."

"I'm sure, ma'am. Next time you plan to drop by, have Mrs. Roosevelt put your name on the guest list, and come to the front entrance like everybody else," the crisply dressed young butler replied, closing the door on Alice and several companions.

Alice's indignation passed in a flash and she began laughing uproariously. "Oh, won't Eleanor be embarrassed, stumbling over herself to apologize at this grievous affront to me. Imagine, a former president's daughter having the door slammed in her face at the White House, and with her cousin, no less, in occupancy!"

The next day when the mail arrived, Alice opened a note from Eleanor. She showed it to a male friend who had been part of the visiting entourage at the White House the previous day.

"What did I tell you? The personification of breeding," Alice said as she commenced reading the note aloud. "I feel terrible that the doorman did not let you bring your friends through the White House this afternoon. He very foolishly did not ask the usher and, when the usher came downstairs, you had already gone. Please another time ask them to ask the usher or someone in the house. My deepest apologies, Affectionately, Eleanor."[1]

With mock alacrity, Alice said, "Isn't that sweet? Only Eleanor can convey such piety. I find it completely tedious...in fact, it reminds me of the conversations she used to engage in when we were young...over ideas like whether contentment is better than happiness and if they conflict with one another. I couldn't give a damn about such nonsense. I'll take a good scandal any day...like those rumors of the pillow fights Eleanor has with her female impersonator friends upstairs in the White House. Now that is not boring. More strength to them, I say! Pillow fights are a jolly form of communication."[2]

She picked up an embroidered pillow from her couch, inscribed, "If you have nothing nice to say, come and sit by me," and gave her companion a healthy whack. Then she collapsed on the couch clutching the pillow in a contagion of giggles.

"Truthfully, though, Eleanor has done quite well. Cousin Corinne told me she found the new First Lady in a corner on Franklin's Inauguration Day, wailing, 'I will have no identity. I'll only be the wife of the President.' It took her a little while to find her footing, but since Franklin can't stand on his own..."

"Alice! That's maliciously cruel, even for you!" complained her companion.

"Balderdash!" Alice shot back. "Franklin doesn't pity himself, so why should we? He's a cripple. So what? He's also President of the United States. Harding's legs worked perfectly well. In fact, he spent a good deal of his time as President chasing ladies into the closet, but he was a mental cripple. So were Taft and Wilson. Franklin may be bankrupting the country with all his socialist programs, but at least he's making an impact. That's not exactly what we expected from our upstream relation. Eleanor's been his legs and ears around the country. Of all the Presidents' wives, not one has used her position as effectively as Eleanor," Alice said admiringly.

"Such uncharacteristic generosity from you, Alice."

"Don't let it get around," she said, brushing off her guest's comment. "It's tea time. One lump or two?"

Tragedy and Triumph

In April 1931, shortly after Alice and Nick celebrated their 25th wedding anniversary, Nick departed Washington for a visit with his friends James and Laura Curtis, in Aiken, South Carolina. Aiken was the winter home of such wealthy citizens as Wintie Rutherfurd, whose second wife, Lucy Mercer, was Franklin's former love. Laura Curtis ran infamous $1000 minimum poker games where Nick drank and played with other Hoover Cabinet notables like the Vice-President, Charlie Curtis (no relation to Laura) and Secretary of War, Dwight Davis, who endowed the Davis tennis cup. Nick's paramour, Alice Dows, had planned to meet him there.

Everyone's plans changed dramatically when the cold Nick was fighting turned into pneumonia. A death watch ensued, for it was widely believed that anyone who had abused his body with as much rum as Nick could not live through such a disease. Alice left Paulina in

Cincinnati, where their daughter was attending elementary school, to be with her husband. Newsmen awaited a sign from the doctor. Hoover asked to be kept informed. Cissy Patterson, still up to her newspaper mischief, ran a front-page photo of Nick with Laura Curtis on his arm in earlier days. The beloved former Speaker died on April 10.

Alice declined a state funeral for her husband. A private car in a government train transported Nick's body back to Cincinnati, accompanied by his valet, several trunks of his wardrobe and, at his wife's invitation, Alice Dows. She was being treated as if she were the widow. The funeral turned into a huge affair despite his wife's wishes.

At the end of the service, Alice Dows walked down the aisle alone, dressed in black with a drawn veil. She laid a bunch of violets on the coffin. The mourners stared in disbelief at the poor taste of her act. Nick's wife, Alice, defied tradition, keeping her veil back from her face. She had not shed a tear in public, a behavior consistent with her upbringing and colored by her complicated relationship with Nick.

Nick's will, typed on a half sheet of notepaper shortly after Paulina's birth, left his wife everything he owned. The estate, thought to be valued at a million dollars, wasn't worth even $200,000 after taxes. No longer the wife of a congressman, Alice's reason for living in Washington had vanished. Reluctantly, she moved to the family home in Cincinnati to be near Paulina's boarding school.

Alice grew up in a family constantly burdened by finances but she always had her own inheritance. Suddenly, she found herself in need of an income. She accepted an offer to write her memoirs in a series of monthly installments to be published in the "family magazine of America," the *Ladies Home Journal*. Curtis Publishing Company's first vice-president, George Lorimer, was a New Deal hater like Alice and hoped to pull off a political coup by publishing her writing. Entitled "Some Reminiscences," the installments later became Alice's autobiography, *Crowded Hours*.

The result met with mixed reviews. The book made the best-seller list but, as Alice described her own writing, it was for "profit, not literature." Some criticized her work as "so lacking in bite that it might have been written by a promotion man for a government bureau." Though Alice was a sparkling conversationalist, her words did not sparkle once translated to paper.

Her writing also lacked the scandal that characterized her life. It didn't besmirch her popular husband's reputation in public, nor convey her true feelings about her stepmother or reveal her sense of loss after her father's death. Alice admired the British stiff upper lip. "Some things are too bad to talk about," she told a friend. "If you must lick your wounds, do it in private."

While Alice struggled through a difficult transition in her life, Eleanor found the years 1930-32 personally productive and emotionally nurturing for her as a woman. Along with her involvement in the Val-Kill enterprises and her teaching, she discovered an unlikely ally and friend. Eleanor liked to drive her own car rather than the state vehicles, but driving by herself made Franklin uncomfortable. He insisted that Earl Miller become her personal driver. Earl was a handsome state trooper, former boxer, swimmer, horseman, marksman and circus performer. At the time, he was 32 with the reputation as a womanizer and Eleanor was 44 years old.

Earl's friends initially described Eleanor as the "old crab," however, he addressed her adoringly as "the Lady." Eleanor's and Earl's friendship churned the rumor mills. He attended her with the care and devotion her sons and her husband neglected. He was fiercely loyal and stood up for Eleanor when her family took her for granted. If Franklin or others took credit for Eleanor's ideas or belittled her, Earl came to her defense. He would remind them that his "Lady" originated the notion or espoused the cause. Eleanor responded to Earl's protectiveness with the warmth and love of a neglected woman. Sometimes their interactions were characterized as a mother to a son. At other times, they acted as if they were engaged in a romantic affair.

Earl and Eleanor took trips alone to the mountains and resorts where they frolicked together. They enjoyed music and put on plays. He gave Eleanor her horse, Dot. Many an eyebrow was raised when Earl took tea with the family. Friends like Marion Dickerson and Nancy Cook expressed indignation over the intimacies between the two.

Similar concerns were raised over Franklin's devoted young assistant, Missy LeHand, who presided over Warm Springs and the Albany Governor's Mansion in Eleanor's absence. For a time, a romance flourished between Earl and Missy; however, it ended when Earl married. Franklin may have encouraged Missy and Earl's relationship to stop the rumors about his wife and her devoted driver. Earl, however, dismissed any seriousness between Missy and him, describing his courtly role as running "interference for the Lady."

No letters survived between Earl and Eleanor, though rumors of a voluminous correspondence existed. There are, however, home movies and family stories. Even at the end of his life, Earl would not reveal any details of his relationship with Eleanor because he refused to cash in on his friends. Their relationship ended abruptly when Franklin was elected President. Earl was not asked to come to Washington with the family. Eleanor allegedly sent an anguished letter to her friend, Nancy Cook, in which she threatened to divorce Franklin and run off with Earl. In a mild panic, Nancy showed the letter to Louis Howe, who tore it up and ordered her and Marion Dickerson "not to breathe a word of this to anyone. Not to *anyone*." Earl dismissed the letter, suggesting that Eleanor had probably "been down in the depths," but he didn't trust anything Marion reported. According to Earl, jealousy among Eleanor's crowd was "phenomenal" as they competed for her attention or Franklin's.

Franklin's resounding re-election as New York's Governor in 1930 set him in position to become the Democratic nominee for President in the 1932 election. Louis Howe had been maneuvering behind the scenes on Franklin's behalf for years towards this goal. By the spring of 1931, Howe had opened up offices for the Friends of Roosevelt.

With the children grown and the path paved for her husband's presidential aspirations, Eleanor was ready to put her considerable political skill to work for Franklin. Though in public, they appeared a devoted, respectful team, in private, he did not discuss his decision to run for President with her. Still, Eleanor played a strong role behind the scenes, directing letter writing campaigns, cultivating political allies, encouraging biographers and advocating progressive social policies for women, labor and children. She continued to travel widely, serving as her husband's proxy. When the public became concerned about whether Franklin's health could withstand the rigors of the presidency, Eleanor replied unsentimentally, "If polio did not kill him, the presidency won't."

She had never relinquished the hope that they could reinvigorate their relationship by forging a shared partnership. Politics could be their instrument to promote the ennoblement of humanity. She expected her husband to share her vision but became increasingly concerned by

Franklin's willingness to sacrifice his principles for pragmatism. When he shifted his position on prohibition, she was seriously distressed that he was being seduced by the naked pursuit of power. But when he abandoned his support for the League of Nations and the World Court, she experienced a far more severe breach.

Franklin had taken a beating in front-page editorials of the Hearst newspaper, the *New York American*, for his support of the League. Hearst reviled internationalism and promoted the isolationist "America First" policy to which cousin Alice had become an adherent. Franklin tried to straighten the matter out by meeting with the paper's editors, rather than delivering a public repudiation of the League. Hearst demanded a public statement and Franklin needed his support in order to secure the Democratic nomination for President. He capitulated in a speech to the New York State Grange, stating that he did not favor American participation in the League of Nations. By acquiesing to Hearst, Franklin infuriated many of his supporters, including his wife.

Such shifts drew into question the strength of his political convictions, reinforcing the charge that Franklin was a political lightweight. After the Grange address, he came under fire from Wilsonian internationalists. He defended himself, arguing that his ideals had not changed, merely his methods to achieve them. To Eleanor, however, abandoning the League represented a severe violation of conscience which threw her into one of her rare Griselda moods. She didn't speak to her husband for three days.

Franklin invited Agnes Leach, former chair of the New York State League of Women Voters, to lunch. He wanted her to make peace between him and his wife. Leach refused. "I couldn't believe my eyes," she said. "That was a shabby statement. I just don't feel like having lunch with you today." Leach's refusal to condone Franklin's shift on his support of the League vindicated Eleanor. She phoned her friend to say, "Agnes, you are a sweet, darling girl. I hear you upset Franklin very much. I didn't know you had it in you."

The Democratic National convention convened in Chicago at the end of June 1932. After the first ballot, Franklin held fewer delegates than the two-thirds he needed to capture the Presidential nomination of his party. He controlled 666 to Al Smith's 201 while Cactus Jack Garner, Nick's successor as Speaker of the House, had 90 delegates. During the

Chapter Sixteen 197

subsequent tense balloting, Eleanor remained aloof and knit while Franklin chain-smoked. By the afternoon of July 1, his team struck a deal. Joe Kennedy, Louis Howe and William Randolph Hearst negotiated for Garner's delegates in exchange for the vice-presidential nod. Hearst had accepted Franklin's complete withdrawal of support from the League of Nations and the World Court. On the fourth ballot, Franklin secured the nomination and pandemonium broke out to the tune of "Happy Days Are Here Again."

Eleanor went out to the kitchen to make scrambled eggs and bacon. Lorena Hickock, a well-respected, award-winning Associated Press reporter and the only woman reporter assigned to Franklin during the campaign, was invited to share some of her eggs that morning. She noticed Eleanor's distant mood, speculating correctly that she was unhappy. The presidency offered her a future in a gilded cage. The fulfilling life she had molded for herself would no longer exist. As the wife of a President, she would have ceremonial duties to attend to which were outside the realm of her public writing, political and teaching careers. Over the next few months, Lorena befriended Eleanor in what became a lifelong, intimate friendship.

Alice attended both the Republican and Democratic conventions in 1932, first seeing Hoover renominated and, then to her astonishment, cousin Franklin nominated. Since Nick's death she had been fending off the Republican leaders hounding her to run for his congressional seat. Other officials wanted her to run for the Senate. Alice refused with the same insistence that she resisted pressure by Dakota Republicans to be made Hoover's running mate. Teddy was still a folk hero in the Dakotas and, if Alice ran, Franklin would be forced to stop trading on the Roosevelt name.

No amount of pressure, however, could get her to budge, even the argument that her assured victory would prevent the Democrats from gaining control of the House of Representatives. Alice offered many excuses—she wanted to care for her daughter, her shyness about speaking in public, dislike of the practice of women "using their [husband's] coffins as a springboard into Congress" and, remarkably, that she didn't have any campaign skills. Many disagreed with such a claim, given Alice's insider knowledge of how power was manipulated in Washington and her campaign forays for Hoover, her brother and other candidates. Some said Alice simply didn't like people. Others

198 Alice and Eleanor

speculated that she was not interested in the rituals of campaigning just as she disdained other political conventions.

The breach between the two branches of the family remained virtually intact during Franklin's 1932 presidential campaign. Alice's relatives rejected the idea of a Hyde Park Roosevelt taking over the White House when Ted, Jr. should have inherited the mantle. The Oyster Bayers united behind Hoover. Edith even emerged from retirement at Sagamore Hill to introduce Hoover at a Madison Square Garden rally. She decided to speak after receiving congratulatory telegrams on the nomination "of her son Franklin." Her appearance thoroughly eclipsed Hoover's at the rally.

Lorena Hickock picked up the scoop of Edith's appearance and shared the news with Eleanor later that evening.

"What do you suppose your Aunt Edith did tonight?" Lorena asked.

Eleanor looked surprised and shook her head, replying "I can't imagine."

"Well," Lorena told her, "she introduced Herbert Hoover at Madison Square Garden!"

"How very interesting," Eleanor said quietly.

Once again, Eleanor did not actively campaign for Franklin as he circled the country promising his "New Deal." Instead, she put her political skill to work for the Democratic candidate for governor of New York, Herbert Lehman, and for the state ticket. However, she travelled when asked and spoke for her husband when called upon. Eleanor represented the essence of Franklin's New Deal. Wherever she went, Eleanor garnered an outpouring of affection and trust from people in all walks of life.

The European community was confused by the election. A United Press story from Paris said that, if Franklin were elected, it would be due to the efforts of his wife, Alice, who nursed her husband day and night for six months and dubbed him, "Fearless Frank." The article prompted a single, unprintable response from Alice.

While she wouldn't run for office herself, Alice promptly stepped up her campaigning with Mrs. Hoover, dispelling her own claim that she had no campaign skills. She even broke her lifelong rule of making no speeches. She got "so carried away...I just had to talk...The Democrats can't get away with blaming the Depression on President Hoover." She

Chapter Sixteen 199

also made her radio debut, arguing that the Democrats, "belittle the intelligence of the average citizen, and I, as an average citizen, resent it." The public sided with the Hyde Park branch of the family in a landslide for Franklin, electing him by a margin of 472 to 59 electoral votes. Alice reacted with such anger she said she could "grind my teeth and blow them out my nose." In private, Eleanor responded to her husband's victory with tears, fearing that she would lose her identity.

Alice told a reporter for the *New York Times*, "There we were, descendants of a popular President, and what happens? A fifth cousin comes along and gets into the White House. Can you think of anything more distressing?" Despite the Roosevelt family's political rift, etiquette dictated that Alice be invited to dine at the White House on Inaugural Day.

Ted, Jr. described his relationship with the new President as "fifth cousin, about to be removed." Before Franklin recalled him from his post as governor-general of the Philippines, Ted, Jr. resigned.

Alexander Woollcott of *The New York Times* labeled the Oyster Bay Roosevelts the "out-of-season Roosevelts." Still, Teddy Roosevelt's mark on the White House was felt, as the executive mansion once again pulsated with vitality and spirit. Franklin told Cousin Susie before the inauguration how he wanted the White House to feel, "You know how it was when Uncle Ted was there—how gay and home-like...Well, that's how we mean to have it!" Rather than Franklin's own children and their pets filling the rooms as Teddy's had 30 years before, his grandchildren and Eleanor's dogs romped through the White House. The family's exuberance placed its inevitable stamp on the mansion and the country.

Alice's mark was felt, too, not as in her flamboyant debutante days but, rather, from two gifts she had given the family. The first was a cigarette holder she gave Franklin when he first came to Washington. It became one of his enduring trademarks, tilted towards the sky as an accent to his upthrust chin. The second was a small, silver tea service that Alice had given Eleanor and Franklin as a wedding present. Every afternoon Eleanor presided over tea on the west end of the second-floor of the White House, which she turned into the family sitting room. She served from Alice's tea set. The teas served in Alice's home on Massachusetts Avenue and Eleanor's in the White House were a vestige and tribute by both women to their beloved political mentor, Auntie Bye.

Bye had died the previous summer, shortly after Nick. All the Roosevelts mourned her passing. Confined to a wheelchair and almost completely deaf, Eleanor's mother-in-law, Sara, was one of the last people to visit Bye. They had been lifelong friends. Bye was present at Franklin's birth and Eleanor's father, Elliot, was Franklin's godfather.

Though Franklin encouraged a gay home life, he knew the country was in a terrible state. Fear paralyzed business and the people were panicky. Over 13 million workers were unemployed. The national income had fallen by half over a four-year period. The new president had to stem the tide of fear. He adapted an appropriate line from Thoreau, which he read in a book that Eleanor had given him as a gift for his first inaugural address. His message became widely quoted, "The only thing we have to fear is fear itself."

By the time he was elected President, Eleanor and Franklin's lives had grown apart. Her dream of a united partnership was only a distant possibility. She still longed to be treated as a confidante, thoughtfully, tenderly and considerately. Franklin, however, had become a magnetic showman who demanded center stage by virtue of his overpowering personality. Soon after his inauguration, Eleanor made one last attempt to grasp the brass ring and forge their individual lives into a double life. As was her custom, Eleanor went in to say good night. She offered to take over Franklin's mail and become his "listening post" to the people. Franklin listened, looking quizzically at his wife. When she finished, he reminded her that Missy did his mail.

Eleanor left the room that night with the final realization that the role she had envisioned at her husband's side was a fantasy. She would need to define her own place as First Lady—making it a real job, not just a ceremonial post. Though initially unclear of the dimensions of her role, she embarked on it with a breadth of experience. Others like Edith Wilson, Nellie Taft and Flo Harding had been influential First Ladies, but none came into the White House with Eleanor's public exposure nor possessed her sympathetic ear attuned to the people's needs.

Eleanor maintained no illusions that any one person could change the world in a short time. She did believe, however, that "...a few people, who want to understand, to help and to do the right thing for the great numbers of people...can help." She hoped her husband's presidency would do just that and she hoped to find her own way to help him. As First Lady, she stood poised on the threshold of an historic presidency. She would soon find her voice as a powerful advocate for great change in society.

Chapter Seventeen

December 18, 1936

Dear Alice:

Someone has told me that you were made uncomfortable last year by receiving invitations to the White House, because, having been brought up in the tradition that you must accept them, you felt you had to come. I want you to know, of course, that no invitation is ever obligatory. It is sent as a courtesy, but I would not want you to feel forced to do anything you do not wish to do.

Affectionately yours,

Eleanor[1]

"Can you believe she denied she ever sent this?" Alice fumed indignantly. "It's an outright lie, and this is the proof!" She waved the handwritten note in front of the reporter seated with her.

The reporter scanned the note, nodding in agreement. "It appears so."

"No one will believe such behavior from the First lady—the woman has a spotless reputation as a 'do-gooder'," Alice replied righteously.

"But it will be difficult to refute this kind of hard evidence," said the reporter.

"True, but the public loves her and devours her self-righteous homilies. Where I, on the other hand, cause their blood to boil," she mused. Alice paused, then released a long, exasperated sigh. "When Franklin was elected, they should have been better winners. They could have said, 'Look here, you miserable worm, of course you feel upset because you wanted this. You hoped your brother Ted would finally achieve this, and now he hasn't. But after all, here we are. Just come if it amuses you.' Instead, they took it all seriously."

The following day, Eleanor recognized the same reporter at one of her special news conferences for women reporters.

"Mrs. Roosevelt, will your cousin, Alice Longworth, continue to be invited to White House functions?"

"Naturally," smiled the First Lady. "Alice is entitled to her opinions, even though she disagrees with my husband. Heavens, he and I don't agree on many things!" A chuckle rippled through the gathering. "Alice has always had her own idea of how things ought to be, as you well know." Another soft laugh filled the room. Eleanor, composed and smiling, continued. "This business about whether she is welcome has gone entirely too far. Alice is a member of the family. If she feels she wants to attend a particular function, she will make up her own mind without interference from any of us. Thank you for your concern. Next question?"

A Public War of Words

During Franklin's presidential years, Alice's relationship with the First Family became increasingly strained. In 1933, however, despite their political differences, their personal relationship remained warm. Alice and Paulina were invited to celebrate the family Christmas Dinner and the children's party on December 25.

In a handwritten note, Alice replied to Eleanor's invitation saying she didn't know whether they would be back in Washington yet. The tone was affectionate. Alice's book, *Crowded Hours*, had recently been published as had Eleanor's book, *It's Up to the Women*. Alice's note contained a reference to both books. "I do think it was too nice of you to cast an eye on my book. I read yours with real interest and I think you are remarkable. There was even something for me there that I took to myself...I'll tell you what it was when I see you." The note contained a reference to something Eleanor had written about Auntie Bye, "I could hear her saying it," Alice wrote. She offered a suggestion that they "put in sealed envelopes what we think [indecipherable] will say about us."[2] Perhaps Alice was referring to the reviewers or the rest of the family.

A few months later, Eleanor and Franklin invited Alice to celebrate her 50th birthday at a White House musicale on February 12, 1934. In typical understated style, Alice said the event wasn't too different from many other birthdays she had celebrated in the house.

With her political cronies, however, Alice spent many evenings at the F Street Club, which operated out of Laura Curtis's home in Washington. Laura, who had been Nick's hostess in Aiken before he died, lost her money in the Depression. By opening the club, she continued to provide an arena where her Republican party friends could gather to eat, drink and play poker. Alice became a charter member and a central figure in lively evening discussions where Franklin's policies were attacked.

Alice drew people disgruntled with the New Deal to her like a magnet, even when she was a guest in the White House. She derided the expansion of the Washington bureaucracy with jibes at all the "alphabet agencies,"—the CCC, WPA, TVA, NRA, calling the nation's capital "The Alphabet Soup Society."

When Franklin informed her one evening that he was about to sign a bill that would save the country $50 million dollars, Alice replied, "That's a drop in the bucket compared to what you are costing the country." When he took the country off the gold standard, Alice appeared at a White House reception draped in gold jewelry. One columnist reported that "If Franklin could have taken her to the Treasury and deposited her, the deficit would have turned into a surplus."

Alice defended her antics. "Eleanor and Franklin shouldn't have minded my making merry of them. I've always laughed about all the family, including myself. I'm a comic character, too."

Always complex, Alice could argue both sides of a conflict with equal passion, depending on her audience. She damned the new President but, if anyone outside the family did so, she would give them her icy glare and remind the offender that Franklin was, after all, a Roosevelt. Members of her tribe were not to be spoken of in a derogatory manner, at least not in front of her.

Alice's barbs became nastier and her imitation of Eleanor more biting as Franklin's occupancy in the White House lengthened. Mimicking Eleanor was always a crowd-pleaser. Alice would tuck in her lower lip and heighten her voice, which made even those who loved the First Lady break into peals of disloyal laughter. She railed not only against the New Deal, but also against Eleanor's left-wing friends.

Alice never referred to her cousin as "Mr. President." To his increasing annoyance, Alice called him, "Franklin." She made him hopping mad at a influential dinner party by claiming, "My poor cousin, he suffered from polio so he was put in a brace; and now he wants to put the entire U.S. into a brace, as if it were a crippled country—that is all the New Deal is about, you know."

She contrasted Franklin's philosophy of nurturing people's dependence on the government with her father's on self-reliance, implying that had Teddy been stricken with polio, he would have willed himself out of his wheelchair through sheer spunk. Eventually, Franklin became so irritated by Alice, he told his son, Jimmy, he didn't want anything to do with "that woman."

Curiously, some members of Franklin's own brain trust felt the same way about his wife. Eleanor was referred to as "that woman" and much worse. She became known as an agitator and was chided for wearing the pants in the family. She was accused of dominating dinner conversations with the numerous causes she promoted. To her consternation, the more Eleanor pressed her agenda, the less committed Franklin became to them. Their conflict was played out in private, while Alice's critique of the First Family occurred in public.

The press latched onto Alice and Eleanor's conflict because it made good news. Alice was quick to criticize where Eleanor's gibes were subtle. At the height of their public bickering, Alice received the note from Eleanor informing her that, although she would be asked to everything at the White House, she mustn't feel she had to come. The disclaimer preserved etiquette without abandoning the family grievances which brewed under the surface. "Perhaps it gave them pleasure not to have me," Alice noted.

Some years later, Eleanor soothed their public conflict by paying Alice a visit at Rookwood. Alice called their meeting "strictly a family affair." She and Eleanor "never allow[ed] politics to come between us." Eleanor told the press she hoped "we in our country will remain as free of prejudice and [as] tolerant as we [she and Alice] have been."

Exploitative journalism hoped for otherwise. Alice needed money and magazines needed name authors to draw their audience. *Ladies Home Journal* hired her to write a monthly column from Washington, expecting Alice's keen political insights to jump off the page. The *Journal* was published by Curtis Publishing Company, which was zealously anti-New Deal. The daring she showed in private, however, once again did not translate to the printed word. Alice's vitriolic repartee didn't survive without the pulse of her personality breathing behind it. Much to her publisher's disappointment, Alice drew her cat's claws in, rarely scratching at her New Deal relations. When the *Ladies Home Journal* was taken over by Bruce and Beatrice Gould, Bruce persuaded Alice to give up her writing for a fee of $2000. In an obvious blow to her ego, Gould proceeded to sign Eleanor for the serialization rights to her autobiography for $75,000. *This is My Story* was published as a book two years later.

Both Alice and Eleanor were private women who did not reveal their pain over personal events in public; consequently, Eleanor's autobiography mentioned nothing about the collapse of her world when she discovered Franklin's affair with Lucy Mercer. She shared the pain of his betrayal only with her most intimate friends. Each woman's restraint demonstrated the strength of her character and breeding, in contrast with the type of titillating "tell-all" tales written by Alice's old rival, newspaper heiress Cissy Patterson.

In December 1935, Eleanor began writing a column for United Feature Syndicate called *My Day*. Alice's publishing friends convinced her to accept an offer to write her own column for the McNaught syndicate, called *Capital Comment*. Her competitive spirit and the financial pressure she continued to experience clinched the deal. The cousins' columns ran head-to-head. Initially, Alice's column was published in twice as many newspapers as Eleanor's. She had a built-in audience of readers who hated Franklin.

Eleanor's column began with homilies, written to offend no one. She documented her visits to various cities and Civilian Conservation Corps (CCC) camps. Yet, as the years progressed, her voice and style developed with the help of her devoted friend and companion, reporter Lorena Hickock. Hick, Lorena's nickname, was not only instrumental in molding Eleanor's writing, she helped Eleanor reshape her image and define her role as First Lady. Though Hick influenced Eleanor's writing style, the ideas in her columns were uniquely her own. They were replete with compassion, insight, common sense and the acquired wisdom of overcoming personal challenges.

Alice didn't have the benefit of someone like Hick to help her writing behind the scenes. Cissy Patterson, her former rival and an unlikely source of support, briefly tried to help. Cissy thought that sitting with Alice, provoking her with irritating questions, would free her to tell great stories. She arranged for her secretary to take down Alice's quotes for later publication, but Alice choked up in front of the stenographer. Cissy even tried having the secretary sit behind a screen, but that didn't work either. She gave up, convinced that paper cramped Alice's style because she couldn't finish her sentences with the gestures and facial expressions that peppered her speech.

Interest in Alice's work waned. One editor wondered, "Why the hell do I roar hilariously when I'm with her and then only smile when her copy comes through?" Eleanor emerged victorious in the battle of the columns. Her "Day" became America's day with dedicated readers across the country. Eleanor earned $75,000 a year, which she gave to charity, far eclipsing Alice's writing. Within a few years, *Capital Comment* faded, but *My Day* continued until Eleanor's death.

Alice failed on the lecture circuit, too. She signed with an agency for $2500 per speech, but the arrangement didn't last long. She gave two speeches, one on "I Believe in America" and the second on the cockroach. The latter was a clear provocation for her agent, Harold Peat, daring him to cancel her contract. Eleanor, meanwhile, had developed her speechmaking skills through the 1920s with Louis Howe's guidance. She was a highly sought-after speaker.

The cousins' role reversal was not lost on the press, but rather, the press fueled it. Alice had been the center of the world, but the *Nashville Tennessean* declared, "It begins to look as if Eleanor Roosevelt is going to make Alice...look like 'Alice-Sit-by-the-Fire'." Alice had been supplanted as the local Washington big shot. She had been anointed a Princess by the press and was then deprived of her crown by a reluctant cousin who was sardonically dubbed Empress Eleanor.

All was not dismal for Alice during the mid-1930s. To her delight, she became the object of a satirical, successful Broadway play that opened on November 26, 1935 at the Music Box Theater in New York. *First Lady* was written by George S. Kaufman and Katharine Dayton, a Washington presswoman.

The real First Lady and her cousin experienced a common struggle in their role as mothers. Eleanor lamented late in life that Sara, Franklin's mother, was more of a mother to her children than she ever was. She had spent years fighting Sara's domination while she struggled to manage her large brood, mostly on her own. Franklin was an absentee father much of the family's early years in Washington and also while he sought a cure for polio. He never liked disciplining his children and, once his political career resumed, he had little time for family life. As adults, the Roosevelt offspring moved in and out of marriages as often as they did occupations, much to Eleanor's distress.

For Alice, raising Paulina alone after Nick's death put a severe strain on her. Not only had she lost her official place in Washington

Chapter Seventeen 207

society, she was unequipped emotionally to handle single parenting. Alice was not a nurturing, supportive mother. Waldie, Paulina's nurse, provided that role in the young girl's life. Many factors may have contributed to Alice's failure, including her own lack of a mother-child bond with Edith, becoming a mother late in life or the child-rearing practices of the day. Ultimately, however, the responsibility lay in her own temperament. Alice repeated many of the parenting errors of her own childhood.

She was a critical mother who withheld affection and denied Paulina her much needed talk about her beloved father. Teddy had done the same thing to Alice, never speaking of Alice Lee. Paulina was a shy girl who stuttered and was as stubborn as her demanding mother. Though she tried to please Alice, Paulina only succeeded in disappointing her.

To the dismay of Alice and her isolationist friends, Franklin won a second term in 1936 against the Republican candidate, Alf Landon. The world was turning to war once again as Hitler took over the Rhineland. Alice's previous anger at Wilson for procrastinating about getting into a war was reversed as she sided with proponents of "America First."

At the start of Franklin's second term in 1937, Alice grabbed a front row seat to witness arguments over her cousin's move to pack the Supreme Court. Franklin wanted to increase the judges from nine to 15 in order to get around the conservative justices who were declaring his New Deal legislation unconstitutional. Alice gleefully watched opposition to his proposal mount and the Judiciary Committee finally send his proposal packing.

Despite the rampant anti-New Deal crowd with whom Alice associated, Alice and Eleanor's personal correspondence continued to express warmth and family concern. While Paulina was boarding at the exclusive Madeira School in Virginia during her teenage years, Eleanor sent Alice a note on October 13, 1939 offering to do anything for the child if Alice were not in Washington.[3] In a note dated October 25, Alice replied, "I appreciate so much your offering to look out for Paulina, but I am planning to be in Washington, so that is one chore you will not have to add to what must be a fantastically full list. But do have a word with her sometime when you are at Madeira to visit your cousin..."[4] In the note, Alice went on to thank Eleanor for her concern over the fact that several young cousins had not been able to "get a

208 Alice and Eleanor

glimpse of the downstairs rooms at the White House" because "Franklin was having a conference...They did not in the least feel that they were being turned away from the old Manse."

Alice continued to exercise political influence in the Republican party long after her husband's death. By the 1940 election, she was promoting an unlikely candidate for the Republican nomination for President, Robert Taft, son of William Howard Taft. The fickle winds of politics had placed Taft right in Alice's political corner, despite the differences between their fathers in the past. Though Robert was a dull politician, Alice agreed with his politics. She worked as hard for Taft as she had for her own father. Wendell Wilkie bested Taft to be the nominee against cousin Franklin.

Robert Taft was an "America First" isolationist, whose supporters included a cast of xenophobic, rabid anti-semites like Charles Lindbergh and Father Charles Coughlin, a radio priest from Michigan, plus members of the Ku Klux Klan and genuine pacifists. These New Deal haters feared the President more than Hitler. John L. Lewis, founder of the new labor organization, the Congress of Industrial Organizations (CIO), the same man who brought labor into Franklin's camp in 1932 and again in 1936, joined Alice's new cronies in opposition to the sitting President. Franklin refused to put the labor leader on his ticket. Consequently, Lewis bolted from the Democratic party and supported Wilkie in exchange for the promise of a major voice in the administration.

Gossip columnists enjoyed speculating that a winter's love had enveloped Lewis the "Welshman" and Alice the "sorceress." Rumors about their liaison were fueled by Alice's own comparison of the labor leader to Senator Borah. Lewis was charismatic, and self-educated, but also a married man.[5] He had originally joined the Republican Party because Teddy Roosevelt had settled the coal miners strike in 1902. Lewis led the coal miners out of the corrupt AFL, originated the sit-down strike, and organized steel and auto workers.

John and Alice shared a sense of humor as "fellow thieves." They had the same birthday. They quoted Shakespeare and the Bible to one another. "He loved making trouble and I loved watching him make it," Alice recalled. "It was natural that we should get together...I was lucky in my middle age, to find a new delightful companion...Marriage? I didn't take it seriously. I wouldn't have married anybody. Once is

Chapter Seventeen 209

enough, but, for me, he was the best company there ever was...We didn't pretend at all. We laughed at ourselves...We could have come straight from the Arabian Nights." They were also united in their opposition to Franklin.

Public figures invariably develop a following of both admirers and critics and such was the case with Alice and Eleanor. Some found their activities laudable, others claimed they were subversive. Both women engendered the criticism of their intimates for commercial endorsements— Alice for Lucky Strike cigarettes in 1937 and Eleanor for doing TV commercials and hosting a television program in the 1940s and 1950s. They were baited publicly, Alice by her old nemesis Cissy Patterson and Eleanor by Westbrook Pegler, a popular syndicated columnist; but neither responded, which outraged their detractors all the more.

Neither woman countenanced the pursuit of power for self-aggrandizement. Both declined to run for public office. Alice disdained women taking over their husband's congressional or senate seats. Eleanor didn't want to be in competition with her children's political aspirations. Duty and usefulness were her ends, not power, wealth or privilege. She did use her position, however, to take courageous public stands on issues like youth employment and racial justice. She even resigned from the Daughters of the American Republic when they refused to allow Marian Anderson, as a black singer, to use their hall for a concert in 1939.

Alice was not alone in weathering the storms of personal controversy in her private life. Eleanor experienced her share. She was named in a 1947 divorce suit by the third wife of Earl Miller, Eleanor's Albany companion. In addition, speculation swirled about Eleanor's personal relationship with her lesbian friends Lorena Hickock, Nancy Day and Marion Dickerman, Esther Lape and Elizabeth Read, and even Eleanor's mentor at Allenswood, Madame Souvestre. Much of the lengthy correspondence between these women has disappeared, like Eleanor's with Earl. Limited though they are, the letters between Eleanor and Hick are intimate in a manner which left one biographer with little doubt about the extent of their relationship.[6]

Amidst the allegations, both Alice and Eleanor pursued their lives undaunted. Eleanor took principled positions on issues and became her husband's conscience for the New Deal, while Alice often took stands out of mischief "to annoy Franklin." She became an officer in the

210 Alice and Eleanor

Washington chapter of "America First." Assured by these isolationists that the Axis powers posed no threat to the U.S., Alice continued her affiliation with them until the entire coterie was dumbstruck by the Japanese attack on Pearl Harbor, December 7, 1941.

The war struck at the hearts of both Roosevelt women, claiming their loved ones as it did so many other American families. In death, there are no privileged mourners, only sorrow. Ted, Jr., Alice's brother, had volunteered to fight for the British but, when America entered the war, he was one of the officers who led the Allied assault on the beaches of Normandy. At age 57, the brigadier general moved from one locale to another under enemy fire, rallying the men he had taken over the sea wall. The strenuous ordeal proved too much for him and he suffered a fatal heart attack. Ted, Jr. was awarded the distinguished Medal of Honor for meritorious service, an honor which had alluded his father. Alice's younger brother Kermit also died during the war in Alaska. She was profoundly affected by their deaths.

The war claimed another, more famous Roosevelt, the President Franklin Delano Roosevelt (FDR). He died of a cerebral hemorrhage at age 63 on April 12, 1945 at his resort in Warms Springs, Georgia. FDR had been elected as the nation's leader for an unprecedented fourth term of office. Eleanor learned of his death while she was in Washington. "I am more sorry for the people of this country and of the world than I am for ourselves," she said after a moment of silence. Her personal sorrow was deepened by not being with her husband when he was stricken. Her absence symbolized their estrangement in their last years and the intimacy they failed to achieve in their marriage. The final indignation Eleanor suffered was the presence of Lucy Mercer Rutherfurd at Franklin's side. Lucy was with him as he sat for a portrait she had commissioned. She was whisked out of sight before Eleanor arrived. Alice had known that the President resumed seeing his former love. Unlike in earlier days, however, she chose not to burden Eleanor with the painful news.

Eleanor had been looking forward to a quiet life after leaving the White House but, instead, plunged into a heavy work load at President Truman's request as a United Nations delegate. Freed from Franklin's shadow, she became a powerful figure in her own right. She argued forcefully that the United Nations should be the cornerstone of U.S. foreign policy. Eleanor felt strongly that as a nation we needed to put ourselves in the shoes of other countries and listen to their needs, not dictate from on high. She put her former advocacy for the failed League of Nations to use, fashioning the United Nations into a powerful world body of the post war era.

Eleanor served as a delegate to the United Nations from 1946-52 and as Chair of the United Nations Human Rights Commission. Her tireless work drafting the *Declaration of Human Rights* left an indelible mark on modern history. The document provides the world with a forceful moral construct, a guarantee of dignity and essential rights for all humanity. Eleanor called it a "Magna Carta for Mankind," fashioning it with her vision, fortitude and diplomacy. It stands as the crowning achievement of her life's work, a testament to her greatness.

By the 1950s Alice was still a rock-ribbed Republican but she had developed a nonpartisan circle of friends who shared one characteristic—power. She dined and had tea with the men who crossed the political spectrum from Joe McCarthy to Fidel Castro to Bob Hope. Both she and Eleanor continued to befriend Presidents in the years after their husbands passed away.

Each had close relations with the Kennedys. Alice loved Jack's style and teased his more serious brother, Bobby. Though Eleanor had supported Adlai Stevenson for the 1960 Democratic nomination, Kennedy came to visit her at Val-Kill. She found him "a brilliant man with a quick mind, anxious to learn, hospitable to new ideas, hardheaded." She took part in his campaign, even though she was already 76 years old, and offered poignant, useful advice to Jackie on her role as First Lady. Kennedy later nominated Eleanor for a Nobel Peace Prize but, given her self-effacing manner, she couldn't imagine why.

Alice was close to the Johnsons, often taking tea with Lady Bird. She admired LBJ, calling him "Old Slyboots" and "a lovely rogue elephant." She described him as a "...masterful man, the greatest I've ever seen at getting things done, and I've seen them all." But she didn't fail to deliver her sharp one-liners even to those she admired. When LBJ insisted on showing the scar from his gall bladder surgery to the press, she quipped, "Thank God it wasn't his prostate."

Alice had a long relationship with Richard and Pat Nixon, beginning in Washington when he was a young California congressman. Eleanor, however, never forgave Nixon for deliberately and falsely labeling his opponent, Helen Gahagan Douglas, as a Communist during the height of the McCarthy investigations for the House Committee on Un-American Activities. The late 1940s were as turbulent a period as the Red scares of Attorney General Palmer's Raids in 1920. Nixon knew Douglas was not a communist, but traded on the xenophobia sweeping the country to gain a political advantage.

Though Alice admired Nixon in his early years, she became disillusioned with his mushiness during Watergate. She had seen plenty of dirty tricks in her time, but what she couldn't abide was softness. Had Nixon destroyed the White House tapes, there would not have been a scandal. She didn't think Jack Kennedy would have "shilly-shallied" the way Nixon did. When he resigned, Nixon quoted from Alice's father's diary. "When my heart's dearest died, the light went out from my life forever." These were the words Teddy had written when her mother, Alice Lee, had died. Alice couldn't see how her father's experience could possibly give Nixon any comfort for it had nothing to do with Nixon's troubles.

Alice suffered her most devastating personal trauma at the end of January 1957. Her daughter died at the age of 31 from an overdose of tranquilizers, barbituates and alcohol. Paulina had been treated throughout her sad life by psychiatrists for nervous breakdowns, depression and suicide attempts. She was survived by her ten-year-old daughter, Joanna, who Alice insisted live with her.

Alice broke in a manner none of her intimates had ever seen. This stoic lady was crushed, wondering over and over whether it was her fault. She was remorseful, ashamed and shaken for her own failure as a mother. Alice had never been sure whether she was loved as a child and chastised herself for not raising her daughter differently.

It was Eleanor who drew the final touching response from Alice on her daughter's death. Beneath their political divisions lay moments of profound compassion and support which did not surface in public. Eleanor wrote her cousin the following note, "I am shocked that this great grief has come to you, and I am glad that you have the small Grandchild. If there is anything I can ever do for you, please let me know. With my deepest sympathy, Affectionately, Eleanor." Alice replied, "For months after Paulina died, whenever I tried to write, I simply crumpled." It was a stunning, poignant confession from the stalwart "perambulatory Washington monument." Yet to the world, Alice squared her shoulders and held her head high as if saying, "Don't you dare pity me!"

While it may seem unusual that Alice bared her soul to Eleanor, a woman who many considered her rival, their lives had been bound inextricably through family and politics. Perhaps Alice was finally able to relinquish the tough veneer which shielded her from life's pain to respond to the unlimited compassion Eleanor extended to others. She may have recognized her cousin's kindred spirit from their troubled childhoods, or their shared experience losing a child, or their common concerns as mothers for their children or problems with their spouses. Perhaps, as Alice had said, she "always liked Eleanor," but life had simply gotten in the way of their ability to communicate. She may have finally been able to acknowledge Eleanor's achievements without feeling threatened or jealous and prided herself that they were both Roosevelt women. Or perhaps, reports of their personal conflicts were greatly exaggerated for their correspondence revealed a warmth and compassion that ran counter to what made good copy for the news.

Few people knew of the touching relationship that Eleanor developed with her doctor, David Gurewitsch, after Franklin's death. The difference in their ages led some to describe it as physically unrequited; nonetheless, they were extremely devoted to one another. David toured much of the world with Eleanor. During her last years, she lived with him and his new wife.

The infirmities of old age caught up with both Alice and Eleanor, yet the spirit of TR ran strong in them both. Each had also witnessed the grace under which their dear Auntie Bye suffered from arthritis in her last years. Alice informed a caller, "You can't live to be my age without having a few diseases...At least I still have all my marbles." She endured a mastectomy at the age of 72, which she kept from even her closest friends. Eleanor remarked near the end of her life, "Inevitably there are aches and pains, more and more, and if you pay much attention to them, the first thing you know you're an invalid." Eleanor recognized what others had seen long before—her similarity to Alice's father. "I think I have a good deal of my Uncle Theodore in me, because I could not, at any age, be content to take my place in a corner by the fireside and simply look on."

Unlike Alice, Eleanor had avoided frivolous, self-indulgent behavior during her early adulthood yet, as she aged, she developed an ability to poke fun at herself. As a young girl she was taught to please, but, as she matured, Eleanor learned the art of deliberate provocation that Alice had employed so effectively. Eleanor initiated press conferences for women reporters while First Lady, telling them, "Sometimes I say things which I thoroughly understand are likely to cause unfavorable comment in some quarters, and perhaps you newspaper women think I should keep them off the record. What you don't understand is that perhaps I am making these statements on purpose to arouse controversy and thereby get the topics talked about and so get people to thinking about them." She also recognized that she "acted as a spur" to her husband "even though spurring was not always wanted or welcome."

Eleanor believed that "Life must be lived. Curiosity must be kept alive." Alice concurred. Her wide interests were evident in the books that filled her house, spilling out of the bookshelves. They covered an eclectic range of topics. Alice read into the wee hours of the morning and didn't rise until noon. "I'm allergic to morning," she claimed. At age 95, Alice was still described as rambunctious as a high-school freshman. Another interviewer called her "a survivor in a town where the word is an anachronism."

Both Alice and Eleanor welcomed death with a lack of fear and with Roosevelt courage, accepting it in Alice's words as "just another special occasion." Alice Roosevelt Longworth died at the age of 96 on February 29, 1980. She did not want a funeral or a memorial service. Irreverent to the end, the boyfriend of Alice's granddaughter told a reporter that Alice had stuck her tongue out before she died. Perhaps the gesture was for him, or God or death itself. When asked to list her occupation on the death certificate, he replied, "Gadfly." Indeed, like the gadfly and cousin Eleanor, Alice used provocation to spur people into action.

Throughout Eleanor's life, she wanted no special treatment. She resisted her infirmities with an iron will, even the aplastic anemia she suffered during her final years. Eleanor developed subterfuges against her nurses, hiding her pills in the recesses of her mouth and refusing to swallow them. Eleanor Roosevelt died on November 7, 1962 at the age of 78. Her simple decency and her profound sincerity found a place in hearts all over the world. She left the world a beloved humanitarian.

Epilogue

Alice's quips:
On herself—"A combination of Scarlett O'Hara and Whistler's Mother."
On the Roosevelts—"A group of Upstart Dutch who made a couple of bucks."
On a politician friend/lover during the 1920s—"Well, if you really want to know, I suppose you could say that I was adept at skating on thin ice and playing with fire. Nice image, don't you think?"
On the 1970s sexual scene—"...if one wishes to talk about bodily functions, my philosophy is 'Fill what's empty, empty what's full, and scratch where it itches'."
On Franklin's Presidency—"Franklin very possibly wouldn't have emerged if my father hadn't emerged, and my father might not have emerged if Czolgosz hadn't killed McKinley. Who can tell? Were it not for Czolgosz, we'd all be back in our brownstone-front houses. That's where we'd be. And I would have married for money and been divorced for good cause."
On her place in history—"Perhaps...perhaps I'll be a footnote."

Eleanor's writing—*Ten Rules for a Successful Marriage* (1931)
1) Have a plan, some central idea, as definite a pattern for your life.
2) Sooner or later money is apt to be a cause of friction.
3) Apportion your time and energy, allowing each [partner to] share joint homemaking duties, as well as individual responsibilities.
4) Let neither husband nor wife strive to be the dominating person in the household. A victory for either...means failure for the partnership.
5) Expect to disagree.
6) Be honest. [With yourself, and with each other.]
7) Be loyal. Keep your differences to yourselves. The less said about your married troubles, except between yourselves, the better.

8) Talk things over...Meet every situation in the open.
9) Avoid trivial criticisms.
10) Keep alive the spirit of courtship.

A Contrast in Style and Purpose
The contrast between Alice's quips and Eleanor's writing reflects the sharp differences in their personalities as well as their style and purpose. Their long lives, though remarkably different, had many similar influences, concurrent paths, parallel problems and influential outcomes. Though by personality the two women were diametric opposites, both found the allure of politics irresistible. During the years each lived in the White House, they attracted the press like bees to flowers, creating a constant buzz of criticism or admiration. They played their political hands deftly with more similarity than difference. Their lives were inextricably entwined, not merely by bloodline, but in a complex relationship uniquely tied to their passionate involvement in life and politics.

Biographers have devoted years of their lives and thousands of pages to the life of Eleanor Roosevelt. She was the famous Roosevelt, eclipsing for a generation of Depression families that other famous Roosevelt, Alice. Eleanor was admired and reviled for her advocacy of labor, women, children and poverty issues. She viewed politics as a vehicle for changing the world. She reached out to the country and the world with compassion, warmth and devotion, much as she did to her intimate friends and family.

"When will our consciences grow so tender that we will act to prevent human misery rather than avenge it?" she wondered. Eleanor Roosevelt transcended personal pain and struggles to form a bond with world privation and suffering. In *The Declaration of Human Rights*, she guided the formation of a statement of universal entitlement that reaches across class, race and political borders.

Alice had no grand plan or cause to which she was devoted. Rather, she operated out of the passions of the day, choosing causes and people to advocate when the spirit captured her. Politics had always been a part of her life, from earliest childhood. Her father and, subsequently, her husband and lovers were all powerful players on the local and national scene. Alice was motivated to play her own political hand in support and later in defense of her father's goals. She was fiercely loyal to his memory, but was also a rogue in pursuit of entertainment. She delighted in the havoc she was able to generate, reveling in gossip and controversy, while disdaining convention.

Where some saw Alice as malicious, others experienced a woman of self-deprecating humor. "People ought to be shaken up," an admiring friend commented. Alice had variously been called a super pixie with low boring point. She was blunt, witty, outrageous, provoking, rebellious, possessing power, energy and much more. Adjectives like earnest, hardworking, loyal, warm and self-doubting described Eleanor.

The revolving doors of the White House whirled Alice in as a debutante and Eleanor as a middle-aged woman. Alice made headlines as a scandalous youth and, though she strove to re-enter the revolving doors again as the daughter of a returning president, the wife of a president or the sister of a president, she was not privileged to take up residence again. She remained forever a guest. Eleanor's occupancy, however, became the longest of any First Lady, ushered out not by vote or choice, but by her husband's death. Neither woman's voice was stifled by her exit through the revolving doors, however. To the contrary, leaving liberated them to explore their own concerns.

What then can one conclude from an examination of the parallel influences and divergent paths these first cousins traversed throughout their lives? From their sheltered, troubled childhoods, burdened by the social conventions of their times, both wielded unconventional political power. They invigorated dialogue, exercised influence and ultimately expanded the role of women in public policy.

Alice captured the country's imagination as a young debutante and continued to hold court throughout her life. From the turn of the century through her husband's tenure as Speaker of the House, she dominated the media for 30 years and beyond. She was an eternal youth in contrast to Eleanor who was grandmotherly even as a child.

Eleanor usurped Alice's place in Washington as "The Roosevelt Woman" from the 1930s through the early 1960s. She promoted a liberal social agenda with unfaltering vision while enduring intense criticism. She inspired countless women to a life of excellence, including the current First Lady, Hillary Rodham Clinton.

Alice was famous for her imitations, her tart quips, her eccentricities, her controversial lifestyle and her fabulous salon. Alice did achieve her youthful ambition of becoming a "Grande Dame." In the intervening years, she was transformed from a self-indulgent princess to, in her own words, "a loathsome combination of Marie Dressler and Phyllis Diller" and, finally, "a symbolic dotage of Queen Victoria with levity."

Eleanor blazed her own trail too, creating and defining a new dimension of the political woman. She travelled a far greater arc of personal change, shedding the mantle of her birth into the privileged class to represent the voice of needy humanity. In addition to her own work for the disenfranchised, she lobbied extensively for the appointment of women to government positions. She achieved a scope of influence that would have astonished her father, yet vindicated his faith in his "little Nell."

As Hillary Rodham Clinton swept past the marble busts of the nation's Capitol to embark on a plan to restructure the American health care system, she was walking down a historic path paved by First Lady Eleanor Roosevelt. During Franklin's first term, she had worked at her husband's behest creating Arthurdale, a model community to relocate miners into a farming community.

Mrs. Clinton expresses a joy in public service that Eleanor concealed. Susan Faludi, feminist author of *Backlash*, wrote an op-ed piece in the December 20, 1992 edition of *The New York Times* in which she shared Eleanor Roosevelt's view that women in politics could either be biblical "Marthas" or "Marys." Eleanor cast her lot with the "Marthas." She presented herself as dour and self-denigrating, never missing an opportunity to discount her influence. Eleanor, who loved her public life, worked behind the scenes burying her feelings in deference to her husband.

Hillary, on the other hand, can afford to spread her arms to embrace her admirers, then consult openly with congressional representatives to craft the nation's new health care system. She has established a public partnership with her husband, in which each looks to the other for counsel and advice. Hillary is the one person Bill Clinton wants to consult in a moment of crisis. Not so with Franklin and Eleanor who became increasingly estranged over the years. Hillary has achieved what Eleanor desired. Wisdom would dictate, however, that Mrs. Clinton learn from Eleanor's experience. First Ladies are vulnerable to double jeopardy. They are political figures without real power.

Epilogue 219

Alice's legacy as a salon mistress has been expanded by current Washington hostesses. Today, women like Pamela Harriman and Katherine Graham openly use their influence to push a political agenda and raise money for their causes. The late night poker players who powerbrokered conventions in the past have relinquished their influence to sophisticated political action committees.

Emily's List and other women's political organizations have benefited from Eleanor's work to elect more women and expand the role of women within the mainstream of the political parties and the government. The three women senators elected in the 1992 election, 60 years after Franklin's first successful presidential bid, owe a debt to Eleanor and her colleagues in the Democratic Party.

The role of women will continue to expand on the local, state and national level as a legacy to both Roosevelt women. Louis Howe was so convinced that Franklin's New Deal revolution would make it possible to elect a woman as president, he asked Eleanor if she wanted to run in 1940. "Tell me now so I can start getting things ready." Eleanor declined, perceptively informing Howe that the country wasn't ready. When it was, however, she hoped the woman would be elected as an individual because of her capacity, integrity and ability as a person, not merely because of her sex. "It's a man's world now...and will be just as long as the women want it to be!" Eleanor exclaimed.

Sometimes in the shadow and sometimes in full daylight, the Roosevelt women exercised their powerful influence in Washington. Their impact was felt across the political spectrum, prodding the nation to re-examine itself and to evolve. It is doubtful that there will ever again be two such close relatives influencing the power elite of our country from such different perspectives for so long a period of history. Alice and Eleanor were remarkable women, each in her own right, who not only witnessed but were an integral part of America's history in the 1900s. While their personal styles were in dramatic contrast to one another, each left an indelible mark which will inspire future generations.

Notes

Chapter One
[1] This incident did take place at Bye's house, however, the final quote was actually attributed to Eleanor's grandmother after the incident. Lash, 1971, p. 72.

[2] Family and friends attributed Alice Lee's death to Bright's disease, an outdated term for kidney disease. However, she may have died from toxemia of pregnancy or preeclampsia. Felsenthal, 1988, p. 32.

Chapter Two
[1] Alice recalled that her family used to say, "after a diving lesson, my tears made a perceptible rise in the tide." Longworth, 1933, p. 5.

[2] Edith had her heart set on Teddy at a very early age. Their families were neighbors in New York and Edith knew his sisters well. It was difficult for her to justify that she had been TR's second choice. "She was one of those people who made up her mind early...she was passionately in love with him," said one relative. Felsenthal, 1988, p. 34.

[3] According to Edith Kermit Roosevelt. Felsenthal, 1988, p. 53.

Chapter Three
[1] This incident occurred on one of Eleanor's infrequent visits to Sagamore Hill. Brough, 1975, p. 6.

[2] According to Alice, her father preferred simple food and plenty of it. Teague, 1972, p. 4.

[3] While Edith did write such a letter to Bye (Brough, 1975, p. 64), the setting described is purely fictional. Teddy actually orchestrated such runs down Cooper's Bluff and the game of stagecoach. Longworth, 1933, p. 6-7.

[4] Mrs. Hall describing Eleanor to Corinne Robinson after Elliot's death. Lash, 1971, p. 59.

Chapter Four
[1] This incident was dramatized from a report by Alice and Eleanor's cousin, Corinne Robinson, Corinne and Douglas's daughter. She hated her obligatory dinners with Eleanor. Lash, 1971, p. 61.

[2] TR's tirades apparently disturbed Mrs. McKinley so much that Teddy would be ushered into the corridor after dinner to continue his denunciations out of the President's hearing. Brough, 1975, p. 90.

Notes 221

Chapter Five
¹Eleanor did make arrangements for her own chaperone through an employment agency in New York. As it turned out, she might just as well have crossed alone. Their trip was rough and the two didn't see one another until the day they landed. Roosevelt, 1961, p. 33.
²Alice and Ted, Jr. did do a jig when they learned of McKinley's assassination. Teague, 1981, p. 62.

Chapter Six
¹This incident is adapted from a similar event recorded in Teichmann, 1975, p. 50.
²Franklin confided in Bye's son, William Sheffield Cowles, Jr., that his failure to make "Porc" was one of the biggest disappointments in his life. Cook, 1992, p. 149.
³Theodore Roosevelt, Sr., Eleanor and Alice's paternal grandfather, was a well-respected New York philanthropist who started the Children's Aid Society, the New York Orthopedic Hospital, the Metropolitan Museum of Art, and the American Museum of Natural History. Felsenthal, 1988, p. 13.

Chapter Seven
¹Alice sent Eleanor a note on December 8, 1905, telling her cousin of her engagement to Nick Longworth. "I'm trying not to announce it until the 17th, so don't say anything about it until then. I hope for a surprise, but am much afraid you are not." Courtesy of Franklin Delano Roosevelt Library, Hyde Park.

Chapter Eight
¹Eleanor did chide Franklin about having a drink with Alice in a Boston hotel outside her room. She wrote to him, "No one would know that you were her cousin. You were seen going to a woman's room. I think it would be a good idea if you and Alice didn't see each other for some time." Teague, 1975, p. 157.
²From a letter sent to Eleanor and Franklin from Alice, December 23, 1907. Courtesy of the Franklin Delano Roosevelt Library, Hyde Park.
³Douglas reportedly told Nick that when he married a Roosevelt (Teddy's sister, Corinne), he had done so in ignorance. It never occurred to him he was marrying into a Presidential family. Teichmann, 1979, p. 65.

Chapter Nine
¹This interaction is adapted from one reported in Cook, 1992, p. 183 and Lash, 1971, p. 162, in which Eleanor sat and wept in front of her dressing table at their new 65th Street townhouse on their first night in the new house. She

cried and cried until Franklin appeared to find out what was delaying her for dinner. "I didn't like to live in a house which was not in any way mine, one that I had done nothing about and which did not represent the way I wanted to live," she replied. He made no effort to console her or comprehend her pain, announcing that he thought her "quite mad." He assured her she would "feel differently" as soon as she became "calmer."

The townhouse had been a Christmas gift from Sara in 1905. She acquired the land the following year and hired Charles A. Platt to design it. The home was modeled after the Ludlow-Parish home of cousin Susie, where Franklin and Eleanor had been married.

Chapter Ten
[1]The dialogue between Taft and Alice was quoted in Teichmann, 1979, p. 84-85.

Major Archie Butt wrote to his mother early in 1909, "Apart from the Monument, Alice Longworth is still the greatest attraction in the Capital." Teichmann, 1979, p. 82.

[2]Major Butt never returned from the voyage. Chivalrous to the end, he went down helping women and children board the Titanic's lifeboats. Felsenthal, 1988, p. 126.

His misgivings about the trip were evident in a letter he wrote to his sister-in-law, informing her that "all my papers are in the storage warehouse and if the ship goes down, you will find my affairs in ship-shape condition." Teichmann, 1979, p. 86.

[3]Butt had reservations about serving for Taft after TR. He was a favorite riding and walking companion of both Teddy and Edith. Edith was partial to him for him impeccable taste. Felsenthal, 1988, p. 126, footnote.

[4]During her debutante years, Alice had found her father's attitude about large families, the purity of womanhood, and the sanctity of marriage humiliating, shameful and embarrassing. In protest of his attitude about birth control, Alice formed the Race Suicide Club. The club was secret, with four founding members, all somewhat older than Alice, who proclaimed that there could not possibly be anything even remotely pleasurable in sex. Teague, 1981, p. 82.

[5]Letter to Isabella Ferguson in Tucson, Sept. 28, 1912 in Cook, 1992, p. 528.

Chapter Twelve
[1]A widely reported quote expressed by Alice regarding Eleanor and Franklin. Lash, 1971, p. 226.

[2]Franklin always referred to his children as the "chicks."

[3]Alice did try to tell Eleanor about Franklin's affair with Lucy Mercer on the steps of the Capitol. Eleanor, as portrayed, would not listen. She reported to Franklin that she left Alice at the door, "not having allowed her to tell me any secrets. She inquired if you had told me and I said no and that I did not believe in knowing things which your husband did not wish you to know so I think I will be spared any further mysterious secrets!" Lash, 1971, p. 226.

[4]Eleanor and Alice had this exchange, but it occurred years later when Franklin was in the White House. He and Alice were chuckling over the incident when Eleanor told her what she thought of the entire affair. Teague, 1981, p. 163; Cook, 1991, p. 223.

Chapter Thirteen

[1]This incident was fictionalized from an account given by Cook, 1992, p. 221. Cissy Patterson pursued Alice's husband and lovers at parties in Alice's home. One evening she disappeared with Borah and the next morning the maid found her hairpins in the library. Alice sent them back with a note to which Cissy replied: "And if you look up in the chandelier, you might find my panties."

[2]Cissy frequently referred to herself by this quote. Cook, 1992, p. 222.

[3]Even though they developed profound political differences, Cissy Patterson never demeaned or criticized Eleanor. She admired her, calling Eleanor the "noblest woman I have ever known. I adore her above all women." According to Cissy Patterson's biographer, the former Countess wanted to be Eleanor Roosevelt. Cook, 1992, p. 222.

[4]Alice frequently entertained people at parties with her Eleanor imitation. Eleanor even asked her to see it at a White House party. Teague, 1981, p. 155.

[5]Pearson, Drew, and Robert Allen. *Washington Merry-Go-Round*. New York, Horace Liveright, 1931, p. 24.

Chapter Fourteen

[1]A direct quote by Alice. Teichmann, 1979, p. 112.

Chapter Fifteen

[1]Dramatized from reports in Teichmann, 1979, p. 134.

[2]Quoted from an article written by Eleanor Roosevelt for *Collier's* magazine entitled "Ethics of Parents," in 1927 which was never published. See Lash, 1971, p. 302.

[3]Eleanor and Franklin's first grandchild was born to their daughter Anna in March 1927 at their home. Lash, 1971, p. 302.

224 Alice and Eleanor

Chapter Sixteen
[1]Letter from Eleanor to Alice, dated March 5, 1939. Courtesy of the Franklin Delano Roosevelt Library, Hyde Park.
[2]Quotes by Alice adapted from Teague, p. 154-55, 160-61.

Chapter Seventeen
[1]Letter from Eleanor to Alice, dated Dec. 18, 1936. Courtesy of the Franklin Delano Roosevelt Library, Hyde Park.
[2]Correspondence between Alice and Eleanor, Dec. 7, 1933. Courtesy of the Franklin Delano Roosevelt Library, Hyde Park.
[3]Letter from Eleanor to Alice, Oct. 13, 1939. Courtesy of the Franklin Delano Roosevelt Library, Hyde Park.
[4]Letter from Alice to Eleanor dated Oct. 25, 1939. Courtesy of the Franklin Delano Roosevelt Library, Hyde Park.
[5]John L. Lewis had been married to Myrta Lewis since 1907. Felsenthal, 1988, p. 193.
[6]Cook, 1992, p. 479.

Works Cited

Brough, James. *Princess Alice. A Biography of Alice Roosevelt Longworth.* Boston, MA: Little, Brown and Company, 1975.

Cook, Blanche Wiesen. *Eleanor Roosevelt.* Vol. One. 1884-1933. New York: Viking, 1992.

Felsenthal, Carol. *Alice Roosevelt Longworth.* New York: G.P. Putnam's Sons, 1988.

Lash, Joseph P. *Eleanor and Franklin.* The story of their relationship, based on Eleanor Roosevelt's private papers. New York: W.W. Norton & Company, Inc. 1971.

———. *Life Was Meant To Be Lived, A Centenary Portrait of Eleanor Roosevelt.* New York: W.W. Norton & Company, 1984.

———. *Eleanor: The Years Alone.* New York: W.W. Norton & Company, 1972.

Longworth, Alice Roosevelt. *Crowded Hours.* Reminiscences of Alice Roosevelt Longworth. New York: Charles Scribner's Sons, 1933.

McClure, Ruth K., ed. *Eleanor Roosevelt, An Eager Spirit.* Selected Letters of Dorothy Dow 1933-1945. New York: W.W. Norton & Company, 1984.

Parks, Lillian Rogers, in collaboration with Frances Spatz Leighton. *The Roosevelts, A Family in Turmoil.* Englewood Cliffs, NJ: Prentice-Hall, Inc., 1981.

Roosevelt, Eleanor. *The Autobiography of Eleanor Roosevelt.* New York: Harper & Brothers Publishers, 1961.

Roosevelt, Elliot, and James Brough. *The Roosevelts of Hyde Park, An Untold Story.* New York: G.P. Putnam's Sons, 1973.

Teague, Michael. *Mrs. L. Conversations with Alice Roosevelt Longworth.* Garden City, NY: Doubleday & Company, Inc., 1981.

Teichmann, Howard. *Alice, The Life and Times of Alice Roosevelt Longworth.* Englewood Cliffs, NJ: Prentice-Hall, Inc., 1979.

www.ingramcontent.com/pod-product-compliance
Lightning Source LLC
Chambersburg PA
CBHW030410100426
42812CB00028B/2908/J